the

gringo

trail

the gringo trail ■ ■

MARK MANN

green candy press

Published by GREEN CANDY PRESS
San Francisco, CA

www.greencandypress.com

The Gringo Trail
Copyright © 2002 Mark Mann
Originally published in the UK by Summersdale Publishers Ltd.

ISBN 1-931160-10-4

Front cover photograph Copyright © David Nicholls
"Breathe" (in the air) - Waters/Gilmour/Wright Copyright © 1973
Pink Floyd Music Publishers Limited

Interior Design and Typography: Yolanda Montijo

Printed in Canada by Transcontinental
Massively Distributed by P.G.W.

To my PARENTS,
for endless support and love,
and to D.

for 'WESTIE'
(shine on you crazy diamond)

▪▪ contents

section 1

the Andes

"Everything that has happened
since the marvellous
discovery of the Americas . . .
has been so extraordinary that
the whole story remains quite
incredible to anyone who has not
experienced it at first hand."

BARTOLOMÉ DE LAS CASAS
A VERY BRIEF ACCOUNT OF THE
DESTRUCTION OF THE INDIES, 1552

Chapter 1
Ecuador: Mama Negra

in-flight entertainment
Mark took his last seventy mushrooms on the plane from London to Quito.

How they let him into Ecuador remains a mystery. He strode across the tarmac – for Mark always marched everywhere – towards the big shed that passed for an arrivals hall, dressed in a purple shell-suit, head and shoulders above all the Ecuadoreans and most of the tourists. His hair was a tangled mess. His pupils were wildly dilated. The veins on his arms and neck bulged. Melissa and I waited outside and watched him (it's a small airport) grinning maniacally at the customs officials and then grinning maniacally at the immigration officials. He couldn't have looked more conspicuous if he'd painted himself fluorescent pink and stuck a sign on his forehead saying 'Stoned'.

They let Mark through. I guess Ecuadorean customs aren't really on the look-out for people bringing hallucinogenic drugs into South America. Anyway, Mark's were safely inside him by the time he got off the plane. His wild eyes and stupid grin could have been simply due to lack of oxygen, stepping off a plane from England into the second highest capital city in the world.

It was a bad sign.

****

Charles de Gaulle Airport
Before leaving England, I'd made both Mark and Melissa promise that *on no account* would we take any drugs across international borders. That lasted an hour into the trip, when Melissa and I changed planes at Charles de Gaulle airport and Melissa pulled out a couple of ready-rolled joints. She pointed out that the fastest way to get rid of them was to smoke them.

'We could throw them away,' I ventured.

Melissa tossed her long brown hair out of her eyes and looked at me sadly. No. You can never just throw a joint away. As we smoked the dope, hiding behind a line of trolleys, the realisation dawned: no one was going to take any notice of anything I said.

Not that I was in charge, as such. It was just that I'd done all the work to get the trip together.

'If you've organised the tickets and the insurance and where we're going and what we're taking and so on . . . what's my role?' Mark had asked.

'You can buy the drugs,' I'd suggested.

Mark had missed the plane altogether, postponing his flight by three weeks while he worked through the two thousand magic mushrooms drying in his front room. That's how Melissa and I came to be in Quito already, waiting for him. I knew that if Mark came to South America, life wouldn't be dull. I also knew that he would be a pain in the arse.

I was right, as it turned out, on both counts.

****

slacker

Mark was probably the most intelligent person I knew. He certainly thought so.

I remember an entire night, a few years earlier, wandering around the Glastonbury festival while Mark explained why sines and co-sines were fundamental to the working of the universe. It all made sense. As he spoke, sines and co-sines leapt into life, danced across the fields and sang through the air. I *cared* about them. I instantly forgot every word. (Well, I was tripping.) Most people who talk about maths and chemistry and stuff like that for more than, say, three seconds are immediately consigned to a social status slightly below that of a fungal infection. But Mark could carry it off, even with guys I regarded as seriously dangerous. Guys who stole cars to get home from the pub. Of course, this had much to do with the fact that he was always the last one standing in any drug-taking contest. That earned you the right to talk about co-sines.

I'd originally met Mark at university, where he'd studied anthropology and I'd studied politics. For the last two years, though, he'd been happily unemployed. In between, he'd been 'northern European sales manager' of an American computer company. What he liked about the job – apart from the huge salary and trips to southern California where 'girls go crazy when they hear an English accent' – was that the 'northern European office' comprised one person and was located in his front room. The very room in which he kept his dope.

The company was taken over. Mark was made redundant. He adjusted to the massive drop in income by cranking up his speed intake so he didn't need to buy food, and not paying any bills. He stopped paying the mortgage, phone, electricity, gas, water and TV license. Nothing happened. A stream of red letters threatened legal action, but his house wasn't repossessed. His phone wasn't cut off. Electricity, water and gas continued to flow from their appropriate taps and sockets. He even got to keep his most treasured possession: his three-litre, fuel-injected Toyota Supra sports car.

While he was still working, he'd assembled a solid wall of television, hi-fi, videos, amps, guitars and speakers, all arranged to direct maximum-volume, state-of-the-art sound and vision at one chair in the middle of the living-room. This was Mark's chair, and prolonged psychological warfare ensued if anyone else dared to sit there. Every other bit of floorspace was piled high with debris: CDs, tapes, old cigarette packets, empty beer cans, half-roached rizla packets, unfinished plates of food, unwashed mugs with mould in the bottom, smelly shoes, dirty clothes, half-inflated footballs, golf clubs, books, comics, a chess board and a game called *Fantasy For Lovers*.

****

acid stories: the erect penis-coloured Supra
One of Mark's hobbies was racing his erect penis-coloured Supra through the narrow country lanes near his house in Kent, on acid, while the rest of us hung on in terror. It's scary enough being a passenger when you're tripping: driving was a minor miracle. We had no idea if he was driving safely, but we seemed to get there alive. As he was often stopped doing 110mph at 2am, stoned and half-drunk, with no tax or insurance, it was another minor miracle that he was never even cautioned, let alone arrested.

'I was just born lucky,' Mark would say.

He pushed that luck to the limit. One time he spun off a narrow country lane at a point where the road contoured around a hill. The car hit loose gravel at 80mph and launched itself into space before crashing down onto the slope below, rebounding over a hedge, uprooting two small trees and disappearing into a field of wheat.

A crowd of passing motorists began to assemble. His friend Tris, who'd been standing on the passenger seat with his upper body through the sun-roof, was sprawled across the roof of the car, either dead or unconscious.

It didn't look good. Mark turned on the radio. It worked. Tris groaned. Not dead. The other passenger, Si, who'd been sitting on the window of the passenger door, was also stirring. Mark tried the ignition. It started first time. He drove off through the wheat, only the aerial visible, and out of the gate on the far side of the field. When the police arrived, he was gone.

Unable to afford the petrol-guzzling Supra, he finally traded it for a Honda 650 motorbike, which was twice as fast and twice as dangerous. Every journey became a TT race. 'And besides,' he said, 'girls go crazy when they see you walk into a pub stroking your purple helmet'.

****

acid stories: the Cheshire Cat

Mark had a lump of wood embedded beneath the skin of his left hand. He acquired it from playing Paintball, a game in which supposed adults run around in the woods firing paint pellets at one other. Asked to raise a team to oppose some chemists, he'd produced a slightly-scary bunch of bikers, minor criminals, speed-freaks, slackers, and me. At lunch, having won every round with embarrassing ease, everyone on Mark's team took a tab of acid. This didn't stop us winning, but it did add an element of confusion to the afternoon. I spent half-an-hour attacking a small plant before I realised that everyone else was having a tea break.

During the next game, Mark slipped. His hand went down to break his fall and a broken branch, sticking out of the mud, pierced his palm. It passed clean through his hand and out the other side. He stood up. The wood extended about six inches on either side.

Mark held his hand up for inspection. The sight made my head spin.

Someone drove him to a hospital. He wandered into the sterile glare of the busy emergency department, still wide-eyed and tripping. A nurse asked him if it hurt. As she spoke, another accident came in. Without waiting for his answer, she stuck a nitrous-oxide mask over his face and raced off. Everyone forgot about Mark. When they finally remembered him, the doctor had to wrestle the nitrous oxide tank away from him.

'I'm afraid this is going to hurt,' he said, as he yanked the wood - or most of it - out of Mark's hand. As it came out, Mark was grinning like the Cheshire Cat.

****

planning

Physically, Mark was a fine advert for a speed-only diet. Tall, lean and muscular, he remained in perfect health. The amphetamines made his veins and muscles bulge like a boxer pumped up for a fight. Still, we both sensed that he needed a change before he sank too deeply into this slacker lifestyle. And anyway, we knew his debts must *eventually* catch up with him.

'What you need,' I told him, 'is to travel.'

What I actually meant was that I wanted to travel myself, and Mark seemed a good companion. Not perfect: he was too selfish and intense. But you had to accept Mark for what he was. He had a vitality, an energy. Mark thought he was Superman, invincible and indestructible, and when you were with him, he tended to make you feel the same way too. Life was a game. Weird things happened, such as the time someone fed his Doberman a tab of LSD and it ejaculated all over the carpet in the middle of a party. He was also, I figured, a useful person to have along if things ever got ugly. If we were arrested, or had to fight our way out of some dark Third World backstreet. Mark could handle that sort of shit – even if he did make it more likely to happen in the first place.

I planned the usual trip to Asia. I spent months researching it. I scribbled timetables on scraps of paper that filled my house: when to see leatherback turtles in Malaysia and Komodo Dragons in Indonesia; how to avoid the monsoon in India while arriving in Thailand in the cool season.

Then Mark saw a programme about hallucinogenic plants in South America.

'Let's go there,' he suggested.

Well, why not? I buried myself beneath another hastily-assembled mountain of guidebooks. I phoned travel agents. I compiled lists of equipment. I pored over maps and planned routes.

Mark went to a field and picked two thousand magic mushrooms.

It was a month before we were due to leave, and Mark still had huge debts. I suggested he go to Amsterdam and make a false travel insurance claim, but he was too lazy. I suggested he sold his bike, but he couldn't bring himself to part with it. Then we hit upon the idea of him going bankrupt. You fill in a form and all your debts disappear. Where was the catch? But there was no catch. With one bound, as they say, he was free. The building society still didn't ask him to move out. The Inland Revenue even gave him a tax rebate.

And, as I knew all along, I had to lend him the rest of the money.

****

luggage
The next bad sign was Mark's luggage.

Melissa and I had staggered off the plane, our rucksacks bulging with the latest expedition-quality, ultra-lite vibram-gortex-qualofil-hydrolite-aquadril-pertex camping gear. We had torches, compasses, guidebooks, thermals, fleeces, gortex overtrousers and the lightest camping stove in the world (not that I could ever get the fucker to work). We had mosquito nets, coils, DEET, anti-malaria tablets, six types of antibiotics, anti-fungal creams, antihistamine cream, eight types of bandages and plasters and wound dressings, sterile syringes and Tropical Medical Kits. We had glucose tablets and concentrated power-bars for mountain survival. We had travel plugs, lightweight travel towels the size of a handkerchief and toothbrushes with the ends cut off to reduce weight. We had Swiss Army penknives, and spare Swiss Army penknives in case we lost our original Swiss Army penknives.

Mark arrived in Quito with a half-empty second-hand backpack. I looked inside. One porn magazine, a large hardback copy of Stephen Hawking's *A Brief History of Time* borrowed from Chatham library, two changes of clothes and two dozen packets of king-size cigarette papers.

'I don't know if they sell Rizlas here,' he explained.

'Where's the tent?' Melissa asked. She'd arranged for Mark to borrow a very good, very expensive tent from a friend of hers.

'Well, John's car broke down on the way to the airport, and the stupid bastard was pissed anyway and turned up late in the first place, so we didn't have time to pick it up. But I've got this.' Mark pulled out a thin silk jacket. 'Did you know that silk is the warmest material known to man? And I've also got . . . this.'

He waved what looked like a small bag made of kitchen foil.

'Astronauts use it. It reflects heat inwards.'

Mark launched into a long, scientific-sounding explanation of different types of heat loss. There was no point arguing with Mark. You ended up either baffled by science, or he went on so long that you simply forgot what you were arguing about.

'I reckon that silver foil thing is crap,' Melissa muttered to me quietly.

****

the Gran Gringo

We were staying at El Gran Casino, a famous travellers' dive universally known as the 'Gran Gringo'. The Big Gringo. There's a hangout like it in most Third World cities. The original; the cheapest. Windowless rooms with damp walls and peeling paint. Collapsed, lumpy beds. Fleas, cockroaches, rats; hippies and junkies – although it was rumoured that the owner's son was a cop and if you smoked dope there you stood a good chance of ending up in prison.

The Gran Casino had some good features: a half-decent cafe, a shady cobbled courtyard and, oddly, a sauna. It stood at the bottom of a long flight of steps that led up to El Panecillo ('the Little Loaf'), a hill topped with a prominent statue of the Virgin Mary. Robbery ruled these steps off-limits for tourists. In the same street was the 'Gran Casino 2', whose bar served basket chicken and had a pool table. It became our meeting place in Quito.

The Gran Casino 2 stood near the corner of a sloping square which periodically turned into a junk market. Wooden stalls creaked beneath piles of scrap metal, broken-down kettles, rusty nails, the entrails of ancient radios, old shoes and clothes. All worn out and seemingly beyond repair.

****

Quito

Quito stretches like a finger along the central valley of the Andes – what Alexander von Humboldt called the 'Avenue of the Volcanoes'. About 12km long, it's rarely more than two wide. That makes it hard to get lost: you just work out how far north or south you are. On either side, the parallel mountains of the Cordillera Occidental and the Cordillera Oriental rise up. Their predominantly green slopes (for here on the equator the snow-line is 5,000m) are interspersed with Humboldt's great snow-capped volcanoes – Cotopaxi, Cayambe, Chimborazo. These are visible on clear mornings, while the grassy flanks of 4,800m Rucu Pichincha seem to rise right out of the city centre.

The Gran Casino stood in the Old Town, Quito's original heart, with its compact grid of colonial streets, churches and plazas. The church of San Francisco, for instance, which was begun in 1534, was the first major Spanish church to be built in South America. It commanded a huge square which street performers turned into an open-air theatre every afternoon. The Plaza de la Independencia, in contrast, was more like a small village square in southern Spain – palms sheltering young couples and weary old men – despite being flanked by the Cathedral and Presidential Palace.

The churches were decorated in the 'Quito School', a baroque fusion of Spanish and native Indian imagery. Gold plastered every altar wall from floor to ceiling. To my mind, it said more about the conquistadores' obsession with shiny metal than anything spiritual. In dimly-lit side chapels, poor Indians knelt in silent supplication before impassive, blue-eyed portraits of Jesus, Mary and various saints, all drawn in the image of the people who had enslaved them.

The Old Town was full of Quechua faces. Short Indian men in felt hats and woollen ponchos struggled uphill, bent beneath the weight of huge sacks. Indian women in their voluminous woollen skirts and pork pie hats tended little pavement stalls.

It smelt of stale piss and dampness. Old 1950s buses that once collected school children in Kansas or Idaho now groaned up the steep, too-narrow streets, belching black exhaust that enveloped pedestrians and turned the historic whitewashed facades a dirty grey. The day after we arrived, we were eating some fried rice at the back table of a Chinese restaurant (Ecuador, like the rest of South America, is full of Chinese restaurants) – when a wall of diesel smoke from a passing bus drifted through the open door. The whole room vanished inside a dense black cloud for a few seconds.

That was the Old Town. The New Town, a couple of kilometres north across the Parque El Ejido, was entirely different. It was modern(-ish), clean(-ish), quiet(-ish) and uncongested. Smarter restaurants, bars, clubs, cinemas, tour agencies offering mountain climbs and jungle trips, banks, souvenir shops and upmarket hotels all catered for the every need of tourists and expats.

Home to a million, mainly Quechua, inhabitants, Quito is a quiet and conservative town, small for a capital. It's not even the biggest city in Ecuador, the busy port of Guayaquil having taken over as the nation's economic hub. There is plenty of hustle and bustle in Quito – street sellers and markets and traffic and so on – but it stops short of the uncontrolled chaos of so many Third World capitals. That suited me just fine. I didn't like cities, anyway.

****

Mama Negra

Mark dumped his bags in his room. We went downstairs for coffee in the Gran Casino's cafe. I mentioned that there was a fiesta called 'Mama Negra' that afternoon in Latacunga, a town fifty miles south of Quito. Mark was keen, and any jet-lag was outweighed by the effect of the mushrooms. It was fiesta time.

The bus was packed with teenagers in their best gear, laughing and joking. Mark sat beside two pretty girls, squeezed into low-cut dresses, with scarlet ribbons in their hair and scarlet lipstick and 2-inch scarlet high-heels, obviously brand new. He offered them some sweets. They giggled.

'Look's like you've scored already,' said Melissa.

We reached Latacunga. The town's buildings were mainly the plain concrete boxes typical of the Ecuadorean Andes. Steel supports protruded from flat roofs in anticipation of imaginary storeys still to come. A vast, hanger-like market-building dominated one end of the main street and Cotopaxi's symmetrical cone loomed ominously over the town. At 5,897m, Cotopaxi is claimed to be the world's highest active volcano: its eruptions buried the town in 1742, 1768 and 1877 and each time the locals stoically (or maybe that should be 'stupidly'?) rebuilt it.

The streets were packed with men in baseball caps and stout women in heavy skirts and red shawls. Their jet-black hair was parted in the middle and gathered into two plaits, giving even the most ancient grandmother an incongruously girlish look.[1] We found a spot where we could see, which wasn't hard for Mark and me as we already stood head-and-shoulders above most of the crowd.

In front of us, noise and colour lit up the grey street. A procession of honking, marching bands and dancers swayed drunkenly past and disappeared around a corner. The men wore lace shirts and ponchos and danced in one line opposite the women, who hitched up their skirts and swirled them from side to side. Everyone looked exhausted from hours of continuous dancing.

Each group was accompanied by a couple of men in drag, cracking whips with mock ferocity. They'd rush threateningly at anyone straying onto the procession route, and kiss them. Other costumed characters mixed with the dancers: demons, slaves, Napoleonic soldiers and strange masked figures called *huacos*. Dressed all in white, they reminded me of Olympic fencers, except instead of an epee, they waved shields decorated with bits of glass, mirrors, matchboxes, medals, buttons and so on.

Mama Negra literally means 'black mother'. The celebrations focus around the parade of the statue of a black Virgin. Just how a black virgin came to be revered in this entirely-Quechua town remains a mystery. One explanation is that she symbolises the expulsion of the Arabs from Spain in 1492. Why the people of Latacunga should feel *that* an event worth celebrating, I've no idea.

In any case, this was no sombre Christian parade, but a Bacchanalian, pagan celebration of a complex allegorical world of strange spirits and beliefs. The Spanish may have tried to stamp out the religion they found in the Andes, but they only succeeded in diverting it, as the Indians took Christian symbols and gave them their own meanings.[2] In this way, something of the old religion of the Andes survives. And we were looking at it.

At the heart of each ensemble, one man shuffled along with a pole strapped to his back, usually bent double and looking fit to drop. And no wonder. Impaled on the pole was an entire pig, ready for roasting, eyes staring blindly upwards. Uncooked chickens, guinea pigs, packets of cigarettes and bottles of rum or *aguardiente* hung from the carcass.

Other bottles passed freely between the marchers. The bands sounded as if they assembled each year without rehearsal, hoping to remember the tune from the year before. Which, I found out later, is more or less what does happen. They make it easier by playing only one tune all day. Marching bands in Ecuador only ever play one tune, as far as I can tell, which consists of a few bars repeated interminably. Even that was a fair enough achievement, considering how drunk everyone seemed.

If the participants were falling-down drunk, then many of the spectators had already fallen. Little groups stumbled past, clinging to bottles of rum and to each other. Mark and I invested two dollars in a superior-looking brand. We wandered through the crowds, swigging rum, dodging drunks and stepping over bodies asleep on the pavement. Three teenage boys waylaid us, slapping us on the back and repeatedly shouting 'you are *gringos, gringos*', just in case we'd forgotten and mistakenly assumed we were Ecuadoreans. The boy in the middle hung limply between his friends, unfocused eyes pointing towards the pavement. The other two insisted that we share some of their rum. To be polite, we insisted that they have some of ours. So, naturally, they insisted we have more of theirs.

Soon, both bottles were empty.

I noticed Mark was no longer walking in a straight line. The next time I looked, he was dancing with a six-foot transvestite dressed in a Shirley Temple wig, a pink nightie and enormous Adidas trainers. The crowd cheered them on. The transvestite kissed Mark.

'Looks like you've scored again,' Melissa joked.

Mark's knees gave way. He crashed backwards in a heap on the pavement.

'And I thought Mark could hold his drink,' I said to Melissa. Melissa was looking down at me from above. I worked out that I must be lying on the pavement too. Melissa started to revolve.

Now I understood why everyone was in such a state. Alcohol hits without warning at this altitude. One moment you're fine, the next . . . unconscious. There's no happy bit in the middle, no hazy realisation that you're smashed, barely even time to make a fool of yourself. Just . . . wham. Knockout.

I sat up gingerly. I was dimly aware of Mark struggling to his feet and careering around behind us in wildly unbalanced circles, after which he came back and sat down beside me.

'I always feel better after throwing up,' he grinned.

'We'd better find a hotel,' Melissa said. We hauled ourselves upright and lent on her from different sides. One 5ft4 woman trying to hold up two 6ft men. First, my weight would send us veering to the right, then Mark's counterbalancing weight brought us lurching back to the left. Around us, other trios performed a similar routine.

'Hey, Mark, there's those girls you were chatting up on the bus,' Melissa said suddenly.

Mark turned his head instinctively to look. Unfortunately, he did so a little too quickly for his stomach to handle. A jet of liquid vomit arched from his mouth and landed on one of the girls' prized red stilettos. She stood transfixed, her smile frozen in shock. Then she burst into tears. We tried to look apologetic as Melissa dragged us hurriedly off into the crowd.

The rest was a blur. I recall a series of run-down hotels, looking in vain for a room. Pandemonium at the bus-station. Melissa forcing us onto a bus ahead of a stampede of Ecuadoreans. Slumping into the seat behind the driver. I remember that he was wearing a brand-new leather jacket, still crisp and stiff. The bus pulled off, lurching over potholes I'd hardly noticed on the way down. They seemed like craters. I was going to throw up.

But where?

The only open window was the driver's. Reaching it meant resting my head sideways on his shoulder. I just made it. Most of it went out of the window, but a few bits dribbled down the back of the driver's new jacket. He didn't look happy. Then, my head still on his shoulder, I fell asleep.

****

a small demonstration
I awoke on the bed of our hotel room. My head was throbbing. Mark was asleep on the floor. Melissa was rolling a joint. Mark came to and discovered that he'd lost his silk jacket. A good start. We wandered out to get breakfast in a cafe: fried eggs, bread and coffee.

On our way back, we passed a small demonstration. A couple of hundred striking teachers were half-heartedly chanting and waving placards. They'd been on strike for six months without pay. Knots of soldiers waited idly with machine guns. Two tanks were parked at one end of the street.

****

angels' bollocks
We spent the afternoon in the hotel, nursing hangovers. Mark decided to pass the time by explaining some religion to Melissa.

'The people here are animists,' he said. 'Well, they're now Christian, technically, but underneath that they're still animists.'

'Isn't that a bit racist?' Melissa said.

'What?'

'Well, calling them animals.'

'Not animals, Melissa. Anim-ists. Look, animists are people who believe that everything has a spirit, or soul. People, animals, plants, rocks, whatever. That's the big difference from Christianity. Christianity basically sees mankind as a special case, superior to the rest of creation. I don't think a Christian would argue that the life of, say, a tree or an animal, is of equal importance to the life of a human. To an animist, all of Nature is equal.

'The Spanish, you see, were more selective about what they admitted into the Kingdom of Heaven. Never mind rocks and animals, 16th century Europeans didn't even credit all humans with souls. It was pretty commonly accepted, for instance, that Blacks had no souls, and so-called 'theologians' debated whether or not the newly-discovered Indians possessed them.'

'What if you were Chinese?' asked Melissa, who was half-Chinese.

'Well, you're half-European, so I guess you'd have had half a soul.'

'Maybe they'd let you in from the waist up,' I suggested. 'With your legs dangling below the clouds?'

'I'm short enough as it is. I'd spend eternity staring at angels' bollocks.'

'I don't think angels have bollocks,' said Mark.

****

Otavalo

Like every other tourist in Ecuador, we went to Otavalo. Half-way there, I woke from a doze to find the bus was overtaking a car that was overtaking two trucks on a blind corner with a sheer drop off one side. A truck was aiming straight towards us, headlights on full beam and horn blaring. I froze in my seat. But just in time, all three overtaking vehicles swerved back onto our side of the road and the oncoming truck thundered past.

That's Ecuadorean driving for you. If you come up behind a slower vehicle, you overtake it. There's no namby-pamby stuff like waiting for a clear stretch of road, or checking for oncoming traffic. After all, we've all got to die sometime. Right?

Otavalo, two hours north of Quito, nestles in a densely-populated, fertile farming region of lakes and volcanoes whose slopes are parcelled up into patchworks of green fields. The town itself is famous for its market. Traders come from all over South America, peddling every conceivable tourist handicraft from jade masks and oil paintings to dope pipes and hippie jewellery.

Mostly, though, the market is famous for the Otavalo Indians' own alpaca wool rugs, weavings, jumpers and ponchos, which have made them one of South America's most prosperous indigenous groups. The girls, short and plump, wear red-and-black skirts, delicate white-lace blouses and gold necklaces. Proud young men fix you with an even, direct gaze. Their hair is black as tar and tied into a long pony-tail, like Red Indian braves in Westerns.

****

Mama Rosita's

The hole-in-the-wall cafe that we adopted, Mama Rosita's, was a typical Ecuadorean eatery. It consisted of four tables, grimy walls with old posters and a sign in English advertising 'Mama Rosita's world-famous pancakes'. The kitchen was a greasy booth at the back of the room.

The eponymous proprietor was assisted – or more often hindered – by two of the shortest women I've ever seen. Since we'd been in Otavalo, we'd noticed some especially tiny people (and most Ecuadoreans are short enough to start with). Maybe they were the product of some genetic disorder, for most seemed retarded as well. They were bottom of the local pecking order, and mainly employed as (no doubt cheaper) substitutes for donkeys. Men well under 5ft tall staggered past beneath double-beds or wardrobes, held in place by a strap running across their forehead and behind the load – a pre-Conquest carrying device called a *tumpline*.

Sitting down, we could still see over the heads of Mama Rosita's two helpers. The two women buzzed around the room, knocking things over and messing things up until Rosita shouted at them in exasperation. She'd send one on some errand – to borrow some salt from a neighbouring shop, for instance, only for her to return with the wrong thing. Then Rosita would scold her again, while her friend pulled silly faces behind Rosita's back – only to stare innocently into space if she looked round. Both women were about fifty.

Rosita herself was a friendly, maternal woman, always eager to tell us what we were eating. We might have preferred ignorance, for her specialities seemed to be either the boiled skin or stomach lining of cows. Luckily, these less-than-enticing delicacies came with soup, rice, potatoes, fried banana, avocado and a glass of watered-down fruit juice. This constitutes a basic set-meal – known variously as *almuerzo* (lunch), *cena* (supper) or simply *comida* (food) – that remains much the same the length of South America. Only the origin and quality of the lump of meat varies, occasionally reaching the dizzy heights of chicken or fish. There was no sign of the world-famous pancakes.

****

the animal market
Saturday was market day in Otavalo. In fact, there were three markets in Otavalo. While the tourists bought their alpaca rugs and ponchos in the plaza, the locals crowded into the market at the other end of town to buy food, jeans and Metallica T-shirts. And then there was the animal market. Out in a grassy clearing on the edge of town, sharp-eyed farmers and their solid, no-nonsense wives inspected an assortment of cows, pigs, horses and donkeys. One by one, the animals were sold and led away quietly. Only the pigs seemed upset. Their new owners – and their wives and children – dragged the reluctant swine through the dust by ropes tied around their necks; a tug-of-war with the pig bucking and digging in its trotters and honking and squealing. It took a half-dozen people to heave a large animal onto the back of a truck – lifting it by the tail and ears – from where it continued to honk in distress. It's said that pigs are the most intelligent domesticated animals.

****

campesinos, mestizos and latinos
The basic Andean mix consists of native Indian (mainly Quechua) and Spanish. Roughly five out of ten people in Ecuador, Peru and Bolivia are full-blooded Indians, known in the highlands as 'campesinos' (which literally means 'peasants'). Three or four are 'mestizos' (mixed-race) and only one is a 'Latino', or 'blanco' – that is, a 'white' person with Spanish/European ancestry.[3]

It's not quite that straightforward. As Ronald Wright says in his book Cut Stones and Crossroads, *a 'mestizo' is often a full-blooded Indian who's moved to a town, learned Spanish instead of Quechua and adopted Western clothes. And some of the elite 'Latino' families in Peru trace their ancestry to liaisons between conquistadores and Inca noblewomen, making them ethnically mestizos.*

Despite this blurring of the edges, it's glaringly obvious that a mainly European-descended Latino elite rules a mainly Indian population. Politicians, landowners, businessmen, judges, lawyers, doctors, journalists and writers are almost all Latino. The more 'Indian' a person, the poorer he or she is likely to be. The more 'Latino', the richer. (This rule seems to apply to South American countries, too, with Bolivia, Ecuador and Peru bottom of the poverty scale and Argentina at the top.)

In short, the Andes are Indian nations ruled by a Latin minority. It's a hidden system of racism and apartheid, and a social order that has changed little since the Conquest, 500 years ago.

****

a walk on the páramo

Leaving Mark in our hotel trying to chat up an Israeli backpacker, Melissa and I went for a walk on the páramo, Ecuador's grassy upland moors. We took a taxi to some lakes called the Lagunas Mojanda. Thirty miles north of the equator, it reminded me of the Scottish highlands. Tough grasses and heather-like moss covered craggy hills and waterlogged bogs. An early-morning mist hung over the lakes.

'And I thought Ecuador was in the tropics,' Melissa joked.

We planned to hike to a small pre-Colombian ruin, Cochasquí, about three hours away, where we could catch a bus back. But at 4,000m, ten-minute climbs became one-hour slogs. We gasped for breath at every step. The 'grass' turned out to be waist-deep and painfully spiky. After four hours, I had to admit that we were lost. A number of vague paths criss-crossed a broad moorland valley. We picked one and slogged on, hoping it would lead somewhere, until we reached a solitary house beside a wooded creek. An old man lent on a gate and eyed us warily.

'Is this the way to Cochasquí' I asked.

'*Si,*' the old man nodded sagely. So at least we were on track.

'How far is it to Cochasquí?'

'*Si.*'

'Do you have the time?'

'*Si*,' he replied.

'What time is it, please.'

'*Si*.'

'Is this the way to Otavalo?'

The old man paused, considered this question for a while, then nodded again. I gave up.

'*Si*.'

We carried on. After a while, three men and a young boy ambled up the track towards us, probably returning from the fields. They all carried machetes. I wasn't used to meeting people with something as large, sharp and deadly as a machete. It doesn't happen to me very often in London.

Melissa wasn't used to it, either. 'Quick, give me your penknife,' she demanded.

'What use will a penknife be against three guys with machetes?' I asked.

'It's alright for you. They rape women, you know,' Melissa said. 'Just give it to me.'

'I still don't see what good a penknife will be,' I insisted.

'It'll be more good than you.'

Melissa had just read a horrific account of some miners in Colombia, or maybe Venezuela. The sex-starved men, stuck in remote jungle, hired a prostitute to come to their camp, where they raped her. Then, to prevent her going to the police, they decapitated her.

'They can kill me, but they're not going to rape me,' she vowed.

The men looked surprised to see us, and asked where we were going. I explained in broken Spanish. Melissa clutched the penknife beneath her jacket. But the men lead us to a little village and waved goodbye without bothering to rape or decapitate us.

A small building in the main square had a sign outside saying 'bus station', so we went inside.

'What time does the bus go back to Otavalo?' I asked.

'Tuesday,' said the woman behind the desk, without looking up. Today was Sunday. Instead, we negotiated an expensive lift from the only car in the village, when we finally persuaded its owner to stop polishing it. We'd ended up over twenty miles off-course. Not bad for a three-hour stroll.

****

the rabies jab

Back in Quito, we decided, in a moment of travellers' paranoia, to have a rabies vaccination. The jab extends the time you've got to reach a hospital, when bitten, from one day to a week, a consideration if trekking in remote areas. We went to the American hospital. As the Ecuadorean system requires, we bought the medicine – which came in a single bottle with ten doses – first, and waited for the doctor, an American reassuringly called Dr Ringenberg. An Ecuadorean doctor passed.

'I'll give you the injection,' he offered, picking up the ten-person bottle. 'Who wants it?'

'That's for ten people.' I pointed out.

'But there's only one bottle here,' the doctor replied, puzzled.

We decided to wait for Dr Ringenberg.

Chapter 2
Peru: buses, bimbos and banditos

'In 1531, another great villain journeyed with a number of men to the kingdoms of
Peru . . . he criminally murdered and plundered his way through the region, razing
towns and cities to the ground and slaughtering and otherwise tormenting in the
most barbaric fashion imaginable the people who lived there.'
BARTOLOMÉ DE LAS CASAS, *A VERY BRIEF ACCOUNT OF THE DESTRUCTION OF THE
INDIES, 1552*

warrior woman
Three weeks before I was due to leave England, I still didn't know if Mark
would be coming with me. It was a grey and overcast autumn day in north
London and some workmen were digging up the pavement outside my
house with pneumatic drills. My doorbell rang and there was Melissa,
standing on my front step in tears.

'I want to come with you,' she said.

'But you don't even know where Ecuador is,' I pointed out.

'Well, it's got to be better than here.'

Melissa had her reasons for wanting to leave London, and love for me was
only one of them.

Melissa was thirty-three – three years older than me – and beautiful. More
beautiful (and healthy) than someone with her past had any right to be.
She looked ten years younger than she was, when she should have looked
ten years older. She was slim and athletic with olive skin, long brown hair
and seductive almond eyes. Half-Chinese and half-Scottish, her Eurasian
looks gave her a dark sensuality.

'Mixed-race girls are always the most beautiful,' she told me.

She was open, friendly and quick to laugh, with an unaffected charm and
a natural smile. This brightness was broken by periods of introspection,
and she would go off on ten day silent meditation retreats, her way of
dealing with the traumas of her past.

It wasn't easy making sense of Melissa. If her life story had been told straightforwardly, it would have been confusing enough. But she made it harder by explaining things in a way that only made sense if you already knew the story. When I first met her, she'd just split up from a long relationship and some tangled association with a martial arts group.

'Well, it's not really martial arts.'

'Oh. So what's it about, then?'

'Cheese.'

'Cheese?'

'Yes, cheese. It's about stimulating the flow of cheese around your body.'

'Must be pretty runny cheese.'

'No, not *cheese*. Chi. C-H-I. Chi. It's the Chinese word for energy. Opening the energy channels in your body. In this case, through movement. It's the basis of all Chinese medicine.'

Melissa explained that her last boyfriend had been sleeping with all her friends. On top of that, she was living in a house with her mum and another man, who had terrible arguments and fights. In the meantime, she'd been studying martial arts with a brilliant and inspirational teacher, who dragged her out into the park at 5am on dark December mornings and made her wave a stick around for hours.

Eventually, the penny dropped.

'So, are these all the same person?' I asked.

'Are who the same person?' Melissa asked back.

'Well, the guy living with your mum. Is he called Peter?'

'Yes.'

'And your ex-boyfriend. Is he called Peter?'

'Yes.'

'And this teacher bloke? Peter?'

'Yes.'

'So, they're all the same person then?'

Melissa considered this proposition for a moment.

'Well . . . I suppose they are.'

She looked surprised, as if making the discovery for the first time herself.

Melissa had unwisely persuaded Peter and her mother to buy a house in Chiswick together, and now the three of them were stuck. The house was full of his fishing gear and her mother's Chinese medicines. The freezer was stuffed with maggot balls and other bait, and when you opened the fridge you were faced with pickled bats' intestines or frogs' skin. Melissa's mum and her ex-boyfriend argued all the time and drove each other mad, and their driving each other mad was driving Melissa mad.

A constant stream of Peter's adoring disciples and assorted New Age gurus, spiritual teachers, Buddhist monks and Indian yoga masters wandered through the house. Apart from the Indian yogi, who got up at four every morning to have a shit before the sun rose and seemed to do very little after that, most of the great spiritual teachers seemed to be screwing around. Melissa explained the New Age to me.

'It's like musicians and groupies. These guys have loads of charisma and energy and dynamism. What they say is often genuinely inspiring. They are attractive – their energy attracts people. That's how they got to be leaders and gurus in the first place. So all these starry-eyed young women latch onto them and keep sticking their big, firm, young, juicy tits in their faces. What do you *expect* is going to happen?' Melissa pushed out her pert A-cups as far as they would go. Melissa loved breasts; she loved to talk about them and look at them, and even to feel them now and again, given the chance. She just didn't have them herself. Small but perfectly-formed, that was Melissa.

'Yes, perfectly formed,' she pouted, 'and at least they'll never be saggy.'

Melissa's parents had divorced when she was fourteen. Her father had been in the Army and she had grown up on a succession of military bases around the world. She'd been to various boarding schools, dropped out of art college and become a junkie, financing her habit by shoplifting.

'I went a whole year without buying anything. Not one thing. I'd just walk into a shop, pick something up and leave. It got to the point where I'd steal anything. I once took a leather jacket out of a shop window – just walked into the display, took it off the dummy and walked out with it.'

She went to live in Hong Kong, city of junkies and junk. She began sending smack to a friend in New Zealand, concealed in duty-free cigarettes, until the friend begged her to stop. She ran a hostel with her boyfriend, which did well until the Triads turned up to repossess the furniture. She worked as a DJ in Hong Kong's biggest nightclub and as an actress in dozens of cheap Hong Kong martial arts films, which are always on the lookout for attractive European girls.

'My big moment was playing the girlfriend of some big kung-fu star. I forget his name. I only had one line, but I was on the poster for the movie, too. I remember being stuck with my dad in a traffic-jam in Hong Kong. On the bus in front of us was this huge picture of me, naked. I had to keep pointing interesting things out to my dad so he wouldn't notice it.'

After the hostel folded, she worked in a Triad gambling club until she was sacked for suggesting to the boss, in Cantonese, that his mother was not the most hygienic of women. 'Du-le-la-mo-chow-hi,' she said, and two men chased her down the road with meat-cleavers.[4] Triad bosses aren't used to being addressed like that by waitresses. She sent a friend to pick up her wages.

She then went to Kho Samui and tried to smoke so much dope that she didn't miss the heroin. After being on the island for a year, she happened to witness the murder of an Australian tourist. The Australian got drunk in a bar and was badmouthing the locals when a Thai boy ran outside, grabbed a rock and ran back in. Suddenly the lights went out. When they came back on, the Australian lay in a bloody heap on the floor. The next day, the manager of the bar came to Melissa's hut and asked her 'if you saw anything unusual last night'. It was time to leave.

Despite a long and varied criminal past, she'd only been arrested once, while at art college in Brighton, for stealing a flower from a display that spelt 'Welcome to Brighton'. As she bent down to pick the flower, sirens wailed and two police cars screeched up, blue lights flashing. Two cops jumped out, threw her in the back of one of the cars and took her to the police station, where she was kept in overnight and eventually fined fifty pounds for 'theft of public property'. The next day she went back to the flower display and fished out the bag of heroin which she'd managed to drop just in time.

Returning to London, she met Peter, the martial arts teacher, and helped him set up his school. She put her charm and vivacious personality to good use, promoting the school and making newcomers feel welcome and answering endless telephone queries. In return, Peter used her as a crash-test dummy, throwing her across various wooden community centre floors to demonstrate moves to his classes. He dragged her up mountains and glaciers in the summer, and took her rock-climbing in Scotland in winter. She stopped being Junkie Girl and became Warrior Woman. After six years, training six hours a day, her movement was strong and graceful and she was leading classes and retreats on her own.

Peter had attracted a tight little circle of devotees. They trained together, lived together, went out together – and then spent their holidays together, at the centre in Wales that Peter and Melissa had set up. It was a regular little suburban cult. And this group had been Melissa's whole life since returning from Hong Kong. She didn't know *anything* else. She didn't know *anyone* else.

'That's when', she said, 'I discovered that Peter was screwing all my friends.'

But Peter had developed his own, unique style. There were no other equally inspiring, dynamic teachers. If she walked out on Peter, she left it all behind: her training, her friends, her home.

It was a tough choice.

And she thought I was odd.

'At least I've done something in my life,' she said. 'All you ever do is read books.'

Melissa kept telling me that we were totally incompatible.

'I'm a Leo and you're a Gemini. You're a rabbit, which is OK, but your chart is all air, which means thinking and words and no feelings. And you're spleen energy in Chinese medicine, which means you're indecisive and absorbing, like a blob. And your birthday is on the 19th – nine and one added together means you're a number one.'

'You're full of number two,' I said, not entirely happy to be called a blob. Melissa believed in horoscopes, Chinese astrology, numerology, tarot, the I-Ching and feng shui.

'But,' she claimed, 'I can't stand all that 'find-the-goddess-within-you' New Age crystal stuff. I went to a witches' coven once, somewhere on the South Downs. These women were all going on about nature and the earth, so I suggested we go out to the woods. They looked horrified. 'But we can't go . . . *outside*. It's . . . dark,' one of them said. All they wanted to do was get stoned and grope each other's tits. Well, they did have nice breasts. Anyway, so much for nature worship. Although, if you must know, my goddess archetype is Aphrodite, who stands for sensuality.'

'It's funny,' she said just before we left. 'I had my horoscope done about eighteen months ago, after I split up with Peter and before I met you. The woman who did it told me I was going to travel. At the time, I didn't expect to go anywhere, but we've already been to Israel, Egypt, France and Spain, and now we're off to loads of South American countries.'

'Very interesting,' I said, not listening. I didn't believe in horoscopes, except as a way to chat up girls. 'What else did she tell you?'

'Someone close to me is going to die,' she replied.

****

two fat ladies

Melissa, with her olive skin and long, dark hair, could have been a Latino herself. Every time we asked for directions in South America, people would look at her and launch into a high-speed stream of Spanish, to be met with a blank stare. Melissa wasn't good at languages.

My Spanish wasn't much better. By the time Mark arrived in Quito, I was able to talk about anything – as long as it involved a bus, a meal or a hotel. Occasionally, I even understood the reply.

We'd decided to leave Quito and head for Peru. The rabies injection had made me sick, but we decided I might as well recover on a bus. I stumbled down to the bus station.

Quito's new bus terminal was called Terminal Terrestre, which literally translates as Earth Station, conjuring up images of futuristic landing pads for high-tech space-buses. Sadly, there was nothing space age about either the terminal or Ecuadorean buses in general – unless you count driving off the edge of cliffs as space travel. It was one of those modern-ish concrete buildings that look run-down about two days after they are opened. Built on three levels, the upper two were full of fast-food joints and stalls selling biscuits, cakes and cheap plastic gifts. In the basement, bus companies vied for passengers from a line of booths. Touts shouted destinations and pushed us towards their window.

I bought three tickets for the night bus to Aguas Verdes on the border with Peru. I congratulated myself on conducting a whole conversation in what I thought was perfect Spanish. Our bus was one of a line outside, their roofs being piled high with rice-sacks and boxes and bundles of all shapes and sizes. I climbed in and flopped into my seat. I congratulated myself, too, on getting the front row – the only place a 6ft gringo can stretch his legs.

Mark and Melissa disappeared to find a quiet corner to smoke a joint. I just wanted to sit and feel ill. But no sooner had they gone, two enormously fat women, mounds of sweating flesh in jogging pants and sweat-tops, hauled themselves onto the bus and demanded my seats.

I mumbled that I'd reserved the seats, but Mark and Melissa had gone off with the tickets. My head throbbed. I felt sick. The last thing I needed was an argument. I tried to ignore the women, hoping they'd sit elsewhere. But a hysterical torrent of high-pitched machine-gun Spanish suggested that they weren't going to go away. I stood firm and waited for some sign of the other two.

Twenty minutes later, Mark and Melissa wandered back. Melissa was demonstrating karate kicks to Mark. They found the bus in chaos. The fat women were screaming at me, the conductor and everyone in sight. A dozen other people, who might or might not have been connected with the bus company, were adding their opinions. I was mumbling '*reservada, reservada*' (or something along those lines) and trying not to throw up.

'Thank God you're back,' I said. 'Show these two lardbuckets our tickets.'

Melissa showed them the tickets. The conductor, the women and the crowd of onlookers studied them in turn. They were passed around and discussed in knowing tones. Finally, the conductor gave them back to me. He pointed at the date. They were for tomorrow.

Humiliation. I yielded the seats gracelessly. The women collapsed into them and began stuffing themselves with the contents of two enormous crisp packets, as if it was a major medical crisis. I summoned up my Spanish and my best show of indignation and turned to the conductor.

'The people at the counter have sold me tickets for the wrong day. I *clearly* asked for today, not tomorrow.' Of course, I clearly hadn't asked for anything *clearly*.

'I am sorry. You must pay again – or come back tomorrow.'

After more discussion, the bus agreed on a 'surcharge' and we slunk off to our reallocated seats at the back of the bus, next to a toilet with a broken door. So much for my Spanish.

'*Ocho, ocho*,' said Mark as we sat down.

'What?'

'*Ocho, ocho*. Eighty-eight. Two fat ladies. In Spanish.'

'Thanks for your help,' I muttered. My head felt like someone was driving nails into it.

We planned to catch the night bus to the border, and then continue down the coast of Peru and inland to Cuzco non-stop – two thousand miles on clapped-out buses. It would take five solid days and nights. It would have cost $200 to fly. It was a mad idea, especially as I was ill before we'd started.

'$200. No way. I can't afford $200,' Mark said, so the bus it was.

We left Quito. Night fell with equatorial suddenness, switching from intense high-altitude glare to total blackness in minutes. Ten minutes after leaving the Terminal it was dark. We crossed a low pass in the western cordillera and the road began to snake down towards the coast. It twisted and fell, not for a few minutes or a half-hour, but on and on throughout the night, the bus perpetually in first or second gear as the driver eased around endless hairpin bends. I struggled vainly to find a position to rest my head without having my temple pierced, each time we hit a bump, by the rusty metal spike that stuck out from the window frame.

Sometime in the early hours we stopped at a vast open-air restaurant. The temperate coolness of Quito was gone, and the air was warm, humid and tropical, even though it was the middle of the night. To the left, a huge speaker blasted out *criollo* pop and salsa to a crowd of smartly-dressed dancers kicking up a storm in the dusty parking lot. I watched them while our driver ate his meal.

The next morning we awoke to humidity and banana plantations. Ecuador is, after all, South America's original banana republic. Huge areas of the coastal lowlands are given over to production of the fruit, mainly for export. Until 1973, when oil took over, bananas were the country's main foreign-currency earner. The plants, with their man-sized leaves, clusters of unripe green fruits and dramatic purple buds, pressed in on the narrow road, leaves brushing the side of the bus.

****

the spoon
We reached the small border town of Aguas Verdes in mid-morning. We found the Ecuadorean immigration office tucked away in a backstreet and got our passports stamped.

'Now throw that dope away,' I said.

Mark and Melissa both looked at me pityingly.

'OK, then smoke it. But hurry up, because the border closes at midday.'

We found an alley and I forced the two of them to chainsmoke spliffs until the dope was gone. I didn't smoke anything. I've got this thing about drugs and borders, you see.

The border was right in the middle of a hectic, noisy market. Here on the coast, men wore T-shirts and jeans and women wore light summer dress-es. Boys pulled wooden carts laden with jumpers and jackets. Women stood behind stalls of plastic toys and cassette players. Above the bustle, a large banner read: *Bienvenidos a Peru. Welcome to Peru.* We pushed our way through the crowds.

As we stepped across the border, a throng of men and boys besieged us with offers of rides to Tumbes, the first town in Peru. One small boy even offered to take the three of us and our bags the thirty miles on his push-bike. He seemed serious. Melissa and Mark grinned stupidly at the chaos.

The cars were monsters. American giants from the Fifties and Sixties, with tail-fins and huge bonnets. For many years Peru had banned import-ed cars. The ones that were there before the ban had been kept going until they literally fell to bits. When that happened, their owners simply carried on driving the bits. A half-dozen of these dinosaurs cruised beside us, the drivers urging us in. *'Tumbes, muy lejos,* Tumbes, very far,' they insisted. Windows and whole doors were missing, windscreens knocked out, wings smashed, lights broken. They were piles of moving scrap, but marginally more likely to get us to Tumbes than the boy on his bicycle. I looked to Mark and Melissa for help, but abandoned that idea when I saw the glazed looks in their eyes and settled on one of the beat-up taxis, for a price of two *soles* each. It had large holes in the floor through which we could inspect the potholes in the road, and no windows. At least it would be faster than the bus.

'Looks like that car from the 'Dukes of Hazard',' Mark joked.

We stopped at the Peruvian immigration office to get our passports stamped again. For some reason, the immigration office was two kilome-tres down the road from the border. Having heard stories about Peruvian taxis driving off with your luggage, I waited in the car until Mark and Melissa came out. I looked at the driver and his mate – who was, I noticed, the largest person I'd seen since leaving England. He smiled men-acingly into his mirror. The driver was clutching a spoon.

When we'd completed the formalities, the driver announced that the two *soles* was only to take us to immigration. The fare to Tumbes was 15 *soles* each. Mark and Melissa sat looking stoned. The driver drove on for a while, then stopped. The road was deserted. He turned to face us.

'15 *soles* . . .' he repeated, punching the air with the spoon for emphasis '. . . each.'

In Quito, we'd heard one of those travellers' tales about an English tourist who'd been robbed in Venezuela. During the robbery, he'd had a fork shoved up his arse to distract him as his assailants made their getaway. Mark and Melissa sat staring at the spoon. At least a spoon was round: if push came to shove (so to speak) it would probably be more comfortable than a fork.

If we got out of the car we faced a long walk and would lose the two *soles* we'd paid in advance. (Yes, I know: *never* pay in advance.) While it only amounted to about £1 each, there was a principle involved. I insisted on the original price. The driver waved his spoon menacingly. Mark and Melissa followed its movement as if hypnotised. Eventually, the driver and I agreed on 15 *soles* for us all and we set off again. Only to find that we were in . . .

. . . the slowest vehicle in Peru. A half-dozen buses roared past as we crawled along. I watched the road bump past through the holes in the floor. The boy on his bicycle would have been faster.

When we reached Tumbes, we discovered the purpose of the spoon. It was to open the boot.

****

Tumbes
Tumbes is a hot, nondescript provincial town, a couple of kilometres from the sea. Its central plaza is shaded by palm trees. There's a church and stalls selling greasy snacks on street corners. It's one of those places that looks neither modern nor especially old. Peru and Ecuador occasionally fight minor wars over the exact location of their border, but nothing to interest the rest of the world.[5] But Tumbes does have some significance in South American history, for it was the first Inca town the Spanish ever saw. And, as every travel book on Peru has to contain an account of the Conquest, this seems as good a place as any to give you mine.[6]

In 1524 Francisco Pizarro – a veteran campaigner who in 1513 had been among the first party of Europeans to hack through the Panamanian jungle and see the Pacific – sailed down the coast of Colombia and Ecuador and encountered a small Inca trading boat laden with produce.

Figuring that the boat must have come from somewhere, Pizarro returned the next year – and reached Tumbes. Two of his men, Pedro de Candia and Alonso de Molina, were sent ashore. They were well-received and reported of a splendid, well-ordered city, with great temples covered in gold and silver. This was what the Spanish had sought since the conquest of the Aztecs: another rich civilisation to plunder.

So, in 1530, Pizarro sailed from Panama for a third expedition, this time with a small but well-equipped fighting force of 130 foot soldiers and 40 cavalry. He reached Tumbes early in 1532 – and found the city in ruins.

Since his last voyage, the Inca Empire had been ripped apart by five years of civil war, following the death of the Inca Huayna Capac in 1527. The Inca died from a mysterious plague that was sweeping his lands. It was probably smallpox, imported to the Caribbean by the Spanish and trans-mitted via Colombia. The fever that killed the Inca also claimed his heir, Ninan Cuyuchi.[7] A war of succession broke out between two other sons: Huáscar, the elder, held the capital, Cuzco, while Atahualpa headed the main army in Quito.

The decisive battle in the civil war took place at Cotabamba in 1532. Atahualpa, the victor, retired to the thermal springs at Cajamarca - by chance not far inland from Tumbes. Here, messengers brought him news of a small band of strangely-dressed bearded giants on the coast. Seeing no reason to fear such a tiny force (after all, his own army has been esti-mated at 80,000) Atahualpa sent an envoy to invite them to Cajamarca.

The conquistadores marched boldly into the centre of Cajamarca and, in a deceitful yet brilliant ambush, took Atahualpa hostage, killing some six thousand Indians without a single Spanish loss. Pizarro demanded his famous ransom for Atahualpa's release - a room filled with gold and twice as much silver. Yet even at this stage, the Inca regarded this as lit-tle more than a temporary inconvenience and carried on issuing orders in the war against his brother.

But once the treasure was delivered, Pizarro had the Inca put to death. By the end of 1533, his small band had marched south and seized Cuzco, the capital of an Inca empire which stretched from southern Colombia to northern Chile and which was able to raise armies of 300,000.

****

the Holocaust
How could 170 men conquer an entire empire? It seems that luck played a part, especially arriving in the middle of a civil war. (For instance, Pizarro was initially welcomed into Cuzco as a hero for having killed Atahualpa - Cuzco being loyal to his brother Huáscar.) More importantly, the military technology of the Old World - steel, guns, dogs and horses - was vastly superior to the Incas' clubs and spears. Of these, guns were the least important. In fact, dogs were more effective.[8] But it was the

horse ('the tank of the Conquest') that was decisive – just as it had been in earlier invasions of Europe from the Asian steppes. While Andean civil- isation developed more or less in isolation, the Spanish brought the tech- nological fruits of the entire Old World. Gunpowder, dogs, horses and cavalry tactics all originated in Asia.

Yet it was disease that really broke resistance to the Spanish. No major American Indian state was conquered until after its leadership had been wiped out by illness. The Europeans brought diseases unknown in the Americas: diseases that had mutated from domestic animals; that had been spread by bad sanitation or by trade with Africa and Asia.

The Indians had no resistance to such infections as smallpox, bubonic plague, measles, whooping cough, influenza, yellow fever or even the common cold. Sickness swept the Americas, even to parts where Europeans had yet to penetrate. Imagine the horror of such a time. Within a single lifetime, maybe nine out of every ten people died, throughout the whole of the New World. Some historians estimate the population of the Inca Empire fell from as much as 32 million in 1520 to 5 million in 1548 – a mere 28 years – and to 2 million by 1600. It was death on a scale that surpassed even the Black Death or the Nazi death- camps. It was the biggest holocaust in history.[9]

****

along the coast
From Tumbes we caught a bus to Lima, twenty hours south. It was another battered crate with no air-conditioning and windows that either didn't open or didn't close. The seats had been unscrewed and moved closer to allow extra rows to be inserted and more passengers crammed in. Two young boys rode 'shotgun', hanging out of the door and touting for passen- gers at every stop.

Women held babies clamped to one, or both, nipples. Chickens poked their heads forlornly through holes in cardboard boxes. A piglet curled up in a basket under one seat. The roof and the aisle and the gaps under the seats and the luggage racks and every other available space was stuffed with bags and boxes and coloured bundles and food. Children wailed and a *criollo* pop cassette blared out. The back window was covered by a lurid life-size transfer of the Virgin Mary. A glittering silver strip on the wind- screen above the driver read 'God is my co-pilot'.

'So that's God, then,' I said, pointing to the slumped form of the fat co-driver, who was snoring loudly in the front passenger seat. 'I somehow imagined someone a bit more impressive.'

'Wouldn't it be safer to let Him do the actual driving,' Mark mused. God groaned and farted in his sleep. The driver crossed himself and muttered a prayer. The ignition made a few painful chalk-on-blackboard screeches and spluttered into life. Diesel smoke billowed behind us. We were off.

The banana plantations of Ecuador's coast had given way to the Peruvian coastal desert. Parched, grey earth ran straight into a grey sea, while a ceiling of low, grey cloud hung permanently above. On the Peruvian coast it rarely rains, but the sun rarely shines. It's just . . . grey. Far to our left we could see the brown foothills of the Andes, hills that would eventually rise to over 6,000m.

Every few hours the desert was interrupted by irrigated corridors of green fields where a river flowed down from the mountains. At their mouths were towns: some elegant and colonial like Trujillo, others dirty and industrial and stinking of dried fish.

****

ancient erections

We made a couple of fleeting stops between changes of buses. The first was in Chiclayo, to visit the superb Bruning Museum. It was full of mis-chievous, exuberant Moche pottery from nearby sites like Sipán and Túcume, vividly moulded into animals and cheerful, everyday people. Farmers, soldiers, priests, cripples and musicians laughed at us across the centuries. Some pots were shaped as couples in erotic embraces or grin-ning men with hard-ons that reached above their heads. No wonder they were smiling. I dragged Melissa reluctantly away from contemplation of their outsized erections.

In Trujillo, I hauled an unwilling Mark and Melissa around the vast ruined city of Chan Chan. The wind whistled across the desert through a waste-land of crumbled grey adobe mounds. Only one restored section hinted at past greatness.

'Chan Chan,' the guide explained, 'was founded by the Moche, contempo-raries of the Romans and Anglo-Saxons, then expanded by the Chimu. When the Chimu were conquered by the Incas in the 1470s, their best goldsmiths, artists, doctors and teachers were sent to Cuzco, so the Incas could learn from them.' Peru's history, far from starting with the Incas, stretches back 4,000 years – making it one of six great centres of early world civilisation.[10]

****

the Nazca Lines

We continued down the coast. We passed the world's biggest left-hander (not a giant homosexual, but something to do with surfing) and a dusty one-street town called Cabo Blanco. My guidebook told me that in 1953 the biggest fish ever caught on a rod was landed here, a 710kg blue marlin. An ancient American mariner got off, with matted white beard and a tangled mass of long white hair. Harpoon in hand, he looked like Neptune himself. Tanned surfers sat in run-down bars.

We spent two hours in Lima, once among the richest cities in the world. A deathly pallor hung over the city and seemed to creep over the skin of its inhabitants too. Traffic clogged the streets. Faded facades hid behind layers of grime and neglect. Squatter slums climbed the bare brown hills behind the city. Two hours was enough of Lima.

Two hours was enough for lunch and a fizzy drink. There are two home-grown fizzy drinks in Peru. One is Inca Kola, which tastes like liquid bubble gum and is a concise two-word summation of the whole country, with its rich history and present-day US commercial domination.[11] The other is an orange drink called Bimbo. I pestered Melissa to let me take her picture holding a Bimbo.

'What are you implying?' she huffed.

We caught the next bus out of Lima, another twenty-hour ride south to Arequipa. The journey was a huge detour: the shorter highland route to Cuzco passed through the stronghold of the Sendero Luminoso – the Shining Path. A Maoist movement, the Sendero aimed to build a power base among the rural peasants, to eventually surround and strangle the cities. Through a mixture of genuine support and intimidation, they controlled the central highlands directly inland from Lima.

A few months previously, the government had finally captured Abimael Guzman, the Sendero leader. A former professor of Kantian philosophy, Guzman was the inspiration behind its mix of terror, Maoist dogma and Inca paternalism. No one knew if the guerrillas would fade away or put on a show of strength to prove that they weren't finished. We didn't want to be around if they did.

So we either had to take buses to Cuzco via Arequipa – a total of about fifty hours – or fly. The flight took one hour and cost $60. The bus cost $25.

'$60?' said Mark. 'I'm not bloody well paying $60.'

So fifty hours on the bus it was.
The southern coast was much like the northern coast; dull, overcast and monotonous. We dozed and woke and dozed to the sound of incessant *criollo* pop, which sounds like bad salsa music speeded-up. During the night I opened my eyes to find that we were roaring along the beach itself, with no sign of a road. This was the Pan-American Highway. On a map, it's the greatest road in the Americas, running from Alaska to Paraguay and broken only by the swamps of the Darién Gap in Panama. Here it was simply two tyre-tracks along a beach.

We drove across the Nazca Lines. These mysterious giant drawings are up to 200 metres long and cover 500 square kilometres of desert. They depict monkeys, birds, spiders and other creatures. Because they are only fully visible from the air, speculation abounds as to how and why they were drawn. Were they vast maps? Astrological calendars? Running tracks for ritual races? Religious designs for the Gods to see? Created by visiting spacemen? Did the Nazca people fly in hot-air balloons? (Some designs found on Nazca pottery seem to depict balloons.)

It cost $50 to fly over the Lines in a light aircraft.

'$50?' said Mark. 'I'm not bloody well paying $50.'

We drove across the Lines in the bus. From the ground we could make out nothing.

****

the fat magician
The boredom of the journey was broken by a constant stream of people selling food. At every stop, a dozen women stormed the bus. Sometimes, to steal a march on their rivals, they clambered in through a window, landing on an unsuspecting passenger. At each stop, the women sold something different: oranges, or chicken and rice steamed in banana leaves, or *empanadas*, or maize cakes called *tamales*. But at any one stop everyone sold the same thing. Hence the rush to reach the passengers.

The buses in Peru were little theatres, or at least speakers' corners. A steady flow of salesmen stood at the front selling horoscopes or pamphlets explaining the secret of good health, or bottled elixirs whose consumption guaranteed it. Such sales were proceeded by lengthy speeches extolling the virtues of the product, and were surprisingly successful. The salesmen would ride the bus for twenty minutes lecturing the captive audience on the merits of their product, then wander up the aisle looking for buyers. Then they would get off and wait for the next bus back. There must be some school somewhere in Peru for bus salesmen – perhaps with some fat millionaire getting rich through newspaper adverts promising 'You too, can earn 50 *soles* a day with the Pedro Sulizman Bus Sales Technique. It can't fail. Only 200 *soles*. Do it now.' There was certainly no shortage of poor, unemployed Peruvians desperate to find some way of eking out a living. '*Señors y señoras*. Ladies and Gentlemen,' they would announce, always with the same formal introduction, 'may I apologise for interrupting your journey. I believe that when you learn about the fabulous (fill in blank) that I hold before you, you will think that it worth a moment of your time.' Did we have a choice?

A second technique was the sweet system, used for charitable appeals – although sometimes the charity was the sales-person's own poverty. The seller would hand a toffee to every passenger. Then he or she would make a long, impassioned speech, usually (as far as I could gather) about 'the poor orphans near the border,' followed by a repeat trip up and down the bus. You either made a donation or returned the sweet. Our favourite sweet seller was a youth, maybe nineteen or twenty, on our way from Arequipa to Cuzco. He was either deaf or had a terrible speech impediment.

'Se-se-se-se-se-se-NOR-e-e-e-e-ES y-y-y Se-se-se-se-NOR-ah-ah-ah-ah-AHS,' he began, forcing out the endings to each word through willpower alone, his eyes screwed shut with the effort. 'Ngha-ngha-murra-gnnaa' he continued. 'The ch-ch-chil-il-dre-dre-dre-DREN a-a-a-a-T the bor-bor-de-de-DER. Ngha-ngha-murra-gnnaa . . .' Even we could tell that most of his speech was unintelligible. The other passengers listened with rapt attention. When he eventually came to a stop there was a short pause while everyone waited to see if he had actually finished. Then the whole bus burst into applause. He sold all his sweets, although I doubt anyone had the faintest idea to what cause they were donating their money. Then he sat happily next to the bus driver and his crew, who made a fuss of him and rustled his hair and imitated his speech good-naturedly, until they let him off in a little village.

And there was the fat magician. An obese, sweaty man, he heaved himself aboard with a great effort somewhere south of Lima. His huge stomach hung over his trousers and reappeared in the gap left by a missing button half-way up his shirt. His fly was broken and undone.

He stood at the front of the bus and pulled scarves out of his sleeve and ping-pong balls out of his mouth, and made cards disappear while keeping up a stream of banter which brought no response from the impassive passengers. Sweat streamed off him. His shirt – already two sizes too small – became transparent with moisture, clinging to his mountainous stomach. As he approached his finale, he noticed a pretty young girl sitting alone in the front seat, wearing a low-cut dress. Grabbing his chance, he proceeded to produce a dozen ping-pong balls from the middle of her cleavage, letting his fat, clammy hand linger just a second longer than necessary each time. The girl recoiled in horror each time she saw his podgy fingers reaching towards her, but there was no escape. He concluded with a flourish and a bow. No one gave him a sol, but he thanked us all for being a good audience anyway and hauled himself off to wait for another bus. It was tough being a travelling magician in Peru. Especially a bad one.

****

back into the Andes

We stopped in Arequipa just long enough to change buses, grab a Bimbo and visit the nunnery. Peru's second city was a pleasant surprise, full of attractive churches and white houses built from the local volcanic rock. Arequipa's jewel, though, is the beautifully-preserved Santa Catalina *nunnery*, perhaps the continent's most impressive Catholic monument.

'You want to visit a . . . nunnery?' Mark looked incredulous. 'Bollocks to that.'

Melissa agreed with him. They spent the afternoon asleep in a guesthouse. I went anyway.

The bus to Cuzco took another twenty hours, climbing inland into the Andes. As we left the coast, the temperature plunged. Other passengers produced blankets from nowhere. We put on our jumpers, then our spare jumpers and so on until we were wearing all our clothes. Then we wrapped ourselves in our sleeping bags, and we were still cold. Judging by the ear-shattering laughter coming through the speakers, the driver was playing a comedy tape. No one on the bus laughed, but it was the only tape he had and he played it anyway. Sleep was impossible.

Near midnight, we stopped at a roadside eatery. Foodstops in Peru all work the same way. The bus disgorges passengers into an until-then empty room, and everyone desperately crowds the counter. You pay and get a numbered scrap of paper. Then you sit and wait for the serving-girl to appear with the food. If you don't get your order in fast, you sit anxiously wondering whether your food will arrive before the driver decides to leave. (The driver, of course, gets served immediately.) When the driver is ready, he simply strides back to the bus and starts the engine – normally just as my dinner was emerging from the kitchen, to be stuffed down in two desperate mouthfuls.

This time I was off the bus before it stopped, diving to the front of the queue. By now, we'd probably been on more long-distance buses than most Peruvians. There was always an air of suppressed excitement, confusion and anticipation on the buses. I'm sure it was the biggest journey many of our fellow passengers had ever made: families with their entire possessions packed into boxes and sacks, perhaps moving in search of work.

My giant plate of fried chicken was delicious. I even had time to wander outside after eating. In the moonlight I could see boulders and the jagged outline of hills. Men pissed against the bus while women squatted in a ditch across the road, discreetly hidden by their wide skirts.

An hour further on, a rockfall blocked the road. In a flurry of confusion, we were told to swap with the passengers of a bus that had made its way down from the mountains. The bus-boys busied themselves unloading the luggage from the roof and hauling it across to the other bus.

Near dawn, the temperature plunged still further, dashing any lingering hopes of sleep. We'd reached a pass and the bus stopped climbing and began to descend. The hard morning light burnt through the thin air. In front of us, the hills fell away to a wide, treeless plain. This was the alti-plano – one of the highest and harshest inhabited regions on earth.

Reddish-brown adobe houses with thatched roofs dotted the flat brown plain. People, mainly women, were already out working patches of thin soil with hand-held foot-ploughs, or herding a few cattle along the road. Once again, they wore the highland *campesina* dress: heavy skirts, layers of petticoats, woollen jumpers and shawls and hats. Only the hats varied from Ecuador. Here the women wore stovepipe hats, like something out of a Rembrandt painting, instead of the pork pie Ecuadorean felt hats. Some even wore two hats, one balanced on top of the other. The women were stocky and tough, the bitter wind and the intense sun etched into their reddish-brown faces.

We reached Cuzco in the late morning.

****

Cuzco

Cuzco lies 3,300m above sea level at the head of a fertile valley, surrounded on three sides by brown hills. It's the most popular stop on The Gringo Trail in Peru. Tourists come – the sensible ones flying from Lima – for Machu Picchu and the other Inca ruins that surround the town.

Despite some Inca stonework in the walls of its colonial buildings, Cuzco is architecturally a well-preserved Spanish colonial city, full of old churches and a cloistered central plaza. Culturally, it remains a Quechua town; a vibrant Andean community with a bustling market that spills out of its cavernous hall into the adjoining streets. It is also one of the few towns in Peru with Gringo Trail nightlife. There are bars full of backpackers, bakeries selling delicious pastries and veggie cafes serving quiche. And it has Peru's best beer, a black stout called Cuzqueña Malta.

Every radio blared out a record by a Swedish pop group called Ace of Bass, alternating with another equally dire euro-disco song called 'Mr Vain'. We'd come half-way round the world to hear the two worst records in Europe. It sounded as if Radio Cuzco could only afford two records, for it played them back-to-back all day until we wanted to pick up the nearest radio and throw it at the wall. If they were going to have Western culture, did it have to be the dross? 'All that she wants is another baby,' the singer chanted moronically. Everywhere we looked, women struggled on with their work with one baby strapped to their back and another semi-permanently clamped to a breast. The last thing they needed was another baby.

****

the navel of the world

When Pizarro first entered Cuzco, one of his men commented that '. . . it is so beautiful and has such fine buildings that it would be remarkable even in Spain.'[12]

Its heart was the Huacaypata ('Joy Square'), twice the size of today's central plaza. Nearby, where the Santo Domingo church now stands, was the great Temple of the Sun, Koricancha, with its sanctuaries to the sun, moon, stars, lightning and the rainbow. Inside, the Spanish were delighted to find whole walls covered in gold; plus gold and silver statues of llamas, shepherds, birds, butterflies, fruit, trees and plants. Like Atahualpa's golden ransom, this treasure was immediately melted down. The conquistadores were more interested in weight than art.

The Incas called Cuzco 'the navel of the world'. It was laid out as a symbolic representation of their empire, shaped like a jaguar and dissected by two canals. The city's four sections represented the Tawantinsuyu – the four quarters of the empire. It was an empire that stretched over 3,000 miles from southern Colombia to northern Chile. Over 40,000km of paved roads – complete with walls, tunnels, causeways, bridges and drainage channels – wound over the rugged mountins. At the time it was probably the largest empire on earth, similar in size to the Roman Empire at its peak. But this glorious imperium was as short-lived as it was vast. Although they traced their dynasty back to Manco Capac, who founded Cuzco around 1200AD, for 250 years the Incas remained a small tribe. The 'empire' was built by just three rulers, and lasted less than a century.

The first was Pachacuti, a Peruvian version of Alexander the Great. Pachacuti assumed the throne in 1438 after repelling an invasion of Cuzco by a rival tribe, the Chanca. By his death in 1471, 33 years later, he'd conquered all of modern-day Peru, made Cuzco a great imperial city, built splendid palaces and temples, constructed a vast network of roads, agricultural terracing, irrigation systems and grain storage facilities, and established a whole legal and administrative system. His son and grandson, Topac Xupanqui and Huayna Capac, defeated the Incas' last Peruvian rivals, the Chimu, and extended the empire into Ecuador, Chile and Colombia. And that was it. After Huayna Capac's death in 1527, the empire plunged into the bloody civil war which was just ending when the Spanish arrived.

****

give and take
The Incas' achievements were impressive: conquering and organising one of the largest empires in history, feeding its subjects, building great temples and a vast road network.[13] Like the Spanish, they were ruthless imperialists who massacred enemy troops after they'd surrendered and slaughtered inhabitants of captured cities. They sometimes flayed captives alive, stuffed their skins and put them on public display, or made war drums out of their stomachs.

Yet there was some exchange (unless you were made into a drum kit, that is). The Incas tried to integrate the people they conquered into their empire. Defeated chiefs were held hostage in Cuzco but allowed to live in luxury if their followers remained loyal. Their gods were assimilated into Inca religion. Great public works built not just palaces and temples, but also irrigation systems, agricultural terraces (to prevent erosion of the steep Andean hillsides) and grain warehouses (in case crops failed).

The Inca Empire was a totalitarian, paternalistic dictatorship, communally-organised without private property – like the state-communism of the Soviet Union without the rhetoric about equality. There was a vast gulf between the Inca nobility and the peasantry, but at least the Inca Empire provided the basics of life: food and security. Both were soon to be taken away.

****

Machu Picchu

There are three ways of getting to Machu Picchu from Cuzco. There's the 'tourist' train, the 'local' train, or the four day Inca Trail.

It goes without saying that no self-respecting 'traveller' would dream of catching the tourist train, even if it didn't cost ten times more than the local train. And something would have been very wrong if everyone didn't tell you that there was no local train; or that tourists *had* to take the tourist train; or that the local train had 'just left;' or that it was illegal for foreigners to take the local train. That only made it more important for 'travellers' to catch the local train.

But we were hiking. The Inca Trail is the most famous trek in South America. It ends with a breathtaking first view of Machu Picchu that is denied to those who arrive by train and traverses some wonderful mountain scenery on the way. What more could you want?

We caught the (local) train half-way to a middle-of-nowhere stop called Kilometre 88. Kilometre 88 isn't actually a station: the train just stops beside a group of four or five wooden kiosks selling coca leaves, and a handful of trekkers climb down onto the track.

We climbed down. Mark bought a large bag of coca leaves for the hike. Coca is a bit of a wonder plant, and great for trekking. Peruvians chew the bitter-tasting leaves, letting a wad sit in their cheek for hours, or make it into tea called mate de coca. It suppresses hunger and altitude sickness, relieves stomach aches, eases childbirth (although none of us expected to give birth in the next four days) and provides energy. It's said that Inca messengers chewing coca could run 150 miles in a day. What it doesn't do is get you high, unless you chew about a tonne of unrefined leaves.

The Trail was beautiful. We hiked over alpine passes, through meadows and cloudforest, along stone pathways built by the Incas themselves, complete with tunnels and stairways. We passed isolated ruins – lonely forts and step-like terracing. Each more impressive than the last, they seemed almost designed to build up to Machu Picchu itself.

We camped alone, beside ruined forts on misty hillsides. Mark treated us to repeated renditions of *The Rocky Horror Show*, plus a hundred versions of 'My Way'. Even eight hours of constant rain on the second day didn't dampen our spirits. Mark switched to 'Singing in The Rain'. The rain dampened everything else, though, as neither Mark nor Melissa had packed their rucksacks properly. My spare clothes just went around the three of us.

'What's at the end of this trek again?' Melissa asked, as we listened to the rain drumming on the roof of the tent. She was probably the only person in Peru who'd never heard of Machu Picchu.

'You'll enjoy the surprise more if I don't tell you.'

There was method in Melissa's continuing failure to find out anything about where we were going. Melissa put her trust in people. She'd stuck with Peter because she recognised his gifts as a teacher. She trusted me to be her guide. No matter how often I placed the Lonely Planet in front of her, it remained unread.

'If you say it's good, I'm sure it is,' she'd say.

'But you can't just . . . trust me,' I protested. The idea of simply taking someone else's word for something, without checking it against every guidebook published since 1932, horrified me.

For Melissa, on the other hand, nothing was an anticlimax, because she had no expectations. It was a great way to travel and I was slightly envious. Her enthusiasm for each new discovery was so genuine and infectious that it made it all more special to me as well. Together, Melissa and I made a complete single person. I got us to places while Melissa, with her vivacious personality and warmth, made friends with every other back-packer in the hostel. The only thing that stopped her making friends with all the Peruvians as well was her continued inability to grasp even the basics of Spanish.

On the last day we reached the Gateway of the Sun, which guards the narrow pass above Machu Picchu. It's a compact little ruin, consisting of the unroofed walls of an arch and what was probably a barrack room. It was misty and drizzling and we could see nothing except this gatehouse and three narrow grass terraces, descending the hillside in steps. We camped on the lowest terrace, the only one that was flat. Our tents were marginally too wide for this terrace, and overhung the edge by a few inches. I crawled inside the tent and listened to the sound of Mark pissing into the void. (Zen question – what *is* the sound of one man pissing into the void?)

In the morning, the mist lifted. It revealed two things. The first was that we'd camped right on the edge of a sheer cliff. The second was Machu Picchu. Even having seen hundred of pictures of it, it was still breathtak-ing: a lost city crowning a hilltop, with almost-sheer drops on three sides, and the sugarloaf hill of Huayna Picchu in the background.

I first saw Machu Picchu in a cinema commercial (for diamonds, I think) at the Streatham Odeon when I was twelve: it seemed so mysterious and exotic with the mist blowing over it, and as remote as the stars.

And now . . . I was here. Like the Pyramids and other world-famous land-marks, it's strange to see the real thing at last. It's at once new and yet familiar. Approaching it as the Incas themselves would have done, along the Inca Trail, I felt its remarkable isolation and inaccessibility, perched precariously on its hilltop eyrie deep in the cloudforest.

We spent the day exploring the ruins. The buildings, originally thatched, have no roofs, but the walls revealed the Incas' majestic jigsaw-puzzle masonry of massive interlocking stones, fitted so precisely that it is often impossible to insert a knife into the gaps. Mark insisted I photograph him in 'compromising'-looking positions with the llama – quite a famous animal that's employed to cut the grass. By eating it, of course. As far as I know, they didn't try to train it to use a lawnmower.

'Wow,' said Melissa, 'it's amazing.' (meaning, I assumed, the ruins, not the position Mark and the llama were in). 'So what is it?'

Nobody really knows. When Hiram Bingham 'discovered' it in 1911, its impregnable position led him to claim that it was the mysterious Vilcabamba. After the fall of Cuzco in 1533, the Inca leader Manco Inca had raised an army of 100,000, narrowly failed to recapture Cuzco, and then established a short-lived independent capital called Vilcabamba, whose exact location had long fascinated historians and archaeologists.

But Vilcabamba is now thought to be further east at Espiritu Pampu. So what *was* Machu Picchu? Of 173 skeletons found here, 150 were identified (not necessarily correctly) as women, giving rise to theories that it was a religious site, and the women were nuns or priestly concubines.

More probably, if less romantically, it was merely a remote outpost that survived due to its very insignificance and remoteness while more important Inca sites were looted and destroyed.

****

the ayllu

'The Spanish defeat of the Inca Empire . . . was more than simply another conquest. It did not just impose another set of rulers in the succession of Andean civilisations. It tore up by the roots the co-operative agrarian society of the Andean ayllus. The old heart of the Inca Empire in what is now Peru and Bolivia was reorganised for the extraction of precious metals. A way of life that today we would call 'sustainable' was destroyed.'
NEIL MACDONALD, THE ANDES – A QUEST FOR JUSTICE (OXFAM, 1994)

Machu Picchu is even more impressive if it really was 'nothing special'.

The Incas were a pre-literate 'stone-age' people who didn't even use the wheel. Their great engineering feats were achieved by superb organisation and an enforced labour system called the mita.

The Inca Empire was a rigid hierarchy, a pyramid stretching down from the Inca himself. At the base of this pyramid was a much older Andean social unit; the village clan or ayllu. The ayllu allowed co-operation on large communal tasks, such as the building of an irrigation canal. The Inca formalised this into the mita, but retained the principle of communal welfare.

The Spanish destroyed the ayllus. They divided the land into estates, called encomiendas, each owned by a Spanish encomendero. Indians within each estate had to support their new Lord. The Spanish crown piously instructed the encomenderos to take less from the peasants than the Incas, but in far-away Peru this half-hearted request was ignored, and the encomenderos worked 'their' Indians to death. The only duty required of them in return was to teach Christianity.

Before the Conquest, the Peruvians had few animals except the llama. But as farmers they were unsurpassed. Using the different micro-climates created by varying altitudes, they cultivated a greater range of plants and medicines than anywhere on earth. Beans, 20 varieties of maize, 240 types of potato, chocolate, peanuts, cashews, avocados, pineapples, squashes, peppers, tomatoes . . . so many common foods come from Peru that it's hard to imagine what we ate in Europe before the Conquest.[14]

The Spanish brought farming techniques developed for Europe's temperate climate to a land of mountains, deserts and jungle, ignoring 12,000 years of local knowledge. They ignored the need for terracing to prevent erosion of steep Andean valleys, or irrigation systems to water the coastal desert. They introduced animals that grazed away fragile pastures. They farmed monocrops – cash crops such as coffee – instead of letting the land recover by mixed planting, crop rotation and fallow years. They destroyed the collective ownership system in which communities farmed both valleys and hillsides at once to guard against floods or droughts at one level.

The effect was disastrous. Today, Peru grows less food than it did before the Spanish arrived.

****

Aguas Calientes

While waiting for the train back to Cuzco, we soaked our aching limbs in the hot springs of the local village, simply called Aguas Calientes. It was a lovely spot, surrounded by verdant jungle hanging off sheer cliffs. The water was like a hot, sulphurous bath. We sat back and stretched our legs out. Even the sight of a fully-formed human turd floating gently past didn't entirely ruin the moment.

There were no seats on the train, so we had to stand for five hours. Mark treated the carriage to a song called 'I'm In Love With The Girl Next Door', whose lyrics consisted entirely of repetition of the line, 'I'm in love with the girl next door, smell my fingers', with appropriate hand-movements. Our fellow passengers sat impassively, thinking their own thoughts. The train chugged through a valley so steep that it was impossible to see the sky without sticking your head out of the window. We reached Cuzco in the dark and headed straight for a bar and a bottle of Cuzqueña Malta.

****

'do not be a-scared . . .'

Next, we caught a night bus to Puno, on the shore of Lake Titicaca. After our five day marathon, a mere overnight ride was nothing. We settled back to get some sleep, this time well wrapped up against the cold. Mark, already too big to fit into his seat comfortably, found himself squeezed in beside a typically solid campesina, constantly breastfeeding one of her three children. He groaned in anticipation of the forthcoming battle for sleeping space.

We stopped for food at around ten. Everyone raced to get their orders in. There was a group of four Israelis at the back of the bus, and the two girls raced off to the toilet – only to re-emerge in shock. The floor of the cubicle was a six-inch-deep sea of shit.

'But we need a toilet,' they told Melissa desperately. Melissa pointed to the row of women squatting on the opposite side of the road. The Israelis looked horrified.

When we got back onto the bus, the other passengers were unusually agitated. A middle-aged woman was seated behind us, wearing Western clothes and too much make-up. Her hair was pinned up into a beehive. She tapped Melissa urgently on the shoulder.

'*Dinero*,' she hissed, pointing to a thick wad of US dollar bills in her hand. 'Money.' She suddenly stuffed the wad into her hair, where it magically disappeared. The man across the aisle fidgeted nervously in his seat and grabbed Melissa's arm. '*Dinero*,' he echoed. He made slashing motions across his throat. We were still baffled. He took out a pair of nail-clippers and thrust them under Melissa's nose. '*Dinero*,' he repeated.

Was he trying to rob us? In the middle of a crowded bus with a pair of nail-clippers? It seemed unlikely. So what was he trying to say? He took his bag down from the overhead rack and opened it just enough so that Melissa and I could catch a glimpse of a gun inside.

'*Sendero*.' he whispered.

He closed the case and stared grimly at us to see if we'd understood. We understood the word Sendero, and it didn't sound good. Just then, a well-dressed man approached from a few rows back. He spoke some English.

'Do not be a-scared,' he said, reassuringly, 'but there are some *banditos*, in Santa Rosita, where we arrive in two hours. Every bus for the last four nights, they a-*rrrob*.' He added an extra roll to the 'r' of rob for emphasis.

'Sendero?' I asked.

'No, not Sendero. Just *banditos*. They notta kill you. They only a-*rrrob* you. Every passenger must give them fifty dollars. If not . . .' he considered this possibility. '*Then*, maybe they kill you.'

'Well, I'm buggered then,' said Mark. 'I haven't got fifty dollars.'

We looked around the bus. Everyone was busy stashing money in torn seats or secret compartments of bags and jackets. Women were stuffing notes into their bras. We were amazed at all the US dollars we could see. It seemed that the staff at the restaurant had casually mentioned the robberies when we'd stopped. 'Funny how the bus company forgot to tell anyone about them when they sold us the tickets,' said Mark.

The bus pulled off into the darkness, still a mass of anxious activity. Melissa poked me in the ribs. 'Give me your penknife,' she demanded.

'I don't think a penknife will do much good,' I said. The conversation sounded familiar.

'Well, it'll be more use than *you*,' she replied. 'They rape women, you know. So just give it to me.' I gave her the penknife. The Israelis were laughing and joking at the back of the bus, so Melissa went back and told them that they were about to be robbed, possibly murdered and probably raped. They shut up. The driver braked. There was something blocking our way. We heard voices outside. The nervous man with the nail-clippers leapt to his feet in panic and screamed.

'*Esta es.*' This is it.

My heart jumped with his. But it was only a bus in front that had broken down. Our driver got off to help. By the time the repairs were complete, two more buses had pulled up behind us in the darkness, and we continued in convoy. We might as well get robbed together.

Two hours further on – at the exact time we'd been told we would be robbed – the driver slammed on the brakes again. In the bus's headlights, I could see a man approaching us with a black balaclava pulled down over his face – and a gun!

'Madre Dios!' screamed the nervous man. It was true. We were being held up. I could see other masked figures outside. The masked gunman kept coming. He climbed aboard . . .

He was a policeman. His balaclava was pulled down to protect him from the biting cold of the altiplano night. He talked quietly to the driver, and waved us on. There was to be no hold-up tonight. Maybe, after robbing every bus for four nights, the banditos felt they'd earned a night off.

****

rally

Morning found us still trundling across the altiplano, craggy hills breaking out of the flat plain.

In mid-morning, we ran into a queue of other buses at a junction in the middle of nowhere. We wandered out to find a motor rally taking place. A small crowd waited without visible sign of excitement. One by one, about twenty fairly ordinary cars emerged from a cloud of dust and trundled past. They weren't going much faster than the bus. The buses started up again, and the last two entrants in the rally came around the corner to find a solid phalanx of buses blocking their route.

The road led to a river, but there was no bridge. The driver jumped out to assess the situation, then climbed back in, shut the door and drove straight into the river. His mate watched the water seep underneath the door and creep up the steps until it just about reached the main floor of the bus. We inched slowly across the river until we rose safely out of the water on the far side.

Puno lay a couple of hours ahead.

Chapter 3
Bolivia: things get worse with coke

'Only the kingdom of Hell could offer so appalling a picture discrediting humanity!'
SIMÓN BOLIVÁR

' . . . for 500 years of exploitation and robbery, racism and genocide, the Spaniards and the would-be Spaniards have kept our country in a shameful state of backwardness . . . '
COUNCIL OF AMAUT'AS, LA PAZ, JUNE 1977

Finsbury Park station (outer life)

I remember the first words Mark ever said to me. It was our first day at Oxford, fresh-faced young students in the city of dreaming spires (or, as a friend of mine puts it, '. . . of dreamy cunts'). I sat down to dinner in our gloomy, oak-beamed 16th century chamber that was our new college's dining-hall. Mark was sitting opposite me. He grinned.

'Fancy some amyl nitrate?' he asked.

I studied politics. Mark began by reading chemistry – a subject he'd chosen mainly because it had allowed him to synthesise LSD at school. After a year he switched to 'Human Sciences' – a mix of anthropology, psychology and biology and, I believe, the only new course introduced at Oxford since 1920. (It's good to know our great educational institutions are keeping up with the times.)

My university career had two noteworthy moments: one was appearing as an extra in a ridiculous film called *Oxford Blues*, which starred Rob Lowe. The other was being 'sent down' (i.e. suspended) for extortion. I was accused of hitting a student who owed me the princely sum of £20. I thought 'extortion' was exaggerating the crime a bit. Otherwise, I passed through Oxford without distinguishing myself in any teams, committees, debating societies, university magazines or clubs, or attending any lectures. The fact that I managed a half-decent degree surprised my tutor so much that he made a special point of telling me how surprised he was.

I then embarked on a career modelled after Orson Welles. Which is to say that I started at the top and worked my way down. Of course, my initial success didn't compare to Citizen Kane, although it did involve publishing a newspaper. Fresh out of college, I was director of my own company: a very small newspaper. We had radical ideas, no money and no experience. It was doomed from the start.

At 25, I was forced to take an actual job, designing and producing magazines. Plummeting meteorically through the ranks of the journalistic profession, I ended up checking a TV magazine for spelling mistakes and trying to think of new ways to describe re-runs of The A-Team.

For a while, Mark lived with me in London. We shared a house in Hackney with a depressed, semi-alcoholic Irishman and a Polish mime artist. The house was a wreck. A surveyor warned me that there was a real chance of my bedroom wall falling off in the night. This was a little alarming, as it held the rest of the house up too. The wall stayed upright, although the toilet did once fall through the floor and land on top of the cooker. Luckily, no one was cooking at the time. Or on the toilet.

Our street had the most arrests per year in London. It was rumoured that the Fire Brigade considered it too dangerous to drive down. Insurance companies refused to insure the area. Dealers sold dope in little plastic bags from our front garden and our windows rattled to the sound of passing car stereos. Hardcore techno and ragga from pirate radio stations. Edgy, aggressive, industrial sounds infused with inner-city psychosis. You heard the thumping bass before you saw the cars. At the back of the house, a railway passed close enough for us to read the headlines of passengers' newspapers.

Next door was a second-hand car dealer. One night, the car dealer's Alsatian guard-dog climbed over our garden wall. Sadly, its chain didn't reach the ground, and we watched from the window as it swung by its neck and strangled itself, thrashing about too wildly to let us rescue it. The man from the RSPCA who came to cut down the body found two fridges, an armchair and a sofa in our garden, lost beneath weeds that reached to the first-floor. We'd long since abandoned the garden – the railway line blocked all its sunlight anyway. The car dealer closed soon afterwards.

Eventually, Mark moved back to Kent to get away from 'trendy north London people' and I moved into a house in Finsbury Park with a bunch of musicians.

One day, I returned to my job on the TV magazine after a week's sick leave, with the distinctive 'panda bear' sun-tan that you can only get from skiing in the French Alps. I thought my plan was foolproof. French public phones have no click to distinguish them from a home phone, and I wrapped my face with a scarf to avoid a tan. My only worry was the occasional shout from skiers passing the phone-box. But it was freakishly hot and I tanned through the scarf. My editor made it clear that promotion was unlikely. It was time for that long trip I'd always promised myself.

The day before I left England, someone died after being stabbed through the eye, at midday, on a crowded platform in Finsbury Park underground station, about 400 metres from my front door. The assailant was a psychiatric patient who'd been kicked onto the streets as part of the Conservative government's 'Care in the Community' mental health scheme, a thinly-disguised excuse for spending cuts. He'd forgotten his medication that morning and was horrified to find out later what he'd done.

If I had any doubts about going away, that put them to rest. South America couldn't be much more run-down and dangerous than home, and if some lunatic was going to stab me through the eye with a nine-inch knife, I might as well see the world first.

****

inner city blues (inner life)
Travel writers often like to pack a forgotten volume by some obscure 19th century explorer, to quote from at relevant moments. I read many books about South America, before, during and after my trip. My favourite title was *The Role of Urine in Indigenous American Symbolism*, closely followed by *Ritual Enemas in South America*, about the use of hallucinogenic enemas in the Amazon. (Hallucinogenic enemas? Now *there's* a concept.) But the book I took with me was Eduardo Galeano's neo-Marxist economic classic, *Open Veins of Latin America*, a book at once savage, scholarly and poetic. Instead of Victorian Harrison Fords hacking their way towards lost cities, Melissa was subjected to lectures about the price of Peruvian nitrate on the 19th century world commodity market. She took it well.

I've always been interested in politics. This was confirmed to me when I bumped into a former junior school friend I'd last seen when I was ten. 'Are you still a communist?' he asked. I was a communist at *ten*? As for his question, I wasn't really sure, although I'd spent three years in the sort-of-socialist printing co-operative in Hackney. As well as our own newspaper, we'd produced leaflets for tenants associations, gays, greens, anarchists, gay green anarchists, squatters, witches, gay green witches, Hasidic Jews and just about every ethnic group going.[15] I sat in interminable 'community forums' which the Hasidic Jews would throw into chaos by denouncing homosexuality as unnatural. Finally, we gave up the struggle and stopped talking to each another.

I spent the next few years in dull jobs, waiting for something else to throw my heart into. But privatising, tax-cutting Britain in the early Nineties was no place for idealists. The Cold War had been won and lost. Communism was dead. An idiotic voting system and the cowardice of the Labour Party kept green issues off the agenda. The ecstasy/rave scene seemed Britain's only dynamic movement but appeared to offer little beyond dancing oneself into oblivion for a night or two. Which is fine. But these were desperate times. They demanded something more.

My friends got careers, steady partners, houses and families. Just as everyone I knew was getting married, I split up with my long-term girlfriend. Then she got married too. I felt alone.

I still thought of myself as normal, and the world as mad – although to my consternation I gradually realised that my friends thought the opposite, on both counts. Still, I felt untroubled by personal demons. I knew the truth. The world – our Western world – was mad.

I couldn't get enthusiastic about a career and a pension. I wanted a spark of some kind, a crusade, an ideal. All around me, I saw a society that had lost its sense of common purpose, of community. Where the future extended no further than next year's balance sheet. An 'unnatural' society in a literal sense: where children grew up never having climbed a tree and unable to recognise the constellations. A materialistic society that had lost sight of the sheer joy of being alive, and replaced it with self-assembly wardrobe units from IKEA.

It was a fucked-up world and I couldn't find any purpose or direction in it.

Maybe I'd find one in South America.

****

the border

We stopped in Puno only to catch a bus out again, to the Bolivian town of Copacabana. Before we left Peru, I finally persuaded Melissa to pose in front of a sign advertising Bimbo.

'If that's what it takes to keep you happy,' she sighed. The bus cruised around town for an hour in an effort to panic stray pedestrians into jumping on board, then returned to the original stop. I've never quite understood this common Third World habit – does anyone decide to go to Bolivia on the spur of the moment, just because they see a passing bus that's going there?

An hour later, we set off for Bolivia.

The crossing-point was a quiet spot on the southern shore of Lake Titicaca. There was none of the chaos of the Peru-Ecuador frontier. The guards stamped our passports without looking. No one ran up to hassle us. A friendly young taxi driver dropped us in Copacabana and didn't even try to overcharge us. Bolivia seemed promising.

****

Copacabana

Copacabana is a popular stop on The Gringo Trail. It's a quiet town with a whitewashed, Moorish-looking church and quiet streets sloping down to the lakeside.

A few mournful-looking *campesinas* sat on the pavement, selling pathetic little pyramids of tomatoes and potatoes. A couple of trucks in front of the church were being decorated with confetti and flowers. Bolivians bring their cars and trucks here to be blessed by Copacabana's miracle-working Virgin, at the same time spilling some *aguardiente* or whisky as offerings to the Aymara gods.[16]

You find the same religious mix on the Cerro Calvario, an isolated hillock on the lakeshore to one side of town. Here, pilgrims puff up a winding flight of uneven steps, past crosses that represent the Stations of the Cross. Half-way up, they also pass a line of stone tables where traditional *brujos*, or shamans, are engaged in healing ceremonies. Wrapped in incense, the table is littered with symbolic offerings aimed at restoring their patient's lost spiritual energy (their 'ajayu' in Aymara). At the top, around the final Station of the Cross, vendors sell plastic models of cars, boats and houses, and bundles of toy money, all meant to increase your chances of acquiring the real things.

From the Cerro, the view over Lake Titicaca is breathtaking: a vast inland sea over 200km long, the far shore away over the horizon and the snowy peaks of the Cordillera Real sparkling in the distance. The nearby hills, dry and brown and dotted with trees and shrubs, reminded me of Greece.

Titicaca is the largest lake in South America and, at 3,800m, the 'highest navigable lake in the world.[17] The Incas believed the lake was the birth-place of the sun, and it's easy to understand why. The sun's rays penetrate the thin atmosphere with such intense brilliance that every detail of the landscape is crystalline in its sharpness.

We took a boat to the Isla del Sol, the Incas' holiest place, to see the ruined temple and the pumas. Half the size of a lion, these cats once roamed wild. Now only three remained, caged for tourists. The temple dated from when the Incas were still a local tribe and looked like the ruins of a small farmhouse, not the birthplace of a mighty empire. But the island was peaceful, with no cars and only a couple of quiet villages and lovely views across the lake to the hills and mountains beyond.

Back in Copacabana, Mark bought a woollen poncho to go with his black felt hat. He spent the rest of the day doing Clint Eastwood imperson-ations.

'You see, my donkey gets the crazy idea that you're laughing at him,' he drawled at the *campesinas* and their little piles of tomatoes. They looked blank.

We met a young American doctor called Dave, who was working in a hos-pital in La Paz. He was in Bolivia to study the deadly 'chagas' disease, transmitted by the bite of a beetle aptly called the 'assassin bug', which lives in thatched roofs.

'The beetle falls out of roof and bites you. It's fatal, and there's no cure. It can take twenty years, but once you're bitten, you're dead. They say a quarter of all Bolivians have the disease.'

'I'm a immunologist,' he continued. 'They brought some patients into the hospital after a crash. I said I'd never done surgery before. They said I was the only doctor they had.'

'By the way, don't sit at the front of the buses,' he warned us. 'We ran into an accident on one of the roads a while back. Two buses. Head-on. As a doctor, I had to help. It was very nasty. The passengers in the front two rows were all decapitated.'

****

the Bolivian navy

I sat at one of the drinks stalls beside the lake and watched the Bolivian navy, which consists of a couple of old gunboats. Later, I joked to another tourist about the absurdity of a country with no coastline having a navy. He didn't laugh. He was Swiss.

Bolivia's navy is maintained not for fear of a Peruvian armada sweeping across Lake Titicaca, but to remind the world that Bolivia did once possess a coastline. In fact, Bolivia was originally twice its present size. Through a series of disastrous wars, it managed to lose its Pacific coast and the nitrate-rich Atacama desert to Chile in 1883, the rubber-producing Acre region of the Amazon to Brazil in 1903 and the forested Chaco region to Paraguay in 1935.

In fact, Bolivia is a bit of a disaster all round. Not only is its foreign policy a catastrophe, but it's also one of South America's poorest nations, with 97% of rural Bolivians below the UN's poverty line.

It's hardly a model of stable government, either. In 170 years since independence, Bolivia has had over 190 different governments. As the mother of one of Bolivia's short-lived rulers is reputed to have said, 'If I'd known he was going to be President, I'd have sent him to school.'

****

the hospederia

Copacabana is full of hotels, but I read that you could stay in the *hospederia*, an old monastery. It was ridiculously cheap, even by Bolivian standards, so Mark and I decided to check it out. It was a beautiful old building, with a lovingly-maintained cobbled central courtyard full of flowers. The rooms consisted of unpainted cement floors and walls. They had no beds, furniture or lighting; not even windows. But it *was* a bargain. A family of eight cooked, ate, slept and lived in the next room. Melissa groaned, then went to light a candle in the church for a sick friend of hers.

'I'm going swimming,' Mark announced.

'It'll be a bit cold, I'd imagine,' I commented absently. I was reading.

Mark waited.

'Well, come on then,' he said impatiently. 'Let's go.'

'Go where?' I asked. 'I'm going to look at the church.'

Mark looked put out. 'I don't want to see the church.'

'But I do. It's got one of the finest gilt altars in Bolivia, apparently.'

Mark looked at me as if I was mad.

'Gilt altar? You want to see a . . . *what*?'

'Look, you go swimming and maybe I'll catch up with you later.'

'OK,' Mark grunted, 'but hurry up.'

'I only said maybe . . .' I began, but Mark was striding off, no longer listening.

I wandered around the church. (Nice gilt altar, by the way.) When I got back to the hospederia, Mark was waiting.

'How was your swim?' I asked. Mark exploded.

'Where the hell were you?' he demanded. 'How could I go swimming? What was I supposed to do with my stuff? I thought you'd been murdered or something. I waited for hours. You just never think of other people, that's your problem.' He'd completely lost his cool. I was perplexed. I hadn't promised to go to the beach. But from then on, I could do nothing right.

****

Potosí

'I am rich Potosí, treasure of the world, king of the mountains, envy of kings.'
INSCRIPTION ON SHIELD AWARDED TO POTOSÍ BY HOLY ROMAN EMPEROR CHARLES V

We left Copacabana next morning, heading south for Potosí. Another bus journey, or in fact two, because we had to change buses in La Paz, Bolivia's capital. We were getting pretty used to buses. It was another overnight ride and we reached Potosí in the crystal light of early morning.

The scenery was as bleak and bare as any we'd seen. This was a high-altitude desert. The stony brown-red hills were bare and although the sunlight was intense, it was a crisp, icy glare that failed to warm us. We were high.

In fact, at 4,070m Potosí is the world's highest city. It is also one of the historical gems of South America, a UNESCO World Heritage site with over 2,000 listed colonial buildings. And, finally, it is one of Bolivia's poorest towns. Its narrow colonial lanes are crowded with heavily-wrapped Indians scratching a living. Its colonial buildings are unheated.

And towering over the town is the great pinkish-grey cone of the Cerro Rico. The Rich Hill.

The Cerro Rico dominates Potosí, both physically and historically. Indeed, it dominates a huge chunk of South American history. For it was at Potosí in 1544, twelve years after Pizarro captured Atahualpa at Cajamarca, that the Spanish found what they'd come for. Or rather, an Indian named Huallpa found it, while chasing llamas. What he discovered was silver – literally a mountain of it.

Until then, the mountain was known as the Sumaj Orcko – the beautiful hill. (The change of name is instructive.) The Indians knew it contained silver: the Inca Huayna Capaj had even attempted to mine it. But, legend has it, no sooner had his men started digging than a thunderous voice boomed out, saying, 'This is not for you; God is keeping these riches for those who come from afar.' The Indians fled in terror and the Inca renamed the place Potojsi, which means 'to thunder' in Quechua.[18]

The Cerro Rico fulfilled every conquistadores' dream. Soon Potosí was famous: the biggest silver mine in the world; one of the biggest and richest cities the world had ever seen. Cervantes had Don Quixote coin a phrase that entered the Spanish language – 'vale un Potosí' (worth a Potosí) to describe anything incredibly lucrative.

By 1573, just twenty-eight years after the discovery of silver, Potosí had a population of 120,000 – as big as London and larger than Rome, Madrid or Paris. It had become the focal point of the Spanish colonies: Chile supplied meat; Argentina supplied textiles and draft animals; Indians from all over Peru and Bolivia were sent as labourers.

The Spanish residents of Potosí lived the good life. The town boasted 36 magnificently-decorated churches, 36 gambling houses, 14 dancehalls, theatres, bull-rings and salons. The finest luxury goods were imported from around the world: silks and fine fabrics from Italy, diamonds and jewels from India and Ceylon, the latest fashions from London and Paris, carpets from Persia, perfumes from Arabia. Famous artists like Holgüin – 'Latin America's El Greco' – worked on its churches. Even the horses were said to be shod with silver.

But for those forced to work in the mines, life was anything but luxurious.

Indians from all over the Viceroyalty of Peru were forced to leave their homes to keep the silver flowing. A decree in 1572 required Indians and black slaves to work and live underground, without leaving the mine or seeing daylight, for four months at a time. They laboured chained to each other; when one collapsed from exhaustion his body was simply hacked from the shackles. Miners had to carry heavy sacks seven hundred feet up flimsy ladders where one slip meant death. The air was filled with poisonous dust. As many as eight million men may have died in the inhuman conditions of the Potosí mines; from accidents, exhaustion, collapsing shafts or silicosis.

****

el Tio
"Bolivians die with rotted lungs so that the world may consume cheap tin. What does the Bolivian miner's bitter life matter to the consumer of preserves or the money-exchange manipulators?"
EDUARDO GALEANO: *OPEN VEINS OF LATIN AMERICA*

We took a trip to one of the co-operative mines that now work the exhausted seams of the Cerro Rico. Since the collapse of world tin prices in 1985 the state mine has closed but desperate miners still search for scraps of silver, using the most basic tools and minimal safety standards.

Our guide was called Julio Cesar. He was in a bad mood because four German tourists had made him wait while they finished their coffee.

'We are paying, so he can wait,' they said.

'Julius Caesar, the conqueror of England,' we joked, to cheer him up. Julio didn't smile. He clearly didn't remember conquering any gringo country. He took us to a shop where he told us to buy presents for the miners: cigarettes, coca leaves, matches, nitro-glycerene and dynamite. I didn't feel entirely safe carrying this explosive mix and thrust it into the hands of the first miner we met.

A dirt road wound up the side of the giant slag-heap that the Cerro has become. At the entrance to the mine, two thatched huts served as changing-rooms and shelters. Julio went into one and produced helmets and Davy Safety Lamps straight out of Dickensian England. Two miners sat on the gravel, chewing coca leaves and drinking home-made whisky. They said they were celebrating the discovery of a new vein of silver. They poured some whisky on the ground. 'An offering to the mountain,' Julio explained. One of the miners pressed a piece of silver into Melissa's hand. His left leg was deformed – the result, he said, of an accident with a drill.

The mine shaft was so low that Mark and I almost had to crawl. Julio explained that the Cerro yields so little now that the co-operatives can't afford to waste time on such luxuries as a tunnel you can stand up in. Makeshift planks of wood supported the ceiling.

'Yes, there are cave-ins, and other accidents,' said Julio, 'but the biggest danger is silicosis. The dust inside the mines is very dangerous. It eats your lungs. After maybe ten or fifteen years you can die.' We were about a mile inside the hill and there was no ventilation except from the tiny entrance. Shadowy figures, lit only by their headlamps, hacked at the rockface with hand-held picks, sweat pouring off their brows. Boys of no more than fourteen or fifteen ran up the loose slopes carrying sacks of rocks half their own weight.

'I worked in the mines for eight years. Now two years as a guide, every day inside the mine. Maybe I too have silicosis. Maybe I too will die,' Julio mused glumly.

'Where are all the miners?' one of the Germans complained. 'You promised us there would be more miners.'

'Yesterday they found some silver, so last night they celebrate. A lot of drinking. So today, not many are working.' Julio explained irritably. 'They do not work only for tourists. Is that OK?' The German mumbled that, yes, it was OK.

Julio stopped in front of a face carved out of the rock, strewn with multi-coloured paper streamers. A brace of cigarettes were balanced in its mouth. This, Julio said, was El Tio. The name literally means Uncle, but its horns betray its real persona. The Devil. The owner of the Cerro itself.

The paper and cigarettes were symbolic offerings made by the miners for protection and luck. But this was a Devil with the sharp features and goatee beard of a conquistador, a European.

'For the miners,' Julio said, 'these mines belong to the Devil, and the Devil is a European.' He paused. 'We miners hate Europeans,' he added.

****
the open veins of Latin America
The Conquest resonates across the centuries. It changed everything: Latin America today can only be understood in the light of this one cataclysmic, epoch-making event.

The Conquest replaced a self-sufficient agricultural economy with one based on exploitation. Potosí was only the start. Next came sugar – before the conquest a scarce and valuable commodity in Europe. Sugar created the slave trade and exhausted the soil of the Caribbean and north-east Brazil. Other mono-crops followed: coffee, cotton, bananas. Cacao in Venezuela. Cattle in Argentina and Uruguay. Rubber in 19th century Brazil.

Then there were minerals: gold from Minas Gerais in Brazil, nitrates from Chile's Atacama Desert, tin from Oruro in Bolivia, Mexican silver, Brazilian iron, Chilean copper. Today, oil is destroying the Amazon. Each fed the demands of distant economies instead of hungry local mouths. They replaced basic food crops. They depended on cheap labour. They tied producers to a world market where prices could crash overnight if the West's needs changed or the supply was exhausted or a rival flooded the market (as Britain did with Malaysian rubber in the last century).

And it was Western businessmen who controlled the trade – in the 19th century they were mainly British, today they are mainly from the United States – while Latin America's landowners and mine bosses squandered their wealth aping the extravagances of Europe's aristocracy.

****
night bus to La Paz
Another nightbus, this time from Potosí to La Paz. The bus rattles along, shuddering over the bumpy surface. These night journeys are merging into one continuous, interrupted dream. Always the same. Waking and dozing in fitful sleep, ambient techno music on my Walkman, legs jammed against the seat in front. Everyone twisting and turning to get comfort-

able, contorted bodies in rows of seats, always a crying baby somewhere. Outside, shadows of dark hills, more sensed than seen. Isolated
buildings, solitary lights – how lonely they feel in the cold black night of
the altiplano.

****

a new world order

*The Conquest didn't just change the Americas. It also created our mod-
ern world. In 1492 Europe, still depopulated from the Black Death,
stood on the periphery of its world. For most of the planet's inhabitants, what happened in Europe was unknown or unimportant. For the
people of the Muslim domain that stretched from North Africa to the
Philippines, for instance; or of such great Asian empires and kingdoms
as China, India and Japan; or of powerful African city-states like Benin
and Mali; or for the Americans themselves – for them all, Europe mattered little.*

*Europe's main trading need was for spices from the Far East, but trade
routes to Asia were controlled by the Arabs – a stranglehold the
Crusades had tried and failed to break. In 1492, after 800 years of trying, King Ferdinand and Queen Isabella had finally driven the Moors out
of southern Spain. But it wasn't until eighty years later, in 1571, that
the Spanish succeeded in wresting control of the eastern Mediterranean
from the Ottoman navy at the battle of Lepanto.*

*In the meantime, a fortune awaited anyone who could cut out the
Islamic middlemen, for a few grams of pepper or saffron or salt were
worth more than a man's life.[19] Forget God or gold. It was the search
for new routes to Asia's spices that drove European exploration. In 1487
Bartholomew Diaz rounded the Cape of Good Hope: in 1498 Vasco de
Gama made it all the way around Africa and opened a new route to
India that bypassed the Muslim world. And in 1492 – the same year the
Spanish reconquered Andalusia – Columbus reached the Americas.*

*Suddenly, Europe moved to the centre of the world-map: both literally
– with a whole new Western hemisphere to balance out the Orient –
and ideologically. The New World dramatically increased the power of
Christianity. In 1492, Britain and Spain had populations of 3 million
each, Portugal about a million, while estimates for the Americas vary
from 40 to 100 million. The conquest made Christianity the most wide-
spread religion on earth (even if most of the Church's new flock
promptly died before their souls could be saved).*

But the main consequence was the beginning of the European-dominated world economy. South America is twice as big as Europe, with enormous mineral and agricultural richness. According to Galeano, silver from Potosí quadrupled European reserves during the 16th century; a massive injection of investment capital which kick-started capitalism. Sugar, with its slave trade, built the mercantile trade system. Together, they financed the industrial revolution, the scientific renaissance, the final defeat of Islam and the colonial invasions of North America, Australia, Africa and Asia.

Ironically, the Spanish were not the ones to benefit. After the Inquisition expelled or put to death their Jewish and Moorish financiers, most of the funding of – and profiting from – the Conquest fell to bankers in Britain, Holland, France and Italy. Spain, with its profligate and in-debt monarchy, remained backward. The Conquest actually hastened Spain's decline as a European power, while heralding Europe's domination on the world stage.

****

La Paz

We approached La Paz in the early morning. the altiplano gave way to El Alto, a vast slum where 96% of babies are born weighing less than 5.5 lbs (the international standard for underweight births).[20] We passed a base of the Bolivian airforce. A sign above the entrance proclaimed 'Fuerza Aeronautica Boliviana' and, below that, in huge letters, the initials FAB. I jabbed Melissa excitedly and did a Thunderbirds impression.

'So what?' said Melissa, 'You and your bloody words again. You think you're so clever.'

She seemed upset. I was surprised. Maybe it was the Bimbo thing.

The flat suburbs of El Alto ended abruptly and we found ourselves on the rim of a vast fissure that fell away to the city centre 400m below. The view is as spectacular as any city-scape in the world. Imagine a town built inside, say, the Grand Canyon, covering its floor and climbing its sides. Towering above the far side of the canyon, the snow-covered massif of Illimani rose to 6,402m and shimmered in the crisp sunlight.

La Paz is the world's highest capital. (El Alto is at 4,000m.) The airport's runway is twice as long as normal because of the lack of air resistance to slow down planes. It's just conceivable that you could step off a plane here and die from altitude sickness, which would be a bad start to any holiday.

The bus lurched over the edge and wound down into the canyon, towards the city centre.

Close up, La Paz fails to match the drama of that initial view. The centre is mainly Sixties office-blocks, while the streets that climb the canyon slopes are covered by the plain 'Andean rectangle' houses, topped by a mass of washing lines and TV aerials.

The main thoroughfare, the Prado, follows the bottom of the canyon, where a river once ran. (The river is now underground.) Steep streets climb away from the Prado: to the left is the old centre around the Presidential Palace; to the right, behind the San Francisco church, is a sprawling network of Indian street markets. In the Prado itself, *campesinas* sit on the pavement, incongruously selling watches or Sony Walkmans or pirated copies of computer manuals. Almost everyone is Indian: yet Indians were not even allowed to walk on the city's pavements until 1952.

In La Paz, unlike most cities, the rich live lower down, sheltered from the biting winds of the *altiplano*. Follow the Prado downhill and faces become more *Latino*, the cars newer, the shops smarter, the clothes more Western. Finally, deep in the canyon, you reach Calacoto, the city's lowest and most exclusive district, where rich Bolivians and expats shop in glitzy malls and live in expensive walled suburbs with armed guards at the entrance.

We checked into a quiet hotel called 'Residencial Illimani', then went for a drink. Inside the bar, a group of businessmen were well on their way to incoherence, wailing along to local songs on a juke-box. Mark put on 'We are the Champions' by Queen, and everyone wailed to that too. Having chosen the song, we felt obliged to join in. All around us, men lay slumped forward with their heads on the table. Some slept. Others sobbed quietly, making no attempt to hide their tears. It was only eight o'clock. One of the businessmen came over to talk to us.

'You look like you're all having a good time,' I remarked.

'*Si, amigos.* But you know, a Bolivian doesn't drink because he wants to.'

'Why, then?'

'He drinks because he has to. Life is tough. We can't afford to go on holidays like you, but sometimes we need a break too.'

Bolivians, he explained, drink not for pleasure or to lubricate social occasions, but expressly to get drunk. This they do very quickly. The bars are full by 6pm. By 9pm they are carting bodies out to the pavement. La Paz may well be the world's most alcoholic city: at night virtually everyone is staggering about in a drink-induced haze.

We left the businessmen singing and weeping and went in search of food. Mark decided on the cheap option of a hamburger from a street stall. A man beside us ordered one too, but was too drunk to find his money, if he had any. To help the stall-holder get rid of him, I paid for it instead. Except that neither I nor the stall-holder could make him understand that he now owned a hamburger. We left him fumbling in his pockets for the umpteenth time while the stall-holder tried to persuade him to just take the bloody thing and go away.

****

bolivision (invisible indians)
Next morning, Melissa and I found a cafe for breakfast. The television in the corner was tuned to 'Bolivision' – Bolivia's main TV network.

'Have you noticed,' I said to Melissa, 'that the actors and presenters are all Latin. And everyone in the news is Latin too – all the politicians, businessmen, pop-stars. You rarely see an Indian face on TV. It's the same in magazines and newspapers, too.'

'It's funny,' said Melissa, 'but I expected South America to be full of, you know, hot-blooded Latin lovers and Latin girls all dancing around on tables in g-strings.'

Yet all around us, eating their lumps of chewy meat, were the round, red-brown Asiatic features of Andean Indians. Long-suffering, stoical features. Short, stocky frames. They stared into their beers or talked softly. No one was dancing on the tables in a g-string. Here in the middle of La Paz, the notion that these were *Latin* countries was so patently untrue that it seemed absurd. How, indeed, did we ever get such an idea?

The answer was there in front of us, on the television. The Indians were 'invisible'. Not on the streets, of course, but when it came to TV or newspapers it was as if they didn't exist. Nor in official documents, where Aymara and Quechua, the main languages of the Andes, have no official status.

Even the names of their homelands hide their presence. Colombia: after Columbus, an Italian who never set foot on Colombian soil. Bolivia: after Simón Bolívar, a *Latino* Venezuelan who spent about two weeks in Bolivia. Ecuador: after an imaginary line. The word Peru does refer to Indians, but not to people who actually came from Peru – it was mistakenly named after the Biru, who once lived on the Pacific coast of Colombia. The Amazon: named after a Greek legend about a tribe of women warriors from northern Turkey or Bulgaria. Indians in general: named after a country on the other side of the planet. The Americas as a whole: named after another Italian, Amerigo Vespucci, an obscure member of a few expeditions to the North American mainland between 1499 and 1502. Latin America – named after the conquering minority, not the conquered majority.

Thanks to Hollywood, we think of American Indians as the buffalo-hunting horsemen of the North American plains, although *they'd* only been riding horses for a short while anyway and there were – and are – far more 'Red Indians' in Latin America than in the United States.[21]

Latin America's conquerors have created a fiction in which the Indians barely exist. They've been assigned the status of beasts of burden: there to work but rarely mentioned in polite society.

****

the real thing
That evening, we all returned to the cafe for dinner. A woman sat on the pavement outside, frying chicken. Inside, we ordered huge greasy fry-ups and big bottles of cheap Bolivian beer.

The room had once been painted white, with a half-dozen battered Formica tables and chairs. It was decorated with a huge poster of a Mexican singer, done up in full *mariachi* outfit with an enormous sombrero and equally-outsized moustache. Next to him was a soft-focus Seventies shot of a topless English blonde and a painting of The Last Supper.

As we ate, we noticed a *Latino* girl at the next table staring at us. Maybe she'd counted two men and one woman and figured that one of us must be spare. She was in her mid-twenties, dressed in impossibly-tight jeans and T-shirt, slightly overweight and more-than-slightly over made-up, with long, black hair and dark, Latin eyes. She wasn't beautiful, but she had a sexual presence. Maybe we'd just seen too many *campesinas* with the bodies of prop forwards and skin as tough as ancient bulls.

The girl lent over and asked if one of us wanted her meal, which she'd hardly touched. She had a deep, husky voice, like Marlene Dietrich in Spanish. She said her name was Jenny. She'd just woken up with a terrible hangover and couldn't face food. It was 7pm.

Mark wasn't turning down anything free. He wolfed down her plate of fried fish, and we agreed to have a drink at a bar she knew called 'La Luna'. And that was were the trouble began.

As we puffed our way up to the bar, Jenny pressed a little bag into Mark's hand.

'A present,' she said. Cocaine, maybe three grams. The sort of present Mark appreciated.

La Luna was a trendy sort of place, with soft orange lighting, black-and-white photos of old film stars on the wall and candles in wine bottles on the tables. It was aiming for a Parisian Left Bank bohemian atmosphere. Drinks were expensive and it was early, and the place was deserted. Mark headed for the toilets. He didn't come out. I followed him.

'I suppose you want some of *my* coke, don't you,' Mark huffed.

****

Bolivian marching powder

Time for a few lines of cocaine (so to speak). Bolivia probably earns more from cocaine than from all its legal exports combined. Although Colombia is the world's 'cocaine capital', much coca is actually grown in the eastern jungles of Bolivia or Peru and smuggled through the Amazon to Colombia, where it's refined and shipped or flown to the States.

Coca has been grown in the Andes for 4,000 years. The Spanish at first tried to ban it because of its use in religious rituals. Then, realising it made the Indians work harder, the Catholic Church went into the narcotics business itself, soon controlling the trade in what it had once called 'the delusion of the devil.' In 1859, the active ingredient, cocaine, was isolated and the West discovered it. (It was, of course, the special ingredient that added life to Coca-Cola until 1906.)[22] But seen from a Bolivian perspective, coca is a typical export, in that Bolivia supplies the raw material but dealers in the West make most of the profit.[23] Still, the plant grows well in poor soil, lasts for up to 20 years, produces up to four crops a year and is worth around ten times what most other crops fetch. And roughly one third of Bolivians now depend on the cocaine industry.

****

a knock at the door

La Luna was quiet so we bought some beers and went back to our hotel room to carry on with the coke. At around midnight, Jenny got up to leave and discovered that she'd lost her wallet. There was a phone in the courtyard, so she called the bar. The wallet was there. Before leaving, she gave us her number and pressed another bag of coke into Mark's hand. She'd definitely worked out how to make herself popular with him. But suddenly, I felt nervous.

'You do realise that Jenny, who we met four hours ago, now knows where we are staying. And she knows we've got cocaine, because she gave it to us. Anyone smell a set-up?'

'Better hurry up and finish it off, then,' said Mark, queuing up another three thick lines.

'At least they don't hang you for drug offences in Bolivia,' Melissa said, rolling up a banknote.

'I knew I could rely on you two to be sensible.'

'Did you know Robert Louis Stevenson wrote *Dr Jekyll and Mr Hyde* in six days by taking cocaine,' Mark told us. 'That's what the story's all about, too.'

'I thought it was about you,' Melissa joked.

'Same thing, really,' Mark grinned, already preparing another trail of white powder. 'My hands should be going all hairy any second now, so watch out.'

Although it gave you a very smooth buzz, the coke wore off surprisingly quickly. Maybe because it wasn't cut with cheap speed and who-knows-what-else, as it would have been in England. A few hours later, I even felt like sleep. Mark and Melissa kept on tucking into the rapidly-diminishing contents of the bag.

Suddenly, I was being shaken awake by Melissa.

'The police. Wake up, quick.'

It was dark. No one was around. Someone was banging on the front gate, which was locked, and shouting. Melissa was running around in a panic.

'I'd better hide this coke somewhere,' Mark said, and disappeared.

The banging continued. No one answered. More banging and shouting, then the sound of the hotel proprietress stumbling downstairs. Melissa jumped into bed with me.

'Pretend to be asleep,' she ordered.

'I was asleep,' I mumbled.

We heard the woman fiddle with her keys. Then the keys in the lock, and the door swinging open. Through our bedroom window, we saw a hopelessly-drunk Bolivian fall face-first through the doorway and land in a heap at the woman's feet. He staggered up again and stomped off to his room, complaining loudly, while the proprietress heroically lived up to her Lonely Planet publicity, which said that she will 'pleasantly admit you if you return after lock-up time.' Melissa got up and went off to find Mark and the coke.

****

shopping

The next day was a supplies day. Our (or at least, my) main reason for coming to Bolivia was to trek in the rugged Cordillera Real. A five day hike runs from Milluni, thirty miles east of La Paz, across two 5,000m passes and down to a town called Coroico. It traverses an incredible variety of landscapes, dropping 3,000m from glaciated mountain terrain through alpine meadows and cloudforest to the tropical Yungas region around Coroico. And it's nearly all downhill. Essentially, it is a descent of the eastern slopes of the Andes from the watershed to the fringes of the Amazon.

'Just think how firm my thighs will be,' Melissa grinned.

Mark wasn't so impressed. Asked to chose between a hike in the mountains and a bag of cocaine, there was no contest. He said nothing.

To be safe, we changed hotel without telling Jenny. The Hotel Torino was right in the centre of town, in the street behind the Presidential Palace. Like the Gran Casino in Quito, it is a backpacker classic. An old building, its four floors all overlooked an inner courtyard. Occupying this courtyard was a cafe that might have been transported from central Europe, with black and white tiled floor and delicate wrought-iron tables and potted plants around an elegant central fountain. In one corner, a quartet in evening dress played chamber music. This genteel cafe, populated by a mix of Bolivian businessmen and scruffy backpackers, was covered with a translucent plastic roof. Above this, a maze of corridors and unexpected stairways sprawled back into what once must have been different buildings. Our room was a plywood cubicle with no windows, and the floorboards in the corridor outside our door seemed to pick up and amplify every footstep from every part of the building.

Before we went shopping, I suggested we settle some bills. Until now, I'd been paying for things up front and Melissa and Mark were meant to repay me at intervals.

Except Mark never volunteered to pay his debts. This was irritating, especially as I'd lent him most of his money in the first place. He scrutinised my list like a horrified hotel guest handed a huge bar tab. It stretched back three weeks. Mark picked out something near the start.

'For a start, I didn't have *two* eggs when we stopped in Lima. And how do you make that meal in Arequipa come to 5 *soles*. Tell me what I ate there that cost 5 *soles*?' I couldn't remember what I'd had for breakfast that morning, let alone what Mark had eaten in Lima three weeks ago. Mark carried on picking holes in my list.

'I notice,' he commented, 'that you keep adding little extras to these figures.'

I was gobsmacked. The idea that I was trying to cheat Mark out of a few odd pennies was just too absurd to contemplate. We were, after all, talking about a couple of dollars or less.

I could see that Mark resented being in my debt. He resented the implicit pressure to be grateful. He was so determined to be stronger and better than everyone else that he felt threatened by accepting help. To him, it was an accusation: a pointing-out of his failure to manage by himself.

'Don't give me that gratitude bullshit. There's no such thing as unselfish behaviour,' he rationalised. 'Everyone expects a pay-off, whether they admit it or not. I'm just honest about it. You lent me that money because you wanted someone along on this trip with a real personality.'

'Listen, Mark, you're just being a self-centred little kid. Just grow up, will you. This whole bloody arrangement is only because you can't be bothered to make sure you change enough money. Well, you'd better change some money today, because I'm not lending you another penny.'

Mark glared at me.

'And,' he said, 'you're always poncing drugs off me. I notice that you always let me score the coke, take all the risks. When are you going to score some gear, then?'

'Look, you two,' Melissa interrupted. 'we'd better get this shopping done.'

We split up. I sent Melissa and Mark off together because I didn't trust either of them to get it right alone. I set off to do my share of the shopping in the markets behind the San Francisco church. I made a detour to the witches' market, where a few stalls in a narrow lane sold lucky charms and dried llama foetuses. A few inches long, these looked like macabre dolls. Buried in the foundations of a new house, they were meant to bring good luck. There were other odd-looking things in jars; plant roots, beads, hair, stones, statues guaranteeing everything from wealth and health to passing exams. I brought a tiny statuette of a copulating couple – a charm which the stall-holder promised would make me irresistible to women. You never know when you might need something like that. ('If you had any charm of your own, of course, you wouldn't need one of those,' Melissa commented when I showed it to her later.) I wondered if they had anything I could use on Mark.

On my way back, I stopped at a sweet stall, manned by a boy of about ten with a runny nose and big round eyes. I asked him for forty bars of chocolate.

The boy looked frightened. First of all, he was being addressed by a big, strange foreign man. And secondly . . . forty bars. Had he heard right? Could he be sure that I was actually speaking Spanish? Forty bars was more than he expected to sell in a week, let alone in one go. He looked around urgently for his mother, suspecting a trick. But he was alone. Tentatively, he offered me two pieces.

'No, I want forty.' I said.

He still wasn't sure he'd heard right. He gave me four.

'No, not four. Forty.' I repeated.

I held up my fingers four times to mime forty. The boy looked at me in panic. He was paralysed with confusion. I began to count out forty of the small chocolate bars.

'No, no, wait for my mother,' he urged. His eyes opened even wider and his jaw dropped.

I didn't want to wait all day. I poured the chocolates into my sack, pressed the money for the forty bars into his hands, waved goodbye and walked off. The boy stared after me, and then stared at the money. I hadn't even haggled. How was he going to explain *this* to his mother?

Melissa and Mark were waiting back at the Torino. They'd brought exactly half of everything we needed. It was all the cheapest, worst quality stuff.

'I'm never going shopping with him again,' Melissa said when Mark was out of earshot. 'The guy's got no idea how much food we need for a week in the mountains, and he just kept saying everything I wanted was too expensive.'

Then we remembered that Mark had arranged to meet Jenny that night at La Luna. She was waiting for us in the bar, in a figure-hugging white blouse and the same painfully tight jeans. I wondered how long it took her to get into them: it couldn't have been easy. Her hair was tied back in Spanish style, held in place with a red velvet bow matching her bright red lipstick. More importantly, she had some more coke. We stopped arguing for long enough to discreetly polish off a few lines. Then Mark realised that he had no money.

'You'll have to go and find some, then,' I said. 'I told you I wasn't going to front you any more cash,' Mark glared at me.

'Where am I going to find somewhere to change money at this time of night?' he asked.

'You should have thought of that earlier,' I pointed out.

Jenny looked bemused, but said she had a friend who worked in a hotel who could change money at this time of night. When we got there, the friend wasn't on duty.

'Never mind,' Jenny said, 'I have another friend in another hotel who can change money.' We checked it out. Jenny went inside to talk to him, came out and shook her head. She considered the situation for a minute.

'Never mind, I have a friend who works in the casino. I think he can change money.' The friend at the casino couldn't do it either. Melissa and I decided to go back to the hotel. I reminded Mark that we were planning to leave at 6am next morning.

'Don't worry. I'll be there,' he growled.

Our alarm went off at 5.30am next morning. It was the only way of telling that it was morning in our windowless cubicle. I got dressed and banged on Mark's door, but he wasn't in his room.

At exactly 6am, Mark strode up the stairs and marched down the corridor towards us.

'I told you I'd be here,' he said.

****

do the bus stop
The guidebook said we needed to catch a bus to the *Plaza 16 de Julio* in El Alto (from where other buses went to Milluni) but not which bus or where it left from. In Bolivia, 'bus stops' are more concepts than physical objects anyway, so I led Mark and Melissa down to the Prado, canvassed some passers-by and arrived at a majority verdict as to where our bus might stop. We dumped our bags on the pavement and I started examining the dozens of buses that were passing. An hour passed. Melissa, getting bored, wandered off. Mark propped his pack up against a wall, sat down and fell asleep.

Once more, I was left to sort things out.

Buses passed, people hanging out of the door and windows. Two more hours passed. Then I saw it. *16 Julio*, scrawled on a scrap of cardboard in the windscreen. I shouted to Mark, who grunted and started to get up. And Melissa . . . Where *was* Melissa? The bus arrived.

'*Si, si,*' said the ticket-boy, 'this is the *16 Julio* bus.'

I spotted Melissa, looking in a shop window on the opposite side of the street.

'Quick, quick, *señor*, get on,' the boy beckoned. I shouted to Melissa, but she was too far away to hear me. The bus left. Mark grinned at me and went back to sleep.

When Melissa returned, I vented my frustration on her. 'Melissa, you thick cow, how can we catch a bus if you're five hundred yards away.' I felt like a parent dragging two children shopping.

Melissa turned on me.

'*You,*' she shouted, 'are a control freak. Do you know that? Everything's got to be your way. You always think you're in charge. Well, fuck you.' Melissa didn't like being told off.

'Well, fuck you too,' I replied. 'OK, Melissa, *you* be in charge. You get us on this bus, then.' I sat down next to Mark, who was asleep again, and got out a book.

Melissa looked at the traffic. I knew perfectly well that she had no idea what bus we wanted. Or even where, exactly, we were going. Melissa knew, too, but she wasn't going to admit it, so instead she stood on the roadside and watched the passing buses. And, then, of course, after three hours without a bus, I could see three buses approaching together, all going to Plaza 16 Julio. I was stuck. I'd resigned my post. But . . . I could see that Melissa wasn't going to stop the buses. I knew the mature thing to do would be to flag one down.

But . . .

The buses cruised past. Melissa stopped pretending she had any idea what she was doing and sat down with a huff on the pavement beside Mark, who was now snoring loudly with his Clint Eastwood hat pulled down over his face. The three of us sat there, not speaking.

After another hour, I asked, 'How are we doing, Melissa?'

'Oh, just fuck off,' she replied. She picked up her rucksack and marched off. I watched her go. For a moment, I contemplated simply abandoning both Mark and Melissa. I shook Mark awake.

'Back to the hotel,' I told him.

'I see even your own supporters are deserting you,' he jeered.

Mark and I checked back into the Torino. The elegant courtyard cafe had turned into a political rally. A huge banner of a *Latino* politician hung behind the podium and rows of chairs were filling up with *campesinos*.

'I'm going to find Jenny,' Mark said.

For a while I watched the rally, wondering if I'd ever see Melissa again. The politician and *campesinos* left and were replaced with a big 'high society' party. The courtyard was nothing if not versatile. I fell asleep to the sound of Abba's 'Dancing Queen'. More crap Swedish pop.

I was woken by banging on the door. It was 2am. Melissa was outside. 'Let me in, will you,' she said. It was good to hear her voice.

'Fuck off,' I said, and pretended to go back to sleep. From outside the door, a barrage of abuse betrayed Melissa's Scottish roots. I heard her stamp off down the corridor.

Next morning, Melissa knocked again. This time I let her in. She was in a good mood. She told me that she and a few other backpackers had been watching the party from the balcony and decided to gatecrash it. It was a birthday party for a rich *Latino* girl, with food and champagne and all the girls in ball gowns and diamonds. The teenagers (who probably wanted nothing more than to be European themselves) were happy to be joined by some real Westerners – even if they were dressed in dirty jeans and hiking boots. Melissa danced the night away to Abba.

At about 7am, Mark wandered back.

'Ready to go?' he asked casually.

We tried again. We had breakfast in the market near the San Francisco church, squeezing through tight rows of crowded stalls to find a spare seat. Short, powerful Aymara girls with long black plaited hair and white aprons stood elbow-to-elbow, next to piles of fried chicken and steaming cauldrons of soup. '*Joven, pase no mas,*' they shouted over blaring radios, 'Go no further.' Around a corner, fruit juice stall-holders peered through tiny gaps in walls of tropical fruit. One girl was so eager for business that she rushed out and grabbed the man in front of us by his jacket, and was dragging him physically towards her stall. Eventually she pulled his jacket right off. 'Are you trying to undress me?' he protested. She let him go and grabbed us instead. She served a drink called a *supervitamino* which consists of about eight types of fruit, carrots, milk, chocolate, peanuts and malt beer, all liquidised and served in a pint glass shaped like a naked woman's torso.

This time, we caught the bus to *16 Julio* within a couple of minutes. Unfortunately it was Sunday, and the connecting bus from *16 Julio* didn't run on Sundays, so we had to pay $30 to a truck driver for the $1 bus trip to Milluni. But at least we were moving.

****

Milluni

The landscape approaching Milluni might have been the surface of Mars. The bare brown hills were streaked red with iron and topped with patches of white snow. (OK, I know there's no snow on Mars.) Milluni itself was no more than an iron-mine with a few rows of barracks to house the workers. It seemed deserted. We followed the path into the hills until we reached a small hydro-electric power station beside a lake. Low cloud enveloped us, blotting out the sun. Peels of thunders rumbled ominously around the mountains.

Mark did not look happy. It was cold. He was feeling the effects of three sleepless nights on cocaine. And he was just beginning to consider what a five day hike through the mountains involved.

'Let's hope you're little silver foil thing keeps you warm,' Melissa joked.

Mark lost his temper.

'I didn't want to come on this bloody trek in the first place,' he snarled.

'So why are you here, then?' I asked.

'When I agreed to come to South America, you never told me it was going to be this fucking cold. You know I'm not interested in wandering around a load of hills.'

'You liked the Inca Trail, didn't you?'

'Exactly. We've already done one trek, so I can't see why you want to do another one. Your basic problem,' Mark said, 'is that you two don't like people. You'd rather be up on your own in some bloody mountain. Well, that's not why I came to South America. I'm a Party Animal.'

Melissa laughed. 'You're a what?'

'A Party Animal.'

'Well, you should have said that before we left La Paz,' I said.

It was a fitting spot for an argument. Its rocky bleakness would have suited King Lear at his maddest. Swirling mist lifted off the lake, then dropped again to swallow the whole landscape, until we could hardly see each other. We paced around, mainly because it was too cold to stand still. Three disconnected figures, pacing and looking in different directions. I felt strangely detached, as if seeing myself on film. I watched Melissa and Mark drift in and out of the mist.

Mark was particularly upset, he was saying, because I'd said I wasn't going to bring my ski-jacket. Because of this he'd left his behind too. At the last minute I'd thrown mine into my pack – and it was now keeping me warm while Mark shivered in his woollen poncho.

I decided that Mark's torrent of ridiculous complaints was simply the irritable after-effects of the cocaine, and ignored him. Mark ranted to Melissa instead. I huddled on a rock a few metres away and listened to his words drifting disjointedly through the fog.

' . . . was going to bring my skiing jacket . . . he told me not to bring it . . . wouldn't be so bloody cold now . . . two to one . . . always outvoted . . . can't even have a decent argument . . . Party Animal . . . specifically told me not to bring my skiing jacket . . . he just likes rocks . . . I'm a people person . . . no fun . . . whose idea was this anyway? . . . my fuckin' skiing jacket . . . what I want for a change . . .'

It was late and getting colder, and we needed to camp. Beside the lake was the hut of the power station attendant. We asked him if we could spend the night in one of a line of deserted rooms that formed a small terrace opposite his house. He said we could. He said he lived here with his wife and children. I asked him if he liked living here, as it seemed an inhospitable place. He said he did. He didn't seem inclined to talk. Maybe that was why he liked this solitary spot in the first place.

We spent the night in the barn. Melissa brewed some instant soup and we got into our sleeping bags and tried to sleep. Mark wrapped himself in his aluminium space blanket and the woollen poncho he'd bought in Copacabana and almost froze to death. In the morning his mind was made up.

'I'm going back to La Paz,' he said. 'I'll leave a note in the Torino to tell you where I'll be.'

'Fine,' I said.

'Fine,' he said. Picking up his pack, he marched back the way we'd come. We watched him disappear into the distance in his poncho and Clint Eastwood hat.

'What are we going to do now?' Melissa asked.

'Do the trek, I guess,' I said.

****

king of the world

Mark disappeared down the path. The clouds were gone and it was a bright morning. Towering over the lake was the huge white bulk of a mountain called Huayna Potosí. Icy-fingered glaciers reached right down to the water's edge. Behind us was another peak, smaller but also snow-covered. Looking past the dam at the end of the lake, the valley between these two mountains fell away steeply. Far below, a silver thread of a river meandered through it.

Melissa looked at me and laughed.

'It's awesome,' she grinned.

Free from Mark's negative energy, we could clear our minds and bodies in the thin, pure mountain air. We crossed the first pass and spent most of the day hiking past a series of glacier-fed lakes, mist swirling around us once more.

We reached the second pass in mid-afternoon, the highest point on the trek. A steep scree-slope led to a low saddle on the ridge that circled the final lake. At over 5,000m, each step was a struggle. I had to stop to catch my breath every ten paces. When I reached the top, though, I felt like the King of the World. All around us lay the silent alpine world of the high Andes; grey rocks, white snow-fields and calm blue lakes. Ahead were forested valleys that led, eventually, to the vast Amazon jungle. It was a landscape on a giant scale.

We camped just below the pass. As the sun went down, the temperature plunged. We slept in all our clothes and woke to find our tent covered in ice. Two giant birds glided overhead: eagles or vultures or maybe even condors.

From here it was, literally, all downhill. Through grassy pastures where wild horses eyed us warily, down into a valley beside a bubbling white stream. As we descended, it got warmer. Having seen nobody in the two days since we'd left Mark, Melissa had just decided it was safe to go topless when we bumped into a solitary shepherd. He looked equally surprised to see us.

We passed a tiny clutch of stone cottages with thatched roofs and low stone walls. Women washed clothes on rocks beside the river, and a couple of children chased a few cattle. Three days from roads in this remote valley, it felt like we had stepped back a thousand years. We spent the night in another tiny settlement, camped beside the river on damp grass behind one of the houses. The owner managed to find a couple of beers to sell us, then returned to chopping wood.

The scenery was steadily changing, from alpine valleys to humid cloud-forest. Dense foliage enclosed the path. For the next two days the path clung to the steep sides of the valley, and breaks in the trees revealed endless folds of forested valleys and hillsides ahead of us.

****

mountains
Silence. Stillness. Purity. People who live near great peaks invariably

regard them as holy, as gods themselves or as the home of gods. Vast forces humble us with their size and their timescale – the upward thrust of the earth and the erosive power of wind and water. Life becomes simple. We become attuned to rhythms of elemental opposites – up and down, day and night, warmth and cold. Life or death. Being, or not-being.

****

turtle

The path continued through the forest, clinging to the valleyside, often steep and wet. Melissa had one nasty fall from a slippery ledge, her landing cushioned by her rucksack. I came round a bend to find her lying on her back in a puddle with her arms and legs waving helplessly in the air like an upturned turtle. The sight was hilarious. 'Stop bloody laughing and pick me up,' she snapped.

In the mountains, Melissa was a different person. Her petite frame disguised reserves of strength and stamina, as much mental as physical. Melissa never gave up, and her first instinct in trouble was always to fight, never to give in.

'It's my Scottish blood,' she explained. 'Take my dad. He's a short, stroppy working-class bastard from Dundee who's always looking for a fight. I'm the same. Just better-looking. I remember the first time I went to Dundee. The whole town is full of short angry men looking for a fight.'

She'd discovered mountains with Peter the Teacher. He'd made her climb ice-walls, hike across glaciers, camp in blizzards. She loved it. She loved being out in wild places where you feel free. She loved the physical challenge of walking for days on end. And she loved the mental challenge of the high mountains – the need for self-reliance and the willpower to struggle on in rain, fog and cold.

'Anyway,' she said, 'exercise and nature is the only way to stay off smack.'

****

nip and truck

On the last night of the trek we reached the house of The Japanese Man. He'd come to Bolivia twenty-two years ago, after twenty years in the Japanese navy. He said it reminded him of his childhood home in the Japanese mountains. He was a small, quiet, nervous man who spoke no English and little Spanish. High on this distant hillside, with only a couple of Indian families for neighbours and a pack of little yapping dogs as com-

panions, he'd built this house. He grew his own food and had lovingly created his perfect Japanese garden, with Banzai trees and miniature
bridges over miniature rivers. A miniature Japan. After forty years, there
was no going back to the real Japan.

He showed us his collection of postcards from previous trekkers, it
being something of a tradition to visit him. Then he disappeared into
the house. We didn't see him again. The view from his garden was
stunning, looking back up the valleys through which we'd come. Thin
wisps of cloud drifted beneath the forested ridges and white mountains peeked out above them. The house seemed to float in a separate
world above the clouds. What was it like to live here, day after day?

The next day we crossed a series of rivers. The footbridges had been
washed away by floods and been replaced by tree trunks balanced
high above raging white water, best crossed quickly and without
looking down. We'd lost so much altitude that, instead of ice on our
tent, we were dripping with sweat. Such a transformation. There
were increasing signs of life and people. In the afternoon I was bitten by a dog. Melissa had been teasing me about my cautious
approach to dogs, so when a tiny lapdog rushed out of a house
towards us, yapping shrilly, I decided to face it like a man. It was,
after all, no bigger than a football – I could have drop-kicked it into
the next valley.

'Show it who's boss,' said Melissa. I strode along the path. It leapt up and
bit my calf.

'You didn't show it who was boss,' Melissa pointed out, unnecessarily.

We reached the road and rode the last few kilometres to Coroico on a
truck. Trucks are a common form of public transport in Bolivia and at
least thirty passengers and their luggage were already perched on top of
the truck's already-full load, hanging on grimly as it swayed over potholes. We threw our gear up and Melissa clambered up the truck's side. I'd
just managed to haul myself up when the truck started off, its initial
lurch depositing me on top of two young girls and their mother. I rolled
over them, and a couple of other people, before coming to rest on my
back in a hollow in the tarpaulin, between an old man and a big basket of
bananas. The old man nodded without expression, as if he saw nothing
unusual in this entrance.

Coroico

Coroico is the perfect place to relax after a hard trek. The village perches on a hilltop surrounded by banana plantations and tropical forest, with panoramic views back up towards the Andes. The climate is beautifully sub-tropical. The local nuns are said to bake the best biscuits and brew the best wine in Bolivia (although the competition isn't stiff in either category).

As always, the food stalls in the market stood side-by-side. As they all sold the same fare, competition for customers was fierce. When we entered, the stall-holders erupted into a bidding war.

'*Hay pescado, hay carne,*' they shouted. Fish or meat. But I wanted pollo – chicken.

'*Si, si, hay pollo,*' one of the girls insisted. We sat down.

'*Que quieres?*' she asked. What would we like?

'*Pollo.*'

She thought about this for a while.

'*No. No hay pollo,*' she said sheepishly. Still, as we were sitting down anyway, she did have fish and meat. She showed it to us. But we wanted chicken.

'*Hay pollo, hay pollo,*' twenty other stall-holders chorused in unison. We settled for fish.

****

the most dangerous road in the world

The bus journey back to La Paz was as memorable as the trip down, although for a different reason. Which is, basically, that the road may well be the most dangerous on the planet.

It was built by Paraguayan prisoners-of-war in the 1930s, many of whom died in the process. Rising from Coroico at 1,800m to the 4,000m altiplano, it winds along the sides of impossibly steep valleys with breathtaking views across the cloudforested hills. For much of the time, it is no more than a notch in a cliff. Not along the clifftop, but *half-way up*. A ledge has simply been blasted to allow the road to pass. Waterfalls drop beyond the road.

Others drop directly onto passing trucks, soaking any rooftop passengers.
The cold shower at least distracts from contemplation of the abyss below.

It always amuses me that tourists will worry about muggers, rapists, plane
crashes and malaria, and will cancel a whole trip at the merest mention of
the word 'terrorists', and yet jump on a broken-down bus on a road like
this without a second thought, entrusting their lives to a Bolivian bus driver who'll drive for twelve hours solid. They wouldn't trust the same man to
carry their rucksack across the street. Getting on a bus is by far the most
risky thing that most tourists ever do in Bolivia.

We did give it a second thought. We debated whether it was safer to be
on the roof of a truck or inside a bus (we chose inside). Inside, you didn't
have to worry about being thrown off as you rounded a corner. But on a
roof, you had some slim chance of jumping clear should it plunge over the
side. And plunging over the side was a real possibility. Every bend was
marked with crosses – jokingly known as 'Bolivian Warning Signs' – that bore
witness to past disasters. Far below, we caught glimpses of metal carcass-
es strewn on the rocks. Other passengers eagerly pointed out the wrecks.

'Two trucks went over there last week,' said the man beside us.

At least going up was safer than coming down. To save drivers having to
make constant hill starts, upward traffic was granted right of way and the
inside passage (although technically the wrong side of the road for
Bolivia). This was significant, because the road was unsurfaced and only
really wide enough for one lane of traffic. To let upward traffic pass,
downward vehicles had to inch out toward the crumbling cliff-edge.
And sometimes it literally *did* crumble, taking the truck with it.
Occasionally, too, a driver simply miscalculated by a fraction and
drove right off the edge.

The other advantage of going up was that drivers couldn't drive so fast.
Because despite the danger, everybody still drives as fast as they can,
roaring along the winding track, slamming on their brakes when they
round a corner to find themselves headlight-to-headlight with oncoming
traffic.

At the top, a line of dogs is chained beside the road. Drivers traditionally
throw them some meat before setting off, as an offering to the mountain
gods. To be on the safe side, they also cross themselves and mutter a
prayer to the Virgin Mary, Jesus, a couple of saints and anyone else who

might be listening, deck their bus out with windscreen stickers asking God to protect them, and decorate the back of the bus with spray-painted murals of famous biblical scenes. These precautions are, I'm sure, very wise. But not nearly as wise as driving more slowly.

We tried to put all this to the back of our minds and admire the stunning views. Luckily, we only passed one crash, and by then the road had levelled out to the relative safety of the altiplano. A bus had driven into a ditch and lay there on its side. A crowd stood around looking at it. If you only pass one crash on a Bolivian bus journey, it's been a good day.

section 2

the Amazon

"In today's world there are two
different, irreconcilable
systems: the Indian system,
which is collective, communal,
human, loving, and which
represents nature profoundly;
and the European-derived
system, which is exploitative,
individualistic and egoistic,
and which destroys nature."

SECOND CONFERENCE OF INDIAN
NATIONS OF SOUTH AMERICA,
TIWANAKU, BOLIVIA 6-13TH
MARCH, 1983

Chapter 4
Ecuador: rumbles in the jungle

Tumbes
At the Hotel Torino in La Paz we found a note.
To The Hill People,
See you at the Gran Casino for Christmas.
The Party Animal

Melissa and I set off back to Quito. Christmas was still three weeks away, so we didn't hurry. We visited Sorata in the Cordillera Real, which claims 'the most beautiful setting in Bolivia'. We hoped to do more trekking but it rained continuously, so we watched *The Mission* on the hotel video and wrote letters. The German hotel manager assured us that it never rained in December.

'Tomorrow will be fine, I promise,' he promised every morning. After a week, we gave up. As our bus climbed out of Sorata, we looked back to see the valley bathed in sunshine.

We visited the ruins of Tiwanaku near La Paz, another reminder that the Incas were merely the final chapter in a long history of Andean civilisations. And we retraced our route through Copacabana and Arequipa and Lima.

We spent a night in Tumbes. It was a Saturday and a couple of lively streets full of bars had that Saturday night feel, recognisable the world over: paid yesterday, drunk tonight, no work tomorrow. Knots of people hung around on street-corners. Young girls strolled arm-in-arm, pretending not to notice the boys eyeing them up. Old men paid more attention to their drinks and memories. Street stands served the delicious Peruvian snack, *cerviche*; raw fish marinated in lemon.

We were sitting having a beer when the four men at the next table invited us to join them. They were eager to talk and insisted that they buy us more beer, but were so drunk that we couldn't understand anything they said. One of them kept intoning mournfully, in English, 'I am sorry, I am sorry,' like a mantra. We didn't know what he was sorry about. He looked as if he might have been sorry about everything: about all the injustice and misunderstanding and hatred and foolishness in the world. Perhaps he was sorry that one of his few opportunities to talk to foreigners had come when he was too drunk to speak properly. His eyes betrayed a desperate desire to communicate but his beer-fuddled mind let him down. His friends grabbed my arm and pointed to the quietest of the four.

'He,' they announced with a flourish, 'is an Inca.' They found this extremely funny. He looked the part: a long aquiline nose and pinched, aristocratic, leathery-brown face. The Inca leant forward unsteadily in his chair, his eyes focused into the middle distance. He gave us a happy, drunken smile and beckoned us closer.

'I . . . am . . . an Inca,' he beamed, swaying gently.

'He is an Inca,' his friends roared with delight and slapped him on the back.

'Yes, he is an Inca,' we agreed. It was one of those conversations. We all wanted to talk but lacked the means. The Peruvians slapped the table and slapped their friend and offered us more beer. 'He is an Inca,' they called after us as we left.

'I am sorry,' the sad-looking one mumbled into his beer.

****

Guayaquil . . . independence

'For the Indians, the Republic was a new way of labelling the policies of the ruling clique. Independence brought no liberty for the Indians.'
MANIFESTO OF TIWANAKA, BOLIVIA 1973

Crossing back into Ecuador, we changed buses in Guayaquil. Ecuador's largest town is a busy industrial port that lacks Quito's charm and is avoided by most tourists. We didn't even get off the bus. Guayaquil has only commanded an international stage once, in July 1822, when South America's two greatest revolutionaries met for the only time. Simón Bolívar, descending from Colombia, and José de San Martín, coming up from Peru, had between them just 'liberated' most of the continent. Now they met to discuss the future of the newly-independent states. But their meeting ended in disagreement (setting an immediate trend of political disunity for independent Latin America) and both men were soon deeply disillusioned with the countries they'd created.

'So did everything change with independence?' Melissa asked.

'No,' I said. 'Independence made little difference to Latin America,

because it didn't change the basic structure of colonial society. It wasn't a real revolution. All that happened was that the Latin elites stopped paying taxes to Spain. Spain had, in any case, already become nothing more than a middle-man in the transfer of wealth from Latin American mines and encomiendas to the north European bankers who'd really financed the Conquest. With Spain eliminated, Britain dominated Latin American trade in the 19th century, just as the USA dominates it today. But for the Indians, still forced into the mines and fields on slave terms, it was no change at all.'

Melissa laughed. 'You need one of those . . . erm, those things people stand on when they make speeches,' she said. 'You know, a soapdish.'

****

finished with my woman . . .

When we arrived back in Quito, Mark was playing pool at the Gran Casino 2 with an assorted bunch of travellers. He seemed happy enough to see us. He looked even happier when Melissa collected a bag of grass from our 'man in Quito'. We went back to our hotel room.

Melissa started to roll a joint, but Mark held up his hand to stop her. He grabbed our towels and stuffed them along the gap beneath the door, then went to the window and scanned the street. Apparently satisfied, he drew the curtains and sat down.

'I think I'm being followed,' he whispered conspiratorially.

'Followed?' we asked. 'By whom?'

'By the DEA.'

Melissa looked blank, 'The *deeyeyay*? What's that in English?'

'That *is* English. The DEA. The United States Drug Enforcement Agency.'

'Oh.' Melissa still looked blank. 'Who are they?'

'Well,' Mark explained, 'the US government sends DEA agents and troops down to South America to 'help' local governments in 'their' fight against narcotics. It's easier than doing anything about the real causes of drug use in US cities – poverty, for instance. Anyway, the American military have got to find *something* to do to justify their existence, now that there's no

Commie Threat.'[24]

'And what's all this got to do with you?'

Mark filled us in on his trip back from Bolivia. After we'd split up in Milluni, he'd found a truck mysteriously waiting at the bottom of the hill, as if especially to collect him. Back in La Paz, he'd looked up Jenny. For a couple of nights they hung out at La Luna, where a Chilean flautist sat at their table playing his compositions with tears streaming down his cheeks. Mark had been so inspired that he'd bought himself a *queña* (an Andean flute).

Then Jenny made a proposition. She suggested they take three kilos of Bolivian cocaine through Peru to Quito. Because little cocaine is produced in Ecuador, it was much more expensive there. She had a contact, a rich Chilean who was certain to buy the lot. One deal, no hassle, and a fat profit. It sounded simple. Mark agreed.

They stayed for a fortnight with Jenny's family in Miraflores, the middle-class suburb of Lima, where Jenny's pretty young sister spent the time trying to seduce Mark. They had no problems crossing either from Bolivia to Peru, or from Peru to Ecuador. But in Quito, Jenny's Chilean friend wasn't interested. He'd just got a 'delivery' from someone else.

Mark and Jenny now had a serious amount of cocaine and no plan for disposing of it. Jenny went to the Avenida Amazonas, Quito's main street, and began offering it to everybody she knew. And, it seemed, she knew everybody. What made Mark nervous was that, on the whole, the people were on the other side of the street. And Jenny had a very loud voice.

They hid a chunk of the coke in their hotel, tucked above a polystyrene tile in the bathroom ceiling. In the morning, it had vanished. Mark decided that it was time to split. While Jenny was out shouting at potential customers, he changed hotel.

Then he noticed someone following him. A tall, close-cropped American in sunglasses, smartly dressed with shiny black shoes. Mark had a theory that you can tell undercover cops because they can't get out of the habit of polishing their shoes. But three days had now passed since he split from Jenny, and nothing had happened. Mark figured that they must simply be following him to see if he would lead them to a Mr Big, or at least a Mr Slightly Bigger. Still, he was being careful not to go anywhere where he might bump into Jenny.

****

Baños

We spent Christmas in Baños. The name means Bath, although it also translates as Toilets. While hardly as elegant as its English counterpart, it's also a resort built around hot springs, which are channelled into a sort-of run-down municipal swimming-pool. The baths are on the edge of town, beneath a moist, vegetation-covered cliff at the foot of a waterfall. The locals use them to wash not only themselves, but also their clothes, often wading into the water fully clad.

There are pleasant walks and thundering waterfalls in the surrounding valleys, and the church contains the inevitable 'miraculous Virgin', but there's nothing special about Baños: it's one of those places that everyone visits simply because everyone else goes there.

It's very much a Gringo Trail town. Buskers and *artisanas* line the main drag – the Calle Ambato. There's an English book exchange, a salsa bar, a blues bar, a bar called the 'Hard Rock Cafe, Baños', a Danish bakery and nightly screenings of arty films in English. You can get pizzas, pancakes, French food, German food, veggie food, filter coffee, tropical fruit-salad and muesli. There's even a Mexican restaurant, in case anyone has come to Ecuador to sample Mexican food.

I tried the local speciality, guinea pig. In Quechua it is called cuy because that's the noise they make. I didn't ask whether that was alive or while being cooked. Roasted on a skewer with its four little legs splayed wide and its teeth barred, it looked worryingly like a rat on a stick.

****

the Mike Snape joke

Mark decided we were going to save two dollars by cooking our own Christmas dinner.

'We have steak,' the butcher told us, pointing to a poster of prime fillet on the wall. For some reason we believed him. The meat turned out to be too tough to chew.

'That's because it's organic and not softened up by chemicals,' Mark said confidently.

'Jesus Christ, how much garlic did you put in here?' Melissa asked.

'Twenty cloves,' Mark said. 'Garlic's good for you.'

To wash down this feast, we bought some rum and a few bottles of good Chilean wine.

'*Producto de Qualidad*,' Melissa read from the wine bottle. 'I've never heard of a country called Qualidad. Is it in South America?'

Mark sighed heavily.

We shared the wine from Qualidad with some other guests at the hostel, including a young Oxford don who had just completed his PhD – two years studying hummingbirds in the Colombian rainforest. Post-graduate studies began to sound like a good idea.

'I'll research chi development with a one-hundred-and-fifty year old spiritual teacher in the Himalayas,' Melissa said.

'Himalaya.' Mark corrected.

'Let me guess.' I said to Mark. 'You'd study hallucinogenic drugs around the world?'

'I'm doing that now,' he replied.

'You could always do what Mike Snape did,' I suggested.

Mark and I went quiet.

'Poor bastard,' Mark said after a minute's silence.

'What happened to Mike Snape?' Melissa asked.

Mike Snape was a postgraduate psychology student with whom we'd once shared a house. He had a goatee beard and a manic gleam in his eye and looked like a jovial version of the Devil. He was researching pleasure. This involved plugging electrodes into rats' brains.

'When you stimulate their pleasure centres,' he explained, 'the rats lose the motivation to do anything. If you leave them plugged in, they starve to death.'

One day, Mike moved out. We never saw him again. We suspected that he'd succumbed to temptation and plugged himself into his Pleasure Machine. We imagined another researcher returning to the college lab after the summer holidays to find a three-month corpse with a goatee slumped on a chair with two electrodes attached to its forehead, the face grotesquely twisted in salivating ecstasy.

But what a way to go.

We finished the rum. I ended the evening in my customary drinking position: face-down and semi-conscious in the toilet. I made a note to keep off rum until I was back at sea level.

****

into the Amazon
The Cofans are a small tribe in the *Oriente*, which is Ecuador's share of the Amazon. We'd heard that their village of Dureno took in visitors for short stays, but only a few tourists had been there.

Cecil, a young black man from Guayaquil who was staying in the Pension Patty (to see some of his own country, he explained, having just left the army) warned us to be careful.

'The Oriente, my friends, is full of *ladrones* – thieves and murderers. It's not safe.'

I replied that, from what I'd heard, Guayaquil itself wasn't exactly that safe either.

Cecil looked aggrieved. 'No, Guayaquil is a good place. It's the country-side where you've got to watch it. That's why I always carry this . . .'

Reaching into his jacket, he produced a knife at least eighteen inches long. He thrust it under our noses. Melissa, who hadn't understood anything he'd been saying, went white. What use was a pen-knife against *that*?

'Especially in the Oriente.' Cecil continued, putting the knife away. 'These *Indios* . . . they eat people, you know.'

'I don't think they do that any more,' I said.

'*Amigos*, you've must understand. These *Indios*, they're not Christians like us. They are still . . . primitives. Stone-age people.'

I asked if he'd been to the Oriente. He hadn't.

We travelled to Lago Agrio with Herbert, a young Italian whom Mark had met in a bar. I thought Herbert was a funny name for an Italian. He was tall, thin and quiet, with long, wavy, blonde hair and a permanently worried look. At home, he was a Tyrrolean shepherd.

'He can't be a shepherd,' said Melissa, 'he hasn't got one of those curly sticks.'

'So, you think all shepherds are old men, no?' Herbert asked.

Well, yes.

'Aah, it is a wery nice job, in fact. In the summer, I look after the sheep of my family. My father has a cabin in the mountains above our willage. It is wery lovely. Also, many walkers and tourists come by. Next year, I hope I am making a tea-house there. In the winter, I travel.'

The bus was full of the usual melancholic, moon-faced peasants. After twenty minutes we stopped outside a yard full of tyres and spare parts, locked for the night. The driver called to be sure no one was in, then waved to his mate, who fetched a crowbar from inside the bus. The two of them jemmied open the gates, broke into the yard and helped themselves to a couple of spare tyres. The passengers looked on, pretending they hadn't noticed anything. Just like a bus full of English people, I thought. The Andean Indians share the English public reserve and that determination to pretend nothing is happening even if there's a naked lunatic waving his genitals in your face.

Equipped with spare tyres, we set off. Once again, the bus zig-zagged slowly down endless slopes, not for half-an-hour or an hour, but throughout the night. The air became warmer, the shadowy vegetation beside the road thicker. The bus-boy put on a video. As a variation on the usual action/violence theme, he'd found one starring ex-boxer Marvelous Marvin Hagler (He had the 'Marvelous' – with one l – officially added.) Hagler was a great boxer but as wooden an actor as, well, Frank Bruno was a boxer. He played a US marine called Sergeant Stone, somehow stranded in the

Amazon. There he teaches a tribe of peaceful Indians to fight the evil businessman who is driving a road through their jungle and using them as slaves. Hagler lectures the Indians about Spartacus, beats up the evil businessman in a muddy puddle and saves the rainforest. Take away the Hollywood-isms and the ridiculous Hagler character (and so far, the happy ending) and this is just about what is going on in the Amazon. I wondered what the other passengers – many of them real Amazonian Indians – made of it. Melissa wondered how the Indian women stayed so perfectly made-up. Mark thought the girls should have been topless. I nodded into fitful sleep.

Dawn revealed a world transformed. We'd only travelled about a hundred kilometres but, like the journey to the coast, the change from the temperate highlands was absolute. The sound of screeching birds and crickets filled the clammy early-morning air. The sweet, sticky atmosphere embraced us, pregnant with humidity. Beside the road most of the trees had been cleared and a few scrawny cattle grazed in long, uneven grass. Small wooden shacks balanced on stilts, lines of washing strung across their balconies, colourful flowers growing around them.

We passed teenagers on old bicycles with buckled wheels and patched-up tyres. Women in flowery dresses; men in shorts and T-shirts and rubber boots; children skipping barefoot. The road had levelled out after its night-time descent. Now there were only a few gentle hills, from the top of which the little roadside shacks and pastures were dwarfed by the expanse of living green behind them.

However much has been destroyed in recent years (and nobody really knows, although a fifth seems a fair guess), the forest remains mind-bogglingly vast. It stretched from here to the Atlantic, 2,000 miles away. Covering 3.7 million square kilometres, it's bigger than Western Europe, yet the only towns of any size are Iquitos in Peru and Manaus and Belém in Brazil. Otherwise, the next large town ahead of us was in West Africa, half-way round the globe.

The river itself is equally staggering. Six and a half thousand kilometres long, its system contains almost one-fifth of the world's fresh water and drains a catchment area of over five million square kilometres. The Amazon discharges more water into the ocean in a single day than the Thames does in a whole year.

****

Lago Agrio

We changed buses in Lago Agrio. The bus station was no more than a muddy yard while outside the streets were half under water from overnight rain. Plastic and paper and rotting fruit and vegetables floated in the puddles. Mud-spattered pickup trucks and battered buses sprayed the broken pavements with brown water. The buildings looked hastily constructed. Functional concrete blocks.

The town lacked beauty, but in the cool of the early morning it compensated with energy. People hustled by carrying sacks, peddling carts, opening shops. Barechested boys in shorts played soccer with empty plastic bottles against shuttered shop-fronts. Mestizos and black youths from the coast. Settlers from the highlands. Cofan and Siecoya and Quichua Indians from the jungle.

The town's official name is Nueva Loja, but everyone calls it Lago Agrio (Sour Lake) after an oil-town in Texas. That tells you what matters about Lago Agrio. It exists solely as a base for oil exploration of the Ecuadorean Amazon, mainly by American companies.

Before oil was discovered in 1967, this region was virgin forest. Now Lago Agrio is one of Ecuador's fastest-growing towns. One day it may acquire a shady plaza with a big church and so on, but for the moment, no one has time for such luxuries. The US oil-men want to turn oil into dollars and go home. The Ecuadoreans – oil-workers, settlers, shopkeepers – simply want to survive.

The bus to Dureno was an open-sided truck with red wooden benches. The driver sat on the front bench and honked a giant horn above his head. The road gleamed with a fresh layer of shiny black crude oil. The roadside houses were more thinly-spread than before Lago, and the forest denser.

The bus stopped. The driver pointed to a muddy path that disappeared into the forest.

****

Cofan Dureno

The muddy path emerged beside the wide, fast-flowing Aguarico river. Two canoes were tied to the bank, but we couldn't see any sign of people or a village. We went back to ask directions from the house we'd passed on the path.

A *mestizo* man appeared at the door. I explained that we wanted to go to the Cofan village.

'I can get you across,' he said. 'But it'll cost twenty thousand *sucres*.'

I offered ten thousand.

'OK, ten thousand.' Locking up his house, he led us back down to the river.

'Which one is your canoe?' I asked.

'Canoe? I don't have a canoe.'

Instead, he shouted. After ten minutes of shouting and whistling, a wooden dugout canoe approached. Feeling somewhat cheated, I paid him the ten thousand sucres.

The ferry man was Laureno, the guide we were looking for. He was a short, plump, supple-looking man – in his thirties, I guessed – with a soft manner and a pudding-bowl haircut. He was dressed, like everyone in the Oriente, in an old T-shirt, rubber boots and shiny nylon football shorts. Unlike most Cofans, though, he spoke some Spanish.

We spent the night in his home, which comprised two raised buildings connected by a walkway. It had clearly been built with care and love, but everything had the rough textures and absence of straight edges of natural materials – timber and branches straight from the forest. Neat piles of firewood were stacked beneath the main house. The surrounding land was cleared and planted with flowers and fruit trees. Chickens and three young children scurried about in the dirt.

The main building was partitioned in two. The back half was a kitchen with a firepit in the middle of the floor. The front was half-covered and half-balcony. There was no furniture. We slept on this balcony while the family slept in the second building. We spread our sleeping mats and mosquito nets and rested. The balcony commanded a lovely view through the trees to the river.

We went for a swim. The current was strong enough so that if you swam upstream as hard as possible, you remained in the same spot. When we got out, Mark's back was covered in a hundred tiny sandfly bites. No one else seemed to have been bitten.

In the morning, Mark's bites were gone. The rest of us had big red rashes. I was mystified.

'Didn't I tell you I was a shaman?' Mark joked.

****

the centre of life on earth
Next morning, after breakfast of rice, fish and bananas, we headed into the forest. Laureno was joined by another Cofan, Delfin – a stocky, thick-set man, with a neat Gregory Peck moustache and a mischievous glint in his eyes. He looked hungover.

Laureno and Delfin hacked away with machetes at the curtain of branches that had grown across the path since it was last used. After two hours we reached our camp, two raised wooden platforms about twenty metres apart in a small clearing. One was for Laureno and Delfin, the other for us. The platforms were covered with a roof of branches, but open at the sides to the sights and sounds of the jungle. Foliage touched the very edge of the platforms.

For the next four days Delfin and Laureno showed us the jungle.[25] They showed us trees. Trees as wide as a house. Hollow trees big enough to sleep inside. Parasitic trees that grew around other trees and eventually strangled their host. We swung, Tarzan-like, from gigantic hanging vines and swam in warm, muddy rivers full of dead branches and rotting leaves. We canoed down tiny streams, ducking under fallen tree-trunks, with vegetation arching over from the banks to create a living tunnel of plantlife. On the ground, beneath the shady canopy of the large trees, the forest floor was surprisingly open and easy to walk through. *Finding* your way was a different matter.

'Don't you ever get lost?' I asked Laureno, after we'd spent a morning following him through an endless maze of apparently indistinguishable trees.

'Yes, sometimes. But sooner or later, I always come to a tree that I recognise. Like that big one there. Just as you recognise buildings in a city. *They* all look the same to me.'

Here, trees are everything: food and shelter, medicine and sign-posts. We began to adjust to being constantly inside the forest. What would it be like to spend your whole life here? To live and die without ever seeing a flat, distant horizon or any open space wider than a river or clearing?

Laureno and Delfin showed us how plants could provide everything they need. Food, medicine, tools, shelter, fire, rope, baskets, decoration, clothes. Many of the medicinal plants looked like the part of the body they cured. One, used to treat arthritis, had a knobbly knot half-way along its stem that looked just like an elbow or knee-joint. Another plant, which Laureno said was for conditioning hair, consisted of a mass of thick and furry dreadlock-like roots.

We learnt how to fish with spears and to weave giant fern leaves into whicker roofs. We fired blowpipes. I was amazed at their accuracy, and managed to hit an orange from twenty paces with my first shot. I tried to persuade Melissa to balance it on her head while I had another go.

Electric-blue butterflies as big as my hand danced past. Shafts of sunlight filtered through the forest's leafy ceiling like beams illuminating a gothic cathedral. Ants' nests as big as cars sent out giant tentacles of busy leaf-cutter workers; insect motorways that radiated from the central megalopolis of the nest, clearing paths through the tangled debris of fallen vegetation on the forest floor.

Every surface was alive. Spiders' webs stretched between leaves. Each decomposing branch or trunk was a sodden breeding-ground for insects and grubs or fungi to feed on. The whole forest was a vast, fecund living organism in which nothing was wasted, and every dying thing was food for new life. Even now, in the dry season, everything was damp to the touch.

At night, after meals of freshly-caught fish, bananas and rice, we lay under our mosquito nets, listening to the electric hum of insects. The croak of frogs and the music of strange birdcalls lapped around our little platform, washing over us like the sound of surf breaking. One bird sounded exactly like a telephone ringing. Once or twice, I was jerked awake by 'the phone ringing', thinking myself back home, only to find I was in the middle of a jungle. Most confusing. Another made a hollow, echoing, fluid 'keer-plop', like a pebble dropped into water inside a cave.

Our second night was New Year's Eve, which we celebrated around a flickering candle with the few bottles of *aguardiente* we'd brought along for the occasion. Midnight passed. Everyone was asleep except Mark and me. Mark went for a walk. After a while, he reappeared and beckoned me to follow him down the path into the forest. As we walked, I felt the enclosing presence of millions of plants. I hesitated, wondering about snakes or jaguars. But Mark was already further down the path, descending from the slight hill on which our camp was built. We continued until the moonlight from the camp clearing no longer penetrated the forest. Darkness.

'Maybe that's my role on this trip. To take you just a little further.' Mark whispered from the blackness beside me. The forest crackled with cicadas and bird calls. The plants swayed gently. I felt as if we'd entered a vast lung; warm, damp and organic, pulsating with life.

'This is the world centre of bio-diversity,' Mark enthused, 'There could be a million different life-forms within a mile of us – all fighting, competing, living off each other, living in symbiosis with others. You name it, and it's probably out there somewhere, close by. Every conceivable evolutionary strategy – there's a plant or animal or insect doing it around us now.

'Imagine the world 'mapped' according to consciousness. Every life source registers a point, brighter or weaker depending on how complex it is. People, animals, insects. Even a plant is conscious, in a sense. It reacts to its environment, and that's all consciousness is, at a basic level. The capacity to absorb and respond to stimuli. All around us – millions of little points of consciousness. There can hardly be a single spot on the planet more 'conscious' than here.

'So this,' he concluded with a flourish, 'is the centre of life on earth.'

As our eyes adjusted to the darkness, we became aware of the shapes of the forest, half-seen and half-felt. Unlike temperate woodlands, which are usually dominated by one or two types of tree, tropical forests explode with different species, some only found within a single area of a few kilometres. And more species of bird, insect and plants have been recorded in Ecuador alone than in the whole of Europe or North America.

We returned to the shelter. I fell asleep listening to the telephone-bird. Everything felt good.

Soon we were shouting abuse at each other again. This time it was hard to even work out what it was about. We'd spent the morning watching Delfin spear-fishing.

'It's funny how the spear looked bent in the water,' Melissa said when we got back.

'It's not 'funny' at all.' Mark said. 'It's caused by the refraction of the light spectrum on contact with water. Basic physics.'

'Yeah, the, er, reflection,' Melissa said absently.

That set Mark off.

Melissa was perfectly capable of remembering important things, like the fact she would rather be here than in London, and which skin creams to use. ('Let's face it. If I had skin like yours,' she told me, 'I'd never get another boyfriend.') But when it came to abstract ideas and science, she switched off. It was like a red rag to Mark.

'You seem to think it's *good* to be deliberately stupid,' he snapped.

'Well, maybe it is. Being the most intelligent person on earth hasn't got you very far, has it?'

If there was one thing that annoyed Mark, it was people who wouldn't accept the power of logic and science. For one thing, it meant they didn't even realise that he was right. Here Mark and Melissa had reached an impasse, for if there was one thing that annoyed Melissa, it was people who thought that you could explain everything logically and scientifically.

Mark decided that he had to explain refraction again.

'Yeah, yeah, yeah, refacty-dacty doo-dah?' Melissa waved her hand dismissively.

'You should *try* thinking, sometimes, Melissa. That's if you're brain hasn't totally wasted away from lack of use. You might learn something, instead of drifting around in a daze all your life. Mark's right, you *are* a bimbo.'

Melissa shot me a glance.

'Erm, I never said you were a bimbo,' I mumbled hastily.

'Yes, you bloody well did,' said Mark. 'You said . . . '

'Look, I don't think it matters what I said.'

Melissa went on the offensive.

'At least I've done something in my life. I've studied with great spiritual teachers, and you've got a long way to go yet. You think you're so clever. What have you ever actually done? Nothing. That's what. All you do is take drugs and mouth off.'

'All *you've* ever done,' Mark countered, 'is wander around like a fucking idiot. It's a bit rich to claim that being too thick to realise when you're walking into trouble counts as *doing* something.'

I butted in. 'You need to learn to give people a bit more respect, Mark.'

'Respect?' Mark sneered. The other thing he disliked was being lectured. 'Respect? For fuck's sake, what *are* you two? Some kind of delicate-fuck-ing-flowers all of a sudden. Learn to take a little criticism, will you? I have to put up with your pretty-vacant bimbo girlfriend and then I have to take all these fucking Mr Holier-Than-Thou lectures about being calm. For fuck's sake, I AM FUCKING CALM.' Mark glared at me. 'I can't make one lit-tle passing comment without you both getting all precious about it and going on and on and on. Well, people have to *earn* my respect.'

I glanced over at the other platform, where Laureno and Delfin were talk-ing quietly. If they'd heard us arguing, they weren't showing it, or weren't interested. Herbert, too, was reading quietly in his hammock, keeping out of the way. Melissa had somehow extricated herself from the argument and disappeared inside her mosquito net, leaving Mark and me shouting at each other.

'If you can't stand travelling with Melissa and me, just fuck off,' I said.

'Doesn't bother me. I managed fine in Peru.'

'OK. In that case, fuck off and stop giving me a hard time.'

'OK,' Mark said. 'Fine. I'll have more fun without you two boring bastards, anyway.'

'Listen, you two,' Melissa interrupted, wandering back, 'Why don't you just grow up.'
'Shut up, Melissa,' we replied together. 'This is *your* fault.'

'So you don't want any of this, then?' Melissa pulled out an enormous joint.

Mark looked at it for a second.

'Maybe we should continue this, erm, little discussion tomorrow.'

Peace descended once again on our little platform in the jungle.

****
Saturn returns
'Why do you hang out with Mark?' Melissa asked me later. Laureno had taken Mark and Herbert into the forest and Melissa and I were fishing for piranhas with Delfin.

'I know Mark's difficult. But at least he's not dull. It's just his way, I guess. That constant competitiveness. The frustrating thing *is* that he is extremely bright, but he never focuses his energy. And he can't ever ask for help, in case it's seen as a sign of weakness. Maybe it's just immaturity.'

'How old is he, again?' Melissa asked.

'Twenty-nine.'

'Aah. *Saturn returns*, you see.'

As usual, I had no idea what Melissa was on about.

'*Saturn returns*. Every seven years,' Melissa explained, as if that clarified everything.

'That doesn't clarify anything,' I said. 'What does it mean?'

'*Saturn returns*? Well, every seven years or so Saturn passes through your astrological charts and brings about a change. At fourteen, say, you become an adolescent, and at . . . '

I could see Melissa counting.

'Twenty-one?' I prompted.

'Alright, I know. Twenty-one. Which might be, broadly, adulthood. In your late twenties, you move through another change. Look at me. I used to be as wild as Mark – drugs, men, stealing, partying. Listen, I've sold smack in Malaysia, of all places. Ten years ago I'd have been going out with someone on-the-edge like Mark, not a boring bastard like you. But now I'm perfectly normal.'

'Look, I wish everyone would stop calling me a boring bastard. It's bad enough with Mark, without you starting. Anyway, what do you mean by normal? You've just escaped from a semi-religious loony cult. And you're standing in the middle of a jungle smoking a joint.'

'Am I?' Melissa looked at the joint in her hand, as if surprised to see it there. 'Anyway, it wasn't a cult.'

'So Mark's going to get into Krishnamurti and T'ai Chi, then?' I asked.

'*Saturn returns* doesn't have to mean maturity. It just means that something will change. Who knows what. But something will happen.'

****

night
Our platform, wrapped in darkness. A single candle burning. Its intimate light defines our small world – mosquito nets, sleeping bags, books, clothes, moths darting around the flickering flame, insects stuck in the hot wax. The raised platform feels like a ship, sailing silently through the forest, slipping between the shadowy outlines of trees and plants. I listen to the hypnotic music of unseen birds and frogs. Laureno and Delfin are talking quietly on the other platform and in the distance I can hear crashes from workmen repairing the oil-road, across the river.

****

oil be damned
'*With petroleum, as with coffee or meat, rich countries profit more from the work of consuming it than do poor countries from the work of producing it.*' EDUARDO GALEANO, *OPEN VEINS OF LATIN AMERICA*

Since 1972, when the first oil-well in the Oriente was built near Dureno itself, over 1.5 billion barrels of crude oil have been exported and oil has become Ecuador's main export. Ecuador's rulers promote oil as the country's economic panacea. Panacea? Hardly. Most of the profits go to US companies anyway, and in the meantime Ecuador's foreign debt has sky-rocketed and its people have become poorer: 67% of Ecuadoreans now live in poverty, compared to 47% in 1975.[26]

The first real study of the environmental impact of oil in the Oriente was made by Judith Kimerling in 1989. She reported that every week 10,000 gallons of oil and 30 million gallons of untreated toxic waste were spilt or deliberately dumped. Since oil production began, the main pipeline had ruptured at least 27 times and 16.8 million tonnes of raw crude had seeped into the rivers and soil of the forest – more than the Exxon Valdez spilled. Little, if any, had been properly cleaned up.

That's not the end of the story. The oil companies build roads, which let in settlers from the Andes and coast. These settlers are encouraged by the government and promised 'empty' land to farm in the Oriente. Like the USA with drugs, this 'solution' to Ecuador's land shortage sidesteps the real problem – in this case the political difficulty of redistributing land in the highlands. It also ignores the fact that people already live in the forest. The settlers, knowing only the agricultural techniques of the highlands or coast, clear the forest for farming. But the Amazon soil is poor. When the stabilising roots of the trees are removed, the thin top-soil is washed away by heavy rain.

All this has taken a heavy toll on the people of the forest. There are only 600 Cofans left in Ecuador, plus maybe 2,000 across the border in Colombia. The neighbouring Siecoya, Siona, Huaorani and Achuar all number only a few hundred. Of Ecuador's Amazon tribes, only the Shuar and the Quichua are not staring immediate genocide in the face.

****

love stallion

'You realise,' Melissa mused, 'that I only put up with you babbling on about politics and oil and stuff because you're such a magnificently well-hung love stallion with fantastic sexual technique and stamina and you take me to greater heights of ecstasy than any man or beast I've ever known, except for a couple of larger members of the cameloid family.' (Or did she say, 'Shut the fuck up, small dick'? I forget.)

****

the shaman's tree

Delfin took us to a special tree. It had low, sagging branches, like a wil-low, that created a cave-like hollow. He said that the old shaman used to sit here, alone for up to twenty days and nights, eating nothing except an emetic tree bark; a cleansing ritual before he would delve into the rain-forest's natural pharmacy of mind-altering plants. Delfin said that when he was seven, the shaman gave him a hallucinogenic brew as a punish-ment for fighting with other children. It scared him so much that it stopped his bullying. 'Wish they'd had that sort of punishment when I was at school,' Mark joked.

Mark asked Delfin what the plant was called.

'Ayahuasca,' Delfin said. 'The plant of visions.'[27]

And what did it do? Well, Delfin said, it made you see visions. And would it be possible, by any chance, for us to try some of it? Purely, of course, in the interest of science. Delfin wasn't sure. No tourists had taken it before. It took eight hours to prepare. He said he would talk to Laureno.

'I'm not doing any psychedelic drugs,' Melissa said.

We asked Delfin about the shaman.

'We have no shaman now.' Delfin said. 'The shaman died a few years ago. We want a new shaman, but . . .' No one wanted the job, it seemed, or really knew how to do it any more.

'I'll do it,' Mark volunteered.

'Es muy duro,' Delfin explained. 'It's very hard. You must spend many years studying and training. You must give up family life and spend many days and nights alone in the forest. You must face fear and evil spirits. You must learn about the plants and their powers.'

A few village boys were keen on the drugs, he said, but the throwing up and a requirement that the shaman remain celibate tended to put off potential applicants.

'And if someone dies and no one knows why, his relatives might say the shaman has put bad magic on him. So they kill the shaman.'

'Still fancy the job?' Melissa asked.

****

technicians of ecstasy[28]

Then God said, 'Let us make Man in our image, after our likeness; and let him have dominion over the fish of the sea, and over the birds of the air, and over the cattle, and over all the earth . . .'
GENESIS 1.26

Mark (who did, after all have a degree in anthropology) told us about shamans. He explained that they are found in the Americas, Siberia, Tibet, Japan, Indonesia, Borneo and Aboriginal Australia. They were once common in Europe, too. Among the Celts, for instance.

'Shamans are, if you like, the 'priests' of animist cultures . . . '

'Animalism?' Melissa asked. 'What's that?'

'For fuck's sake, Melissa. I've already told you this once. It's animism, not animalism. From the Latin, anima, meaning soul. I think you get these things wrong deliberately, just to wind me up.'

'OK, then, tell me. What is 'animism-from-the-Latin-anima-meaning-soul', when it's at home?'

'You see, you can listen. If you remember, animism is basically nature-worship. It seems to have been a more-or-less universal first religion throughout the world, but today it only remains where life is still dominated by nature. Hunting, volcanoes, drought, floods and so on. It isn't an organised religion – there's no central authority; no Church; no scriptures or dogma – but it's remarkably consistent wherever it's found. Its defining belief is that everything – people, animals, plants, whatever – has a soul, or spirit.'

'Animists divide reality into two: the normal physical world and the (literally) spirit-ual. This is a timeless parallel dimension where things appear as their spirit alter-egos. The physical and spirit worlds are two sides of the same coin. The spirit world reveals, if you like, the inner life. For instance, if you cut down a tree, its inner 'pain' might be expressed by its angry spirit in the spirit world.'

'But what's a shaman?' Melissa interrupted.

'I'm coming to that,' Mark said in exasperation. 'But you just asked what animism was . . .'

Mark took a deep breath.

'OK, then . . . a shaman acts as the link between the normal world and this alternate reality, 'journeying' between them while in 'ecstatic' trances, which are attained by taking psychedelic plants or repetitive drumming or chanting, or hours of dancing, or similar techniques. I'd call it 'tripping' basically. The purpose of these journeys is usually healing, as the shamans search for the inner causes of a problem. Although shamans use herbal and plant medicines, they believe serious illnesses must be cured by finding the 'inner' cause . . . '

'A bit like spirit mediums, then, like in voodoo,' I suggested.

'Not quite. The difference is that a shaman is active. He or she journeys to the spirit world to fight spirits or seek their help. Mediums are passive. They wait for a spirit to 'possess' them.

'Anyway, whether you take all this literally or symbolically is up to you. But to my mind, what the animist world-view expresses – with its multitude of spirits and the magical parallel reality – is a sense of the 'sacredness' of Nature itself. The crucial thing is that it's not just humans who have souls, but everything. To animists, the whole natural world around us is charged with a magical, divine life-energy. The sacred is located within Nature, not somehow outside it, as with our own God. It's a crucial difference. The Western conception of God reflects the Western belief that humans are intrinsically superior to the rest of Creation: that the natural world has been given to us by God purely for our benefit. If you ask me, it's this belief that sowed the seeds of today's environmental crisis.'[29]

****

vine of the soul
'in this world of yage, there is no way in which shit and holiness can be separated.'
M. TAUSSIG – SHAMANISM, COLONIALISM AND THE WILD MAN

Laureno agreed to let us try some ayahuasca. He said it was prepared from a small bush, ground up and boiled for eight hours. Delfin said there was a sort-of half-shaman (a *'poco-shaman'*) in the village who knew how to prepare the potion. Herbert was easily persuaded.

'You don't get a chance like this everyday,' he said.

'I'll just watch you three,' Melissa said. 'You know I never do psychedelic drugs.'

We spent the day in Laureno's house while the *poco-shaman* prepared the potion. Delfin and Laureno went to build some shelters for us, about a mile downriver. By the early evening they'd constructed two benders of branches, with floors of giant leaves, built in the river bed itself. As it was the dry season, the river was low, exposing wide stretches of sand and shingle.

'You must go away from the village,' Laureno explained, 'in case you scare the children.'

'Scare the children?' Mark joked. 'What does he think is going to happen to us?'

'I don't think I want to take any psychedelic drugs,' Melissa repeated.

Delfin led us to the shelters. The *poco-shaman* emerged from one, resplendent in a feather head-dress and feathers amulets and a knee-length blue smock, beneath which he wore a pair of Levis. (Missionaries made the Cofans adopt the smocks, called *cushus*, in the 1920s, instead of going naked.)

The *poco-shaman* set the pot down on the sand, and called us forward one at a time. Mark, as always, went first. Melissa went next.

'Well, I don't want to be left out,' she said.

The *poco-shaman* filled a coconut husk with a thick whitish syrup. Before each of us drank, he sprinkled a few drops of water over our heads and mumbled a few words in Cofan. Delfin said it didn't work without the water. We each drank another bowl. Mark managed a third before the pot was empty. The *poco-shaman*, and another Cofan man, drank two bowls. Delfin didn't take anything.

'Just in case things go wrong,' he said.

'Did he just say 'go wrong'?' Melissa asked nervously.

'What about this other guy?' Mark asked.

'Oh, he just wanted to try it. He's never taken it before.'

Delfin explained what to expect. 'You will see flowers, plants and insects attacking you.'

This didn't sound surprising, considering that we were in a jungle, surrounded by flowers, plants and insects attacking us. Herbert looked pale. The thick liquid was inside us. No backing out.

We waited.

'It looked a bit like semen,' Mark joked.

'You can see why it took him eight hours to produce a bowl that size then,' Melissa said.

'At least it didn't taste like semen . . .' I said.

'And how would you know?' Melissa asked.

' . . . I don't suppose.'

'I could have filled that pot in one go,' Mark said.

Nothing happened.

Herbert sat on the sand looking apprehensive. After about an hour, I asked Delfin about the two Cofans, who were sitting gazing into space. 'Are they seeing anything?'

Delfin asked them.

'Yes, they say they are seeing flowers.'

'Ask him what happened to the plants and insects,' Melissa said.

'You must try not to throw up,' Delfin told us.

Herbert threw up. I was beginning to experience a strange sense of dislocation. Somehow, things weren't quite normal. Now it was starting. I looked shakily at the others.

'I think I'm getting something,' Melissa said. Herbert threw up again. Mark grinned. I wandered a little way from the shelters. In the open river bed, unlike the forest, we could see the sky. It was a clear, starry night. I felt a stabbing gut-ache and squatted just in time to blast out a jet of liquid brown shit. At the same time I threw up, a jet of liquid yellow vomit. Whatever else it was doing, it was giving me a good clean-out. I was finding it hard to co-ordinate my movements. My legs felt like jelly. I staggered back to the shelters and flopped face-down onto the leafy mat.

I lay there for hours. Or was it minutes? At some point Melissa came and lay down beside me. I was dimly aware of Mark and Herbert in the other shelter.

I felt feverish. Everything was spinning. I was pinned to the ground, all physical energy drained from my body. I shut my eyes. Wild geometrical patterns burst like bombs inside my closed eyelids. Kaleidoscopic explosions emanated from a mystical centre. Waves of electric zig-zags scrolled remorselessly past, like psychedelic white noise on a mistuned TV screen. And organic shapes, too. The shapes of the forest. Leaves and branches that danced and swayed. Flowers bursting open. In fast-motion. In slow motion. Inside each flower, another flower. Flowers within flowers within flowers.

Movement around me. Someone walking around outside? Close? Far away? Or was it just my imagination? An animal, even? It was, after all, a jungle out there. Strange how the makeshift shelter now felt so secure and protective, its thin arbour of branches defining a boundary between the familiar and safe and an unknown world beyond. I lay stretched out, stomach-down, my cheek resting on the mat of giant leaves. They felt smooth against my skin, almost like plastic; still strong and green.

Delfin looking down, asking if I was alright. A mumbled answer, yes.

More genuine, if fleeting, hallucinations. One scene emerging from the swirling patterns each time I closed my eyes.

A face.

Gazing at me. The leathery face of an old Indian man, close-up, like those old black-and-white photos of Sitting Bull and others. White man's romanticised image. Sad, impassive, wise. Then I was seeing into the distance, far away. A more distant Indian figure – was it the same man? – climbing a long flight of steps carved into a cliff. The steps climbed out of the luminous emerald forest, but I couldn't see where they led. Towards the sky.

The distant figure on the steps looked back. Waiting for me to follow?

I opened my eyes. I focused as best I could on the spinning world around me. Closing them again, the patterns coalesced into the same image. In my stomach, I felt a knot of tension rising. Something conscious (my ego?) fighting to regain control, shouting warnings. Should I climb the stairs? Was the vision about to reveal something wonderful, transcendental, terrible?

Ego screaming, 'Don't let go.'

I snapped my eyes open again. For a moment I made an effort to focus on my surroundings. Herbert and Mark lying opposite me, in the other shelter. I closed my eyes. The image of the Indian was gone, replaced by the more random patterns I'd seen earlier.

Somewhere in my mind, I'd decided. I wasn't ready to follow the Indian on the stairs, to give myself over entirely to the trip. I felt the knot of tension recede. I felt safe, relieved. And yet at the same time, disappointed. Was the Indian figure beckoning me to a higher plane. Further. Further into the trip. Further from the safe, normal world. Maybe to a place from which there was no return.

Shamans say those who seek knowledge must conquer terror.

The terror of ego-loss.

Ego screaming, 'Don't let go.'

I'd been afraid.

Afraid to let go.

****

cartoon drunk
Delfin is standing over me, saying something.

'We must go back to Laureno's house. It's going to rain.'

I'm weaving about like a cartoon drunk. My arms hang limply. My chin is slumped forward on my chest. I can't seem to hold my body upright or to co-ordinate my movements. Mark and Melissa seem more in control. Even

Herbert looks like he's got it together. Mark and he are laughing.

'The stars are spinning around,' Mark is saying. Or something like that.
'. . . arrooouuaand'. His words float and echo and stretch and hang in
the darkness.

'Zey are moving so fast,' says Herbert. 'Zey are all blurry.' . . . bluur-
reeee.

Head hanging forward, staring at my feet and at the pebbles on the
ground. Smooth, egg-sized, round pebbles. I want to lie down again.
Walking is an effort. Whose feet are these? I'm hanging onto Melissa,
watching the others ahead, coaxing my limbs to respond. Thank God for
Melissa. The others are far ahead. Vanishing. Soon we'll be abandoned in
the forest.

We've been walking for hours.

For all eternity.

I lie spreadeagled on my sleeping mat on the floor of Laureno's house,
watching the roof and then the walls burst with energy and patterns and
listening to the strange calls of the night.

It's morning.

I look around groggily. I'm back in the normal world. Well, I'm in a jungle, but right now that feels pretty normal. Laureno brings us breakfast.
Rice, tinned fish and bananas, all fried. Someone is digging, planting a
fruit tree in front of the house. We eat quietly and contemplate the forest.

****

it's all one big single sausage
I'd picked up a book on shamanism in a second-hand bookshop in Quito. I
read a bit of it to the others. 'A universal aspect of shamanism,' I read,
'is a feeling for the sheer 'alive-ness' of the universe . . . The whole
universe is ablaze with energy. All forms are perceived as interconnect-
ed, with a universal life-force underlying all.'[30]

'A uni-wurst ablaze with Energy? Yes, this is vot I am feeling last night,'
Herbert said.

'A uni-wurst?' Mark joked. 'Does that come with sauerkraut?'

'Vot?'

*'From vot . . .' I began. 'Sorry, from what I understand, Eastern reli-
gions are the same. They say everything is an illusion: temporary forms
of the underlying, universal life-force.'*

*'Just like quantum physics talks of an interconnected universe in which
objects are temporary arrangements of pure energy,' Mark added. 'As
Fritjof Capra explains in The Tao of Physics.'*

*'Fritjof?' Melissa said. 'What sort of a name is that? Anyway, all this
'uniwersal' stuff sound like Buddhism to me.'*

*'That's the whole point,' said Mark. 'It is. Shamanism, Buddhism, what-
ever. Eastern religions also have animist roots and, like shamanism, they
emphasise direct experience. Meditation and shamanic trances are just
techniques to suppress our egos and simply feel the underlying energy.
Nature. The Void. Atman. God. Call it what you like. And tripping.
Getting mashed up on acid or E and full-volume, hypnotic pumping vibes
with lots of upward chord progressions: that's a shamanic technique.
That rush, that euphoria. You know, Western religions – Judaism,
Christianity – are the only ones not based on this experience.'*

'So what are they based on, then?' Melissa asked.

*'Well, there are a mystic Jewish and Christian traditions, but they've
always been on the fringes. Mainly, Western religion relies on texts. In
the Beginning was the Word, and all that. And the Christian sacrament – the wine and wafer: the blood and body of Christ – its an
empty ritual: a symbolic affirmation of faith. The shamanic sacrament
– taking ayahuasca, for instance – is a direct re-connection with the
divine, magical energy of the universe. A connection with nature.'*

*'Maybe that whole body-of-Christ thing derives from shamanic magic
mushroom rituals?' I suggested. 'It's the drug-taking ritual without the
drug itself.'*

*'Quite possibly. Anyway, I think everyone gets flashes of this energy. It's
probably what born-again Christians mean when they say they've been*

115

filled with the Holy Spirit. And I reckon that's why people who have near-death experiences often think they've seen God. When we think we're about to die, maybe our ego lets go. It's all about ego-loss. Letting your self go. Merging with the Infinite.'

****

the other Dureno

Our stay with the Cofans was finished. After breakfast, Laureno and Delfin punted us downstream to the other Dureno, the settlers' town, a shabby one-street place of corrugated-roof shacks. I wanted to buy everyone a beer, but the store had none left. Laureno said they didn't drink, anyway.

This settlers' Dureno had an air of impermanence. Its wooden and tin shacks looked hastily thrown together by people with more pressing concerns than interior design. Most of the people who lived here had only moved to the Oriente in the last few years, economic migrants from the coast or highlands. The Cofan village had nothing more, materially, and I wondered if I was being romantic, but to me Laureno's house had the feel of a real home, surrounded by flowers and fruit trees, connected in a much deeper way than this settler village to the forest around it.

Maybe I was being romantic. Since the first Texaco oil-well came on-line near here in 1972, the Cofans have witnessed the poisoning of their rivers, the disappearance of the animals they hunted and the loss of their freedom to move through the forest. Their communities have been hemmed in by roads and settlements such as this. Their way of life has been all but destroyed.

We went our separate ways. Delfin and Laureno said goodbye and returned to their boats. The bus heading west to Quito arrived and Mark and Herbert got on. Melissa and I said good-bye to Herbert: we never saw him again. Mark said we'd find him in the Gran Casino.

Melissa and I were alone, waiting for the bus east, further into the jungle, to Cuyabeno.

****

Cuyabeno

Cuyabeno is a chunk of primary rainforest, inhabited only by a few Indian communities, that's been made a national park for its rich eco-system and wildlife. Its centrepiece, reached by a two day canoe trip, is a group of small lakes called Lagunas Grandes. (Obviously named by an estate agent.)

It also contains oil and is the site of some of the worst oil spills in the Amazon. So much for being a 'protected area'. But to us it looked pristine. It might have been the garden of Eden itself.

The bus from Dureno left us at the park office, a wooden shack on stilts surrounded by a half-dozen similar houses. It was closed. There was no one around. After a couple of hours, two park officials roared up the dirt road in a jeep.

'No, there are no guides here,' they said, and walked off. An hour later they reappeared with a stocky Indian man in his forties, in a T-shirt, shorts and rubber boots.

'Modesto will take you,' they said. 'He's only a fisherman, but he knows the way.'

Modesto beamed at us. Twenty minutes later, we were on our way. We had a few tins of sardines and some rice in our packs. Modesto had nothing except Fernando, a fresh-faced boy of about eighteen with a ready smile. We glided downstream into the late afternoon in Modesto's wooden dugout, and then set up camp on a muddy riverbank, where we shared our spartan rations and hid from the night's storm in our tent. Modesto and Fernando slept under a sheet of plastic.

Next morning was sunny. Fernando paddled us gently downstream, ducking under fallen tree-trunks. We could see no further than the dense green walls of trees that flanked the narrow, mud-red stream. Birds of all sizes and colours perched around each bend. Moments of eerie silence were punctured by bursts of squawking or the excited chatter of spider monkeys high in the canopy. Trees crackled with the deafening electric hum of crickets.

Ecuador has, if you're interested, over 1,500 known species of bird. My guidebook said there were 45 types of parrot, 19 different toucans, 167 different flycatchers, 133 tanagers, 110 antbirds, 43 cotingas and 120 species of hummingbird, plus an eagle big enough to snatch a monkey off a branch. More than 400 species of bird have been identified in Cuyabeno itself, as well as spider monkeys, tapirs, peccaries (a type of wild pig), jaguars, anacondas, caimans, freshwater dolphins and rare manatees or 'sea-cows'.

Neither Melissa nor I could tell an antbird from a cotinga to save our lives, let alone one species of antbird from the other 109. (Are they a cross between a bird and an ant?) But we recognised a few birds. Yellow-billed toucans, with their jet-black bodies and outsized yellow beaks. Pairs of parrots. Large birds that looked like turkeys swooped from branches and glided in front of us, inches above the water. They landed on low branches on the opposite bank, which sagged under their weight. There were sharp-eyed herons and kingfishers, with their long thin hook-beaks and spindly legs, perched on rocks in mid-stream. As we drifted along, the forest on either side would explode with a great rustling of birds and a wild cacophony of screeches and squawks that warned us off their territory.

Modesto hacked away with his machete at fallen branches to clear a passage for the canoe, pausing occasionally to point out a bird or some spider monkeys. Once, he pulled up alongside a huge anaconda lying coiled in shallow water at the river's edge, so still that Melissa almost trod on it.

Modesto's main preoccupation, though, was fishing. The river was full of fish, from piranhas to giant two-metre pike. Poised and still at the prow of the canoe, home-made wooden spear in hand, Modesto scanned the river while Fernando paddled. Suddenly, he would let fly at a dark object beneath the surface. Mostly he missed, but by nightfall we had an ample dinner of fresh fish.

We passed only one Indian family, fishing on the riverside. That evening we reached the lakes. Modesto took us to some half-built wooden tourist cabins, hidden amongst the trees on an island. He suggested that we go for a swim. As Fernando had spent most of the afternoon pointing out piranhas, we eyed the cool black water of the lake with a mix of anticipation and trepidation. We were hot, dirty and sweaty and in need of a swim. But . . . there were those piranhas.

'No piranhas here. Good swimming.' Fernando reassured us. We dived in. As we did so, Fernando began splashing his paddle energetically on the other side of the canoe.

'What are you doing, Fernando?'

'Piranhas come to this side,' Fernando explained. We were out of the water before he finished the sentence. Fernando had a good laugh at this.

I noticed that he didn't swim himself.

After dark, we went caiman-spotting. Modesto rowed the canoe into the middle of the still, black lake and let us float. Silence and darkness enveloped us. A complete, natural silence. On this moonless night it was a complete, natural darkness as well; something as strange to me as real silence. Caimans slide off the muddy banks into the water as we passed, disturbed by our presence. We shone our torches at the shore and pairs of devil-red reptile eyes reflected in the beams.

Suddenly, there was a mighty splash beside us. Something leapt out of the water towards the boat. I felt a blow to the chest.

Melissa screamed.

The thing fell thrashing to the floor of the canoe. We shone the torch down to see a flying fish flapping about helplessly. This time the four of us had a good laugh.

Paddling upstream next day was harder, so I lent Fernando a hand. Modesto maintained his statuesque fishing pose up front. After lunch it began to rain, but the warm tropical downpour hardly even cooled us. We gave a lift to three Indian men who hailed Modesto from the bank. They all had big flappy ears and in-bred toothy grins. And they all carried battered shotguns. As they sat in the canoe and stared at us, I eyed their beaten-up rifles uneasily. We were, once again, in the middle of nowhere and heavily out-gunned. Melissa was obviously coming to terms with this sort of thing, because she didn't even ask me for my penknife.

We reached the park office just in time to hitch a ride on the back of an empty truck. As the lorry hurtled along, we realised that our platform had no sides and nothing at all to hold on to. Every time it cornered, we were flung across the open platform. The equatorial sun was setting fiery red behind the poor little roadside farms and the jungle around them, but we were too busy trying to stay on the truck to take much in.

section 3
Colombia

"The human murder by
poverty in Latin America is
secret; every year, without
making a sound, three
Hiroshima bombs explode over
communities that have become
accustomed to suffering with
clenched teeth. This systematic
violence is not apparent but is
real and constantly increasing;
its holocausts are not made
known in the sensational press
but in Food and Agricultural
Organisation statistics."

EDUARDO GALEANO, THE OPEN
VEINS OF LATIN AMERICA

Chapter 5
Highlands: cowboys and indians

Locombia

'How was the jungle?'

Mark was beside the pool table in the Gran Casino II, as he'd promised, chalking his cue. He introduced his opponent, a rugged, long-haired New Zealander called Campbell. I ordered a couple of drinks from the bar. Behind me, I heard a loud thud, and looked round to see Campbell lying unconscious on the floor beside the pool table, pool cue in hand. Everyone else in the bar turned to look, too. Mark dragged him out into the fresh air.

'Too much dope,' Mark explained.

We spent a few days in Quito. Mark decided that he would stay in Ecuador on his own for a while. He and Campbell were considering visiting Vilcabamba in southern Ecuador. The town was famous among travellers for the hallucinogenic San Pedro cactus. We agreed to meet up in a month in Barranquilla, on the north coast of Colombia, for Carnival.

'We're going to Colombia,' I told Melissa.

Here, at last, was a country Melissa *had* heard of.

'Colombia?' she asked. 'Isn't that a bit, er, dangerous?'

A country averaging 30,000 murders a year – one-tenth of all murders in the world – with the highest murder rate on the planet, nine times that of the United States. A country which controls 80% of the world's cocaine trade. A country with ten different guerrilla groups, together forming the biggest guerrilla movement on the continent. Where the continent's bloodiest war claimed 300,000 lives as recently as the 1950s and 1960s. Where coke dealers sell you drugs and then turn out to be policemen. Where thieves are said to inject sweets or cigarettes with a tasteless, odourless drug called *burundanga* and then offer them to unsuspecting tourists, who wake up two days later lying in a ditch with no money, credit cards or clothes. Some victims, it was rumoured, had woken up with one kidney missing. Dangerous? Why would she think that?

We crossed the border back-to-back so we would see our attackers coming.

Nothing happened. We looked at each other and held our breath. We caught a bus to Ipiales, the first Colombian town, and found a hotel. We checked in and went out to eat. Still nothing happened. We went to sleep and woke up with our normal complement of internal organs. The next day we went to visit Las Lajas, a mock-gothic church built in the middle of a dramatic gorge. It was on all the local tourist posters and was, no doubt, the site of a miracle. Still nothing happened. No one shot us, threatened us, held us up or tried to offer us cigarettes, drugged or otherwise.

Yet Colombia *was* different.

The highlands of Ecuador, Peru and Bolivia form a unit: the Inca Empire which embraced them all defined the rough limits of the Indian world of the high Andes. Throughout this predominantly Quechua region there is a continuity; of people, scenery and culture.

In Colombia the countryside changes. The Andes are still formidable barriers to travel, but here they are softer: rolling, fertile hills instead of snow-capped mountains. There are flowers everywhere, hanging from baskets on every balcony and beside every fence. And the farmhouses we passed looked more Spanish, with red-tile roofs and whitewashed walls.

And instead of stocky *campesinas* in pork pie hats and heavy skirts, we saw more *Latino* faces. The girls were slimmer and prettier (and got slimmer and prettier as we travelled north) with long, dark eyelashes and flowing black hair. It felt, at last, as if we were in Latin America.

There's a historical reason for this. In the old Inca lands, a handful of Europeans owned huge *encomiendas* or lucrative mines, but there was never substantial European immigration. In Colombia, a gentler climate, fertile land and an easier passage from Europe attracted more settlers, who farmed and intermarried and produced today's mainly *mestizo* society.

Colombia seemed both richer and more Westernised. In Ipiales, people dressed more smartly. There were more cars and they were in better condition. There were office blocks with tinted glass fronts and better quality goods in the shops. Without the traditionally-dressed *campesinos*, who look oppressed just standing at a bus stop, the divide between rich and poor was less obvious. There is plenty of poverty in Colombia, but you have to look a little harder to see it.

You don't have to look very hard, on the other hand, to realise that Colombians are blessed (or cursed) with a touch of madness. In Colombia, crazy things happen and no one seems to notice that they are crazy. It is the country of Gabriel García Márquez, of cocaine, rum and salsa. Of René Higuita, goalkeeper of the national soccer team, who gave the ball away on the *half-way* line in one World Cup, missed the next because he was in prison for kidnapping, and famously back-heeled a shot off the line in a match against England with both feet *above* his head.

Unlike the phlegmatic people of the Andean republics, the Colombians take any excuse to laugh, shout, argue, party, fight, romance. They are genuine, hot-blooded *Latin* Americans. They sometimes alter the name of their country to spell *Loco*-mbia. Loco means mad in Spanish.

****

a little geography
Colombia has its stops on The Gringo Trail, although the trail is thinner here. As in the countries to the south, the trail runs north-south along the Andean spine. But in Colombia, the highlands split into three north-pointing fingers – the cordilleras Occidental, Central and Oriental – divided by the great valleys of the Magdalena and Cauca, rivers that flow north to the Caribbean.

On either side of these central highlands lie hot, undeveloped lowlands. On the Pacific coast are the jungles and plantations of the *Choco*, with its mainly black population. In the south-east, around Leticia, is the top corner of the Amazon and in the north-east, tucked underneath Venezuela, is a vast flat savanna known as *los Llanos*, Colombia's cattle country. In the far north, the highlands fall away down to the hot Caribbean littoral, the land of Gabriel García Márquez and historic cities of Santa Marta and Cartagena.

Apart from Leticia, tourists rarely visit the eastern and western lowlands, which are largely controlled by the guerrillas and drug cartels. Road links are poor and can become impassable in the rain. Instead, a trickle of travellers head north to the Caribbean via San Augustín and Bogotá. And that was our plan.

****

San Augustín
The express bus north from Ipiales was a revelation. A modern Mercedes, as comfortable as any in Europe, with air-conditioning and all its windows.

The tyres had treads on them. This lasted until we changed buses in Popayán. Then the local buses reverted to battered crates with torn seats, missing windows and baggage piled on the roof. The scenery made up for it. Lush rolling hills, prettier and more inviting than the harsher landscape of the *altiplano*.

San Augustín nestled among these green hills. It was a sleepy place, full of old whitewashed houses with red-tiled roofs and green wooden shutters and flowers hanging from their balconies.

The streets were quiet. There were a few old bangers, but most people either walked or rode horses. It was like a real 'Wild West'. Horsemen galloped past in ponchos and leather cowboy hats and tasselled leather chaps, leaning back in the saddle with stirrups forward and reins in one hand, cowboy style. They'd stop outside a bar, tie the horse to a post and march into the saloon through swing doors. You half-expected to see them fly out again in a hail of bullets. Outside every bar, lines of horses waited patiently. Often their owners were carried out over the barkeeper's shoulder and dumped on their back. They were then untied and trotted home, rider slumped unconscious in the saddle.

As we got off the bus we were hailed by a local tourist guide. His name was Stefano and he could show us everything. He helped us unload our bags from the roof of the bus.

'You want horses? You want to see the statues?' he asked. San Augustín was famous for the hundreds of mysterious stone statues on the surrounding hills. That was why tourists came here.

Maybe, we said.

'You want ganja? Cocaine? Girls? Magic mushrooms. I can show you a good hotel.'

Stefano was friendly, in his early thirties with a ready smile. He'd moved here from Cali.

'My friends said I was mad. They said 'Stefano, you're crazy. There's nothing there. Just some peasants.' But now . . . they come to visit me, and they don't want to go back to Cali.'

San Augustín was that sort of place. You came for a couple of days and stayed a couple of weeks. It was a popular stopover for backpackers. Stefano himself was making a decent living taking tourists on horseback to visit the statues. He enjoyed his work. He got to ride horses. He got to meet *gringas*. He was happy.

We promised Stefano we'd hire our horses from him, but his choice of hotel was sandwiched between a market and a nightclub. Instead we stayed in the *Posada Campesino*. It was also known as *Hogar Donaldo*, which loosely translated as *The Donald Duck Home for Disturbed Children*.

The Donald Duck Home for Disturbed Children was a small family farm, twenty minutes walk from town along a red-dust lane lined with other farmhouses. Flowers hung around the front door.

'If you miss your mother, this is the place to stay,' said Susie, a Canadian girl sitting at the table in the courtyard as we came in. The house opened backwards onto a three-sided courtyard. Cats, dogs, chickens and pigs poked around for food. The bedrooms had high, ancient beds and heavy floral curtains. The owner was a matronly, energetic lady called Doña Silviana, who served home-cooked meals and made pizza in a wood-fired oven in the backyard.[31] When we went for a walk, Doña Silviana would fuss and cluck and give us sandwiches and make us promise not to get lost and check that we were warmly wrapped up. Susie was right. It was just like staying with mother.

It was called *Hogar Donaldo* because in the day-time Doña Silviana, not content with running a farm and a guest-house, also took in local children from what she called 'problem homes.' Every morning a dozen infants would arrive, sit timidly and burst into tears when their mothers left. By the afternoon they were tearing around the yard, chasing chickens and each other. Then they would burst into tears again when their mothers came to take them away.

One afternoon, Melissa caused a minor sensation in a pool hall, not just by playing pool but by actually potting the balls. Eventually the size of the audience began to unnerve her.

'I can't perform properly in front of fifty guys,' she complained.

No one could believe that a woman could play pool. The pool halls in Colombia are such out-and-out male preserves that the urinals are right next to the tables. If you could shoot backwards you could play a shot and piss at the same time. At least you didn't have to worry about your opponent cheating when you went to the toilet. We noticed that Colombian men had to hit every shot as hard as possible. I guess it was a macho thing. The trick was to give them easy tap-ins, which they always blasted right out of the pocket.

****

statues

Some days we went riding with Stefano to see the statues. There are hundreds of them in the surrounding hills. Carved into delightfully comic animals and imaginary monsters, they comprise one of the archaeological treasures of the Americas. Yet almost nothing is known about the people who created them, except that their culture clearly lasted many centuries. The statues offer only tantalising hints. For instance, many depict men with jaguars' teeth. Others show men wearing penis-sheaths. Such 'rainforest' imagery (also found in other Andean sites) suggests that the Andean highland culture which led to the Incas may have come from the Amazon.

San Augustín lies near a unique point in South America: a three-way watershed. From here, rivers flow north along the Magdalena to the Caribbean, west to the Pacific, and east via the Amazon to the Atlantic. The easiest north-south migration route from the Caribbean follows the Rio Magdalena to San Augustín, crosses this watershed and heads south along Amazonian tributaries or into Ecuador's central valley. San Augustín thus controls one of the continent's major trade routes, and one that may have played a central role in the early history of the continent.

Such are the fragments that make up so much of South America's pre-Conquest history.

****

visualisation

Sitting outside the *Hogar Donaldo*, I asked Melissa how she beat cancer.

'Visualisation,' Melissa explained.

'What?'

'You have to convince yourself that you can beat a disease. Then it just sort of. . . . does it on its own. I don't know. But just wishing isn't good

127

enough. You've got to believe it. You use a . . .' Melissa paused. 'What's that word when you compare something to something else. An anthology?'

'Analogy.'

'Yes, an anomaly. Like the good cells in your body are an army fighting the cancer cells. You have to picture yourself free of disease. Or course, there was other stuff too. I did loads of acupuncture and meditation and special diets. But visualisation was the key, I think.'

'It sounds simple,' I said.

'No, it's hard. Most people can't convince themselves, deep down, that they can *really* defeat a disease without science and doctors. They don't realise the power of the mind and body to cure itself. Maybe it can't work for everyone. But you can achieve a lot through will-power.'

And Melissa had.

****

Tierradentro

Nearby was Tierradentro, another archaeological zone. The village was surrounded by dozens of burial chambers, thought to be 2,000 years old. Another mysterious legacy of another unknown culture. Even the name was mysterious: *tierra-dentro*. The 'land within'. The tombs were earth caves entered by giant spiral steps, with geometric patterns on the walls. The village itself was simply two intersecting streets. The fact that the 'restaurant' turned out to be in someone's living room was part of its charm.

Like San Augustín, the beauty of the surrounding hills tempted us to stay for a few extra days. The hills around Tierradentro were more rugged than San Augustín's, and we hired donkeys rather than horses to visit the tombs. However hard I kicked my donkey, it wouldn't go faster than walking pace. Then it stopped altogether and I had to drag it the rest of the way.

Melissa was suffering from too much horse-riding. Her backside, lacking natural padding, was worn raw from days in the saddle, leaving a bright red circle like a chimpanzee on heat. When we left Tierradentro, Melissa had to pad her seat with every jumper she had. For the next week she slept on her stomach. It was just as well we hadn't succumbed to the romantic-sounding idea of buying our own horses and riding them to Ecuador. Stefano had helped two English girls do just that a year before.

The girls wrote to him from Quito to say they'd made it *and* sold the horses for a profit.

Tierradentro was *muy tranquillo* – very peaceful. It would have been easy to stay longer. But we had a deadline of sorts, to meet Mark in Barranquilla for the carnival. Each journey establishes its own momentum, and it felt like time to press on. We caught a bus to Bogotá.

****

Bogotá

Colombia's capital has a bad reputation. To most people, it means drugs and murder. Neither Melissa nor I liked big cities much anyway. Our only reason for stopping in Bogotá at all was to get hiking maps for two mountain regions further north, the Sierra Nevadas of Cocuy and Santa Marta.

Bogotá lies in a wide valley in the middle of the country. It has a pleasant climate. Green hills flank the city. It feels almost European, full of high-rise flats and office blocks, shopping arcades and heavy traffic. It didn't seem too dangerous.

The taxi-driver who picked us up at the bus terminal thought otherwise. We showed him the address of the hotel we wanted to go to. He refused.

'No. You cannot go there. I will not take you. You will be killed.'

We insisted. He began to get agitated.

'I cannot take you there,' he repeated. Instead, he took us to a hotel in a different part of town, which cost five times as much as the one we'd selected. We said it was too expensive. He took us to another, equally expensive. I explained patiently that we wanted the original hotel.

'Ah, I know another one. Very nice. Safe.'

It was getting late and we were getting annoyed.

'Look,' I said, 'just take us to the hotel like we asked, or we're not paying you.' That did the trick. Grumpily, he took us to the hotel, making throat-slitting motions to indicate what was about to happen to us. We got out and paid him.

'Hey, what about all the time I've wasted trying to find you a decent hotel?' he complained.

'Do they play cricket in Colombia?' Melissa asked as he drove away.

'I don't think so, why?'

'It's just that I thought that was the signal for lbw.'

The hotel was a dump, all right, like most cheap places in the middle of cities. But at least we weren't robbed or murdered. Getting the maps we wanted, however, proved beyond us. The only maps in Colombia that are good enough for hiking (with contour lines and such details) are military ones. Even these are not perfect. They're based on aerial photographs: if the photo was taken on an overcast day, the map had white gaps where cloud concealed the topography. But they were all there was. You had to go to a special office to order them, then return the next day to collect a photocopy.

The office had moved. No one could tell us where it had gone. We spent all day looking for it and found it just after it had closed. The next day we arrived early. But when we took the maps to the desk, the clerk told us that they were restricted areas and they needed special permission to issue them. The authorising office for the permit was on the other side of town.

Across town, the soldier at the gate wouldn't let us in unless I had a jacket and tie. I didn't. He called an officer. The officer said those were the rules. No jacket, no entry.

No entry, no maps.

Having failed to get the maps, we tried to locate *Inderena*, the government agency that ran the national parks, to get a permit to visit the Sierra Nevada de Santa Marta. The office had moved. No one could tell us where it had gone. We spend another day looking for it. Finally we tracked it down, near the President's house, the streets lined with soldiers and police.

'You have to ask for permission in Santa Marta, not here,' said the man in the office.

That evening I was reading the newspaper. A headline read:

'Bogotá taxi drivers shot and killed five passengers in arguments over fares this month.'

****

El Dorado
The best thing in Bogotá is the Gold Museum. As well as containing beauti-ful pieces – the early Colombians were masters at working gold – it explains the 'pre-Columbian' history of 'Colombia'.

Colombia was part of an intermediate area between the two great cultural centres of Peru and mesoamerica (ie Mexico/Guatemala). The country's broken geography led to regional cultures instead of a single empire: there was San Augustín and Tierradentro, the Tayrona Indians near Santa Marta; and the Muisca around Bogotá.

It is from the Muisca that the legend of El Dorado – literally 'the golden one' – arises. At the Laguna de Guatavita, a meteor-crater lake one hour north of Bogotá, Muisca chiefs were painted from head to toe in gold and rowed to the middle of the lake, where they dived into the water in a ritu-al said to confer divine power. In 1578, one Antonio de Sepúlveda, hoping to recover the gold that had washed off the Muisca chiefs over the years, cut a chunk out of the side of the crater and drained the lake. He found 10 grams of gold and died bankrupt. Two more equally unsuccessful attempts were made, one in the 19th century and one early this century by an English company

We left Bogotá and headed north. It wasn't the danger. It wasn't even an especially unpleasant city. But all it offered was an imitation of a European city. If you want a great city, try Paris or Rome, Berlin or Prague. South America's treasures are not its cities, but its vast mountains and jun-gles. These awesome wild places were our personal El Dorados.

****

Güicán
The green Colombian Andes occasionally break out into compact alpine regions with permanent snow. The Sierra Nevada del Cocuy, a couple of hundred miles north of Bogotá, was one such region. A six day hike through the Sierra started from Güicán, a pretty village high on a mountainside.

Everyone in Güicán looked in-bred. In isolated villages like this, it may

come down to a straight choice between the relatives and the farm animals. The relatives are not always first choice. Peasant-donkey liaisons
are a Colombian joke, much like the Welsh and sheep.

Behind the village, a single massive slope ended with the Sierra's main
north-south ridge. On the far side of this, out of sight, a vast escarpment
plunged down to form the giant wall of a hidden valley. The trek circled
this massif by crossing a pass to the north, following the valley beneath
the escarpment, then climbing back over a southern pass. It was said to
be the best trek in Colombia.

There was only one problem.

Guerrillas. They used the northern pass as a route between the highlands
and *los Llanos* to the east. A couple of weeks earlier, they'd attacked
Güicán itself and killed a shopkeeper. Soldiers patrolled the town. Their
commander wasn't worried by the guerrillas. He tried to reassure us.

'These *banditos* are just peasants. Yes, they use the first pass sometimes.
But don't worry. If you meet them, they probably won't kill you. They will
just rob you of everything.'

South Americans, I was learning, aren't very good at reassurance.

****

guerrillas in the midst

*With the fall of the Shining Path in Peru, Colombia can boast the conti-
nent's last guerrilla conflict. It began in 1948 with the murder of Liberal
politician Jorge Eliécer Gaitán. Over the next nine years, 300,000 people
were killed in La Violencia, a civil war between the two main political
parties, the Liberals and Conservatives. In fact, most of the fighting
revolved around local power struggles. Ideologically the parties differed
little. Their leaders came from the elite and supported the status quo.
Gradually, however, some Liberals began demanding real reform. The
Liberal leaders, fearing they might lose control of their party, hastily
patched up their differences with the Conservatives and set up the
National Front, a power-sharing arrangement that lasted from 1957 until
1986 (although it officially ended in 1974). But the more radical Liberal
supporters couldn't accept that they'd been dying in their thousands for
nothing. And so the guerilla movement was born.*

Colombia is a land of isolated regions, and the guerilla movement was also fragmented. There was the M-19, the Maoist EPL (Ejército Popular de Liberacion), the Marxist-Christian ELN (Ejército de Liberación Nacional) and FARC (Fuerzas Armadas Revolucionarias de Colombia), the largest group with an estimated 12,000 to 17,000 combatants. The guerrillas rarely attack tourists or 'civilians', preferring 'strategic' strikes such as army units, oil-wells or businessmen. Increasingly financed by narco-trafficking – which many observers suspect is replacing their political agenda – they are too entrenched in local strongholds to be easily defeated, too divided to threaten the state.

But the spectre of terrorism is used to justify appalling human rights abuses. Army or army-backed death squads kill more people every year in Colombia than in the whole of Pinochet's 17 year dictatorship in Chile. A United Nations report described Colombia as 'a land of murder and torture where the military kill civilians at will.'

In 1986, FARC agreed a cease-fire and launched the Unión Patriótica (UP), winning 14 seats in the National Congress. Four of these 14 Congressmen were killed in their first year. So far, more than 2,500 UP members have been assassinated, including several Presidential candidates.[32]

I've sometimes found myself wondering why – given that most Latin American countries are now 'democratic' – they don't vote in parties that represent their poor/Indian majorities. The history of the UP demonstrates why. Genuine attempts to challenge the ruling elite through the ballot-box are still met with violence. It takes a brave person to stand for a party like the UP. (Or even to vote for one, as few people believe that their vote is really secret.) Violence still underpins the power structure in Latin America, just as it has done ever since the Conquest.

****

Hans, Fritz and Seventy

In our hotel, I began painting my army-surplus poncho white in case we met the *guerrilleros* and they mistook me for a soldier. I'd painted a large white peace sign on the back, and was trying to convince Melissa (and myself) that our chances of bumping into terrorists were pretty slim, when eight giant Austrians walked in. They were all about 6ft6 and were led by a tiny Colombian woman who barely reached Melissa's shoulder. The Austrians were kitted out in expensive gortex jackets and colourful fleece jumpers, as if we were in a European ski resort. As we were the only other guests in the hotel, the woman introduced herself. Her name was Gloria. She said she was guiding the Austrians up to the highest peak in the range, Ritacuba Blanco, and invited us to join them.

The Austrians were a senior citizens hiking club. They went hiking every weekend in Austria and this was their annual overseas trip. An adventurous choice. They introduced themselves.

'I am Thomas, unt zis is Hans, unt zis is Fritz . . .' I didn't think Austrians really had names like Hans and Fritz. I waited for him to add something like 'Achtung' or 'Englisher schweinhund', but instead he introduced the last member of the party.

' . . . unt he is Seventy.'

He said it as if that was his name. Seventy confirmed for us.

'Yes, I am Seventy,' he smiled.

Seventy explained that every decade he liked to set himself a special challenge. When he was sixty, he'd climbed a 7,000m peak in the Himalaya. For his seventieth birthday, he was aiming a little lower, for Ritacuba Blanco, the highest peak in the Sierra, was only 5,330m. But then, he said, he was not as young as he used to be.

The climb was a two day trip, staying at a mountain hut along the way. It was more of a walk than a climb, but the last section involved trudging up a glacier, something I'd never done. Unlike the Austrians, we had no ice-axes or crampons. But if Seventy could do it, then so could I.

The Austrians not only had ice-axes and crampons, but meters to measure their heart-rate, the altitude, the distance walked and the amount of energy used up in the last five minutes. They probably had meters to tell them when to look at their other meters. Gloria raced ahead. We stuck with her most of the way, but near the top the altitude hit me and every step became a battle. I forced myself to count thirty steps between rests, then twenty, then ten. As the paces fell, the length of each rest increased. As I gasped for air, the Austrians trooped past. Still, the summit was higher than I had ever been and I felt a glow of achievement. Melissa was waiting at the top.

'The views make it all worthwhile,' she laughed.

I looked around. We could see nothing but cloud. I could only just see

Melissa. The mist had blown in exactly as we reached the summit. On a clear day, we would have seen 100km across the plains of *los Llanos*.

****

wisdom

Melissa was happy. She always was in the mountains. Despite her slightness and her pretence of helplessness (carefully cultivated, I suspected), Melissa was tough. A survivor. She took what life threw at her and came up smiling. She'd bounced back from serious illness and heroin addiction and unfaithful partners.

'But none of them actually *left* me,' she pointed out, 'and they all begged me to come back.'

Melissa had remained vital, healthy and without bitterness. She always seemed much brighter and fresher than the other women backpackers we met, yet she was ten years older than most of them. Maybe she had a dodgy portrait in an attic somewhere.

'These kids, eating badly, getting stoned, doing nothing . . . of course they look shit,' Melissa reasoned. 'I'm in touch with my body, that's why I look so good. That and my placenta skin cream.'

For me, Melissa was a rare find, a beautiful woman who could beat most men at pool and climb mountains. And roll spliffs faster and better than anyone I knew, except perhaps Mark. And she was prepared to go out with me.

'The difference between you and me,' Melissa explained, 'is that you live your life through books and words. You think you can learn everything from a book. You should learn that wisdom and knowledge are not the same thing. That's the mistake people like you and Mark make. You know the facts about everything, but knowledge is worthless unless you have the wisdom to use it properly. Wisdom means knowing what's important, listening to your inner self, knowing when to be calm and still. It's not about how many statistics you can quote or whether you can work the latest computer. So there,' she said, sticking her tongue out at me.

'You can be quite articulate when you want to be,' I commented.

'Yes,' said Melissa, grinning like a schoolgirl praised by her teacher. 'I can.'

'Maybe I'll have to stop calling you 'Bimbo'.' I mused.

'Yes,' Melissa said happily, 'you will.'

'Well, let's not get carried away,' I decided, 'you've only said one smart thing . . . Bimbo.'

Melissa let fly with the orange she was peeling. It caught me square on the nose.

When my eyes stopped watering, I could see Melissa in front of me look-ing apprehensive.

'I'm sorry, I meant to miss,' she said.

****

el lechero

The Austrians trooped off with their meters to conquer and record other peaks. We spent a few more days hiking and camping in the Sierra. The scenery was awesome. We felt like Jack in the Giant's castle, intruders into a world on a different scale, walking past enormous cliffs and scat-tered boulders as big as houses and weird plants called *frailejónes*, which resembled man-sized pineapples.

We camped beside glacial lakes where not a single blade of grass grew. The only colours were the white of snow and cloud, the grey rock, and the blue of lakes and sky. Not even an occasional bird flew overhead. The only sounds were the fabric of our tent flapping in the wind and, every so often, a mighty crash when a huge chunk of ice broke off a gla-cier and smashed onto the rocks below. The echo reverberated around the mountains for an age.

In the mornings our tent was covered in ice, just as on the trek in Bolivia. Melissa was in her element. She led me up another glacier to the ridge. Without crampons, I reverted to stone-age technology and found a couple of sharp stones to use as ice-axes in case I fell. (The idea is that, if you fall, you dig the axe into the snow and hang on to stop yourself sliding down the icy slope.) Melissa skipped off ahead, step-kicking a path into the softening midday snow. She laughed back at me as I crawled tentatively up in her wake, my two rock-daggers poised to dig into the snow.

'You can't spend all your life worrying about whether you're going to fall,' she shouted.

Her words echoed off the cliffs. I reached the ridge. This time we were above the clouds, which cloaked the valley below us. The peaks and cliffs of the ridge floated above this cotton sea. Looking back, a string of lakes shimmered like green emeralds embedded in the rock.

We descended to a remote *hacienda*, La Esperanza, for the night. In the morning, we returned to Güicán on *el lechero* – the milk-truck that collected milk from the farms. At each stop, the farmers' wife and daughters waited with their plastic containers. The young driver jumped out and poured their milk into metal drums in the back of the truck, taking more or less time at each farm depending how pretty the girls were. The soft perfume of the milk reminded me of childhood. We perched on the milk drums and tried to avoid the milk that slopped across the floor. *El lechero* collected not just milk, but everything else, too: letters, parcels, eggs, chickens, passengers. Even a cow. There was no ramp and it took the driver and the farmer and a dozen passengers and much grunting and groaning to lift the frightened animal onto the truck. The cow stood next to Melissa, looking bemused.

****

Capitanejo

Our next stop was to be the Arhuaco Indian village of Nabusímake in the Sierra Nevada de Santa Marta. We had to change buses in Capitanejo, in the valley below Güicán. Although only 50km away, Capitanejo was 2,000m lower with a totally different, oppressively hot, climate.

Our bus left Capitanejo at 3am. There was no bus station, so we sat on our packs in the street, trying to doze against a wall. Other passengers sat and waited. Around 2am, I noticed smoke drifting out from underneath the door of the locked cafe opposite us. No one was taking any notice. But the smoke was definitely getting thicker. I nudged the man beside me.

'I think there's a fire,' I said.

He sleepily followed my finger and looked at the smoke for a few seconds. Then it registered. He leapt to his feet and ran off up the street. Moments later, another man came charging towards the cafe. He lurched drunkenly, fiddled with the lock and flung open the door. A cloud of smoke poured out. Flames danced out of a grill or toaster. He dived into his back room, dragged out a crate and proceeded to douse the flames with Coca-Cola. After about thirty bottles, the fire was out. Swaying unsteadily, he contemplated the mess, still clutching a couple of empty Coke bottles.

****

Nabusímake

Rising to the 5,775m summit of Pico Simón Bolívar, Colombia's highest peak, the Sierra Nevada de Santa Marta is an isolated massif, separate from the main Andes. Overlooking the Caribbean, this is the highest coastal range in the world. The drop on its northern side, from almost 6,000m into the sea in only 45km, is greater than the summit-to-base height of Mt Everest. It's also steeper than Everest. The seaward northern side is wet and densely forested, while the rainshadowed southern slopes are dry and brown,

Hidden in a remote valley on these southern slopes is Nabusímake. On our map, it was still marked as San Sebastián de Rábago. But the change of name was important. Nabusímake is the main village of the Arhuaco Indians, one of the few indigenous groups left in Colombia. They once occupied a much wider area but have been pushed ever higher into the Sierra by *Latino* settlers and *marimbos* (drug-producers) and by fighting between guerrillas and the army. And even here, they weren't left in peace, for missionaries insisted on saving their souls.

In 1982, the Arhuacos decided they'd had enough. They threw out the missionaries and changed the village back to its original name. But their problems didn't go away. In 1990, three Arhuaco *mamos* (elders), were on their way to Bogotá to protest about army harassment when they were dragged off the bus by soldiers, tortured and murdered – an act that surely proved their point. An investigation accused two officers from the local battalion. Neither was punished.[33]

Getting to Nabusímake proved more difficult than expected. We caught a bus to the busy town of Valledupar on the dry cattle plains of *los Llanos* at the foot of the Sierra. It's a poor, rarely-visited, remote region, known mainly for its music – a rough-and-ready Colombian country music called *vallenato*, all raucous singing and high-tempo accordion playing. We spent a night in Valledupar. There was little reason to stay: the only interesting thing I saw was an electricity pylon with about five hundred illegal cables hotwired to it. I don't know why this one stuck in my mind, because it's a common sight throughout South America.

From Valledupar a Landrover *colectivo* (a shared taxi) took us into the foothills of the Sierra to Pueblo Bello. The town scarcely deserved its name, consisting of one long, dusty street flanked by a few tatty shops. It was another place with a frontier feel and men wearing cowboy hats.

In Pueblo Bello, we saw our first Arhuacos. They were the most striking people we'd seen. Tall, with flowing black hair, they walked the dusty street with an almost-arrogant disdain. They were dressed as I've always imagined Anglo-Saxons or Celtic Britons, with leather sandals and tunics and trousers of heavy undyed wool, and a short sword strapped to their waistband in a leather sheath. The Arhuacos call themselves 'elder brothers' and refer to the rest of us as 'younger brothers'. They believe it to be their duty to look after the younger brothers, whom they regard as children with no idea how to live properly. Dirty settler towns like Pueblo Bello can only have reinforced this belief.

From Pueblo Bello, it was a three-hour drive to Nabusímake. Or an eight-hour walk. Jeeps left every three or four days and there was a rumour that one was going tomorrow. A young Englishman called Robert, from Devon, was staying in our guesthouse, with his Colombian wife Marcela. They'd met while he was working as a chef in a hotel in Cartagena.

We were chatting to them when four men walked in; a young Colombian and three older *gringos*. The Colombian carried himself with a self-satisfied swagger. He introduced himself.

'I am Raphael. I am taking these Canadians tourists to Nabusímake tomorrow. If you need a lift, I will arrange it.'

We chatted to the Canadians. They were good ol' country boys. Two of them, Pierre and Jean, were French Canadians. The third was called Randy. He was a backwoodsman with a long droopy moustache and a whiny hillbilly twang. He looked and sounded like the cartoon cowboy who always fails to shoot Bugs Bunny. This was the first time they'd been out of Canada, and they were finding it a bit of a shock. I asked how they ended up in Colombia, which seemed a brave choice for a first overseas trip. They said they'd seen an advert for a cheap charter flight from Montreal to Cartagena.

'We jus' thought, hell, why *not* Colombia,' said Randy.

I could think of quite a few reasons.

Pierre asked if we thought Raphael was overcharging them. They'd paid thirty times the normal bus fare from Santa Marta, just for Raphael to get them here.

'The thang was, we came on the bus anyway. We thought he was gonna git us a car.'

The Canadians had paid him an all-in fee for the whole trip. The less he paid, the more he had left. Added to which, Raphael had never actually been to Nabusímake before. He was a cowboy, in the less complimentary sense of the word. But being a good-looking city boy, Raphael clearly felt a cut above the country bumpkins in Pueblo Bello. He made little effort to conceal his contempt for them, or his high opinion of himself.

'I, Raphael,' Raphael announced, 'have arranged the lift tomorrow for nine in the morning. The driver wanted to leave at seven. That is too early. I told him. We will leave at nine. We are paying, so we decide when we leave. These country people . . .' He shook his head.

The next morning we assembled at half-past-eight and went to find the jeep. It had left at seven. No one was going to Nabusímake for the next three days.

'Don't worry,' Raphael reassured announced confidently. 'I will find another jeep.' There was a truck, but its driver wanted three times what the jeep driver had asked. Raphael refused to pay. The driver refused to go for less. Of course it was more expensive, he explained. He was making a special journey, there were no other paying passengers and he had nothing to sell in Nabusímake.

'Let's get going, Raphael.' the Canadians said. 'Pay the man.' Raphael refused. By eleven, everyone was fed up. Pierre told Raphael it was 'pay-up or money-back' time. Raphael gave in. I ran off to fetch Robert, Marcela and Melissa. When we got back, the truck had gone.

We decided to walk. After all, we were in good shape. We'd climbed a 5,000m mountain in Güicán only the week before. But the sun was high and walking in the heat is very different from walking in the cool highlands. After a couple of hours, we were drained. But we'd come too far to turn back. We struggled on and prayed for a change in the weather. In mid-afternoon, it started to rain. Hard. Robert and Marcela had no jackets and were soon soaked.

'Well, we did ask for rain,' said Melissa.

We prayed for the rain to stop, but this time our prayers went unheeded. The road climbed steadily through forest. We were soaking wet and getting cold. I had a painful blister on the end of my big toe. It was getting late and we had one tiny tent between us.

We were wondering what to do when we heard horses behind us. We turned to see two Arhuaco men emerge from the sleet, understandably surprised to see us. They didn't speak much Spanish but, realising that we were looking for shelter, they motioned us to follow them. We trudged after them until we reached a group of huts. The men pointed to one and said we could stay there.

The two men disappeared into the rain. The hut was a small, round, thatched building. Not only was the roof thatched, but so was the wall; a wooden framework of branches stuffed with twigs and brush. Inside, it was a single room, empty apart from a wooden bench, a bundle of firewood and a small firepit in the centre of the floor. We caught glimpses of a few people in the nearby huts but no one took any notice of us, so we went in and spread our wet gear out to dry.

Then we built a fire. Soon the hut was lost in a cloud of choking smoke. Tears streamed out of our eyes. I had to stick my head out of the door to stop them stinging. We were trying to edge close enough to the fire to cook some rice when a little girl of about eight peered in, wide-eyed at the strange people inside. We smiled and waved to her. Melissa offered her a piece of chocolate. The girl hesitated, retreated, re-emerged at the door, then finally summoned up the courage to come inside. She looked at us incredulously. She stared at our sleeping bags, our penknives, our rucksacks, our fleece jumpers, our waterproof jackets and our boots. She examined the picture of Nabusímake in our guidebook with fascination. She looked hopefully at our rice and bread and fish and chocolate.

But when she saw our fire, she looked at us in disgust. Who were these strange people who came from far away with all these strange things, and yet couldn't even build a fire properly? She leaned across and, with a couple of quick prods, rearranged the fire. The flames darted neatly upwards. The smoke funnelled into a tidy plume and drifted up into the ceiling. The hut emerged from its haze. The little girl muttered to herself and ran off to play outside.

In the morning it was dry. We were only a couple of hours short of Nabusímake. The path reached a high point, then dropped gently into a valley. It was like entering a lost Shangri-la. Ahead of us were the mountains of the main Sierra, hidden in cloud. We passed more huts like the one we'd stayed in. Horses, pigs, chicken and cattle wandered freely across unfenced pastures. A gentle stream bubbled through the meadows, flanked by a few trees. It looked like a park.

Nabusímake itself stood at one end of this valley. Thatched stone cottages and narrow cobbled streets were all encircled by a low dry-stone wall and a dry ditch, like the village in the 'Asterix' books. We could have been stepping back a thousand years. Except for a 20-high aerial in the main square. There was little sign of activity, for the Arhuacoss don't actually live in the village.[34] Each family owns a house but comes down for festivals or meetings.

A man emerged from a large house, holding a bottle-shaped leather gourd. He was grinding something inside it with a thin stick. A dozen other men wandered over and stared at us from across the wall, all grinding away absently-mindedly with their sticks and gourds.[35] Finally, an old man came out and announced that we could stay in the valley, but that the high mountains were forbidden.

We were disappointed, but not surprised. I'd heard that the Arhuacos consider the peaks sacred. They spend days in the high wilderness communing with their gods and have no desire for an influx of climbers and hikers. They also believe that all life disturbs the balance of nature and that payments or offerings must be made to compensate for such disturbances. I guess they didn't trust 'younger brothers' like us to respect this balance. So the peaks were off-limits.

Still, the valley was a charmed place. A *Latino* woman rented rooms in her farmhouse, a pretty stone cottage beside the stream. We explored the foothills and the village and swam in rock pools. Robert, who was diabetic, kept collapsing in the middle of streams. Occasionally, Raphael and the Canadians galloped past on horseback, Raphael kitted out like Prince Charles at a polo match.

The Arhuacos remained enigmatic and distant. They greeted us politely but showed little desire to talk. When we went to the village store, the shop-keeper carried on scraping coca for half-an-hour before serving us. They were more interested when we asked to buy one of their bags.

The Arhuacos are famous in Colombia for their woollen shoulder-bags, called *mochilas*, which are knitted by the men and are extremely fashionable in Bogotá. Melissa loved them and bought two. From then on, everyone we passed would point to their *mochila* and offer it to us for sale. The guidebook warned us not to take photos of the Arhuacos, nor to offer anyone alcohol, edicts which we piously obeyed.

We spent two days looking for a waterfall.

'What did the waterfall send you?' An old man asked on our way back.

'It sent its love,' said Marcela.

The old man considered this reply for a while, then nodded thoughtfully.

After a week, there was a jeep back to Pueblo Bello. It was the first vehicle we'd seen since we'd arrived. The Canadians were already inside. There was no sign of Raphael.

'That boy was nothin' but a darn crook. We told him where to stick his gahdin' service. An' we did jus' fine without him, too,' Randy drawled.

'Gee, those guys look great, don't they,' he added. 'Ah sure hope the photos turn out.'

'I thought the Arhuacos didn't like their photos taken,' I said.

'Well, no one told us. But them fellas sure seemed happy enough about it.'

Not only that, but they'd sat around their camp fire at night, everyone getting drunk and having a ball. They'd even invited a couple of Arhuaco elders to Canada.

If the walk up was hard, the ride back was worse. I was feeling sick. For some reason, I only seem to get sick before long, bumpy bus trips. And this one was very bumpy. The road seemed as if it had been hit by an earthquake. This was because it really *had* been hit by an earthquake, two weeks earlier. There were huge gashes across the road, chasms big enough for a car to fall into. Whatever surface the road once had was now reduced to loose rubble. The driver carried two

planks of wood to cross unavoidable gaps. The jeep was stuffed full.
Every time we hit a bump (which was about every ten seconds) my head
smashed against the metal roof. It was three hours of pure misery.

Chapter 6
Caribbean: Carnival!

Santa Marta

The bus to the coast was downright luxurious. It was its maiden voyage and signs splashed all over the bus station trumpeted it as the latest in comfort and reliability. Someone even cut a ribbon. I was settling into my seat and discreetly picking my nose when a photographer jumped on board and took our picture for a publicity shot. I have nightmares of returning to Colombia to find my face plastered over every bus terminal, with one finger jammed up my left nostril.

We arrived at Santa Marta at dawn. This time we'd left the highlands for good. It was 7am and, here on the Caribbean coast, already baking hot. We caught a taxi to the 'Miramar Hotel'.

'*Costeña* girls are the most beautiful in Colombia,' the taxi-driver announced. After a moment's reflection he waved his hand grandly and added, 'the most beautiful in the whole world.' Learning that we were English, he launched into a prolonged description of a soccer match between Colombia and England in 1965 or thereabouts. Colombia, he said, had come back from a Bobby Charlton goal to draw 1-1. The taxi driver became more and more animated as he approached the Colombian equaliser. 'Goooooooaaaaal' he shouted, grabbing the wheel just in time to avoid an oncoming car.

The Miramar was another classic Gringo Trail cheapie. Every backpacker in Santa Marta headed here, although there must have been twenty hotels in town that were both cleaner and quieter and just as cheap. The Miramar looked like a prison. A gringo prison. The front gate (from where it was just possible to 'mira' the 'mar' – to see the sea – at the end of the street) was protected by a heavy iron grill, which was closed at night, either to keep the locals out or the gringos in. Inside was a half-covered courtyard. The reception desk was in the front, covered half. Beside it were a few battered armchairs and a TV tuned to a US satellite movie channel. There was a constant buzz of activity around the reception. Backpackers checked in or out or waited to use the phone. People chat-ted to the manager or assembled for trips to Tayrona Park. Touts and guides hovered, for the Miramar functioned as the local tourist office: if you wanted to know anything, or needed a guide to take you anywhere, the Miramar arranged it.

In the middle of this swirl of activity, the calm eye of the cyclone, sat the Miramar's chubby manager, playing speed chess while simultaneously answering an endless stream of questions and issuing instructions to his staff. The standard of chess was high, too. Colombians manage to turn even something as sedate and cerebral as chess into a test of machismo. Moves were banged out without pause. Pieces were slammed down with a flourish. Spectators crowded around and murmured approval or disapproval after each move. The players appraised each other cagily, like prize-fighters.

Further back, in the open section of the courtyard, was a cafe that served juices and beer and omelettes and played The Doors and Bob Marley. This was the place in town to meet other backpackers and swap travellers' tales. And to take cocaine. People vanished into the dorms and emerging wide-eyed and runny-nosed, while an elegant silver-haired Colombian sat near the front gate and flared his nostril suggestively as you passed.

The Miramar did have two drawbacks. It was impossible to get any sleep, and it was always full. Melissa and I found another hotel in the next street: a one-storey corner building with flaking paint called 'El Prado'. This had only four rooms, all seemingly made of cardboard, and an ant-infested kitchen. It felt more like a family house than a hotel. It was run by an old man, who didn't say much, a cat and Alberto – an enormous, sweaty youth who fell in love with Melissa and greeted us like long-lost friends whenever we came in. Alberto spent most of the day lying in a hammock in the back yard, hidden behind lines of drying clothes, reading Hare Krishna books – not because he was a Hare Krishna but because, being free, these were the only books he could afford.

Chess was popular at El Prado, too. I played an old man who made such weird moves with such speed and bravado that he was clearly a genius or an idiot.

Luckily for me, he was an idiot.

****

jugo de maracuyá
There wasn't much to do or see in Santa Marta, even though it was founded in 1525 and is the oldest town in Colombia, and Simón Bolívar died here in 1830. The Miramar and El Prado were in the town's original colonial heart, a ten-block square of quiet, treeless streets on the sea-front, isolated by two main roads and a railway line. The town's business activity

had moved to the newer centre, away from the sea, leaving the old quarter to slumber peacefully in the heat. Street kids lay on the pavements and slept off glue-sniffing bouts, or else begged food from restaurants along the sea-front promenade. At night, whores lent idly in doorways.

In the evening, the promenade was the place to be. Young couples strolled through the avenue of palm trees behind the beach, and cocaine dealers sat around waiting for customers. Behind the palm trees, the cafes and restaurants turned up the salsa and cranked into life. One open-fronted bar had live vallenato bands every night. The singer wailed sad drinking songs to the accompaniment of accordions and violins.

'If you want to dance,' a Colombian told me, 'you dance to salsa, but if your girlfriend walks out, then you get drunk and listen to vallenato.' It was the music of the *marimberos* – the marijuana growers and smugglers who in the Seventies had briefly turned Santa Marta into a boom town.

Most people in Santa Marta were *mulatos*, of Afro-Spanish descent.[36] Here on the Caribbean, everyone seemed to have mixed with everyone: Spanish, Indian and African. The result was the *costeños*; friendly, laid-back, vibrant and just a little crazy. The *costeña* girls *were* beautiful; tall and slim with mocking, defiant brown eyes, smooth coffee skin and long dark hair.

The narrow beach in front of the promenade was surprisingly clean. Flabby middle-aged men and beautiful young girls jogged along it while a group of youths practised *capiera*, the acrobatic Brazilian martial art. Out at sea, two huge oil-tankers dominated the bay.

The best thing about Santa Marta was the fruit stalls, like the eponymous Fruit Palace of Charles Nicholl's book. The girl who worked at the stall outside the Miramar squeezed her eye-popping figure into skin-tight leggings and a lycra top of distorted black-and-white squares that looked like it might give you a migraine if you stared too hard. But I found myself fantasising about the drinks, not the girl. The stalls served more varieties of tropical fruit than I knew existed. Each had a row of wire baskets containing such familiar fruits as bananas and pineapples, plus stranger treasures: purple golf-balls, things like hairier kiwi-fruits, yellow starfruits, large melon-like globes and other mysteries. My favourite drink was *jugo de maracuyá* – passion-fruit blended with milk, sugar and ice hacked from a large chunk that sat melting on the pavement. The stalls hot-wired power from the nearest electricity cable to run the blender and served

the result in giant, brightly-coloured plastic jugs. The drinks were liquid
paradise and days in Santa Marta revolved around frequent stops at the
fruit stalls.

If we wanted coffee, vendors wandered the streets with racks of thermos-
flasks selling *tintos* – lukewarm, sugar-laden expresso shots in tiny plastic
cups, brewed in the morning and stewed all day.

****

coffee
*'It's funny that you can't get a decent cup of coffee in Colombia, of all
places,' Melissa said.*

It was time for me to climb back onto my soapdish.

*'It's not that surprising. Coffee, after all, is a cash-crop grown for
export.[37] The good stuff is shipped straight out. It's symptomatic of an
economic system that exists for the benefit of the West rather than for
the good of local people. Even in economic terms, most Colombians don't
really benefit from exporting coffee. Local coffee-growers only see about
a tenth of the money from the coffee we buy. The rest goes to exporters,
shippers, roasters and retailers – all mainly Western multinationals.*

*'And coffee is typical. It's still the same system set up by the Conquest.
Even today, most of the region's exports remain either raw materials like
oil, bananas, coffee or even cocaine, or output from foreign-owned fac-
tories located here to exploit cheap labour.[38] Raw materials and cheap
labour: strip away the fancy modern economic terms like Structural
Adjustment and Comparative Advantage and 'Free' Trade, and Eduardo
Galeano's two Open Veins are still bleeding.'*

'What's Structural Adjustment?' Melissa asked.

'Well, it's an economic policy that . . . '

But I'll spare you that bit.

****

poverty
A statistic in today's paper, from a new UN Development Report. The
assets of the world's richest 358 people equals the income of the poorest
45% of the planet's population: 2,300 million people.[39]

****

Isla de Salamanca

The biggest party in South America was approaching. Carnival. Two hours bus ride along the coast from Santa Marta, Barranquilla's carnival was said to be the second-biggest on the continent after Rio de Janeiro. Two hours was enough time for a few hundred people to die in the inevitable blood-and-guts movie that accompanies any Colombian bus journey. Out of bore-dom, I counted them. Sixty dead before the first line of dialogue.

The road followed the coast along a thin spit of land known as the Isla de Salamanca, which separated the ocean from a large freshwater lagoon called the Ciénaga Grande de Santa Marta. The road had cut the lagoon off from the sea, and thus killed the mangrove swamps that once lined the coast, for mangroves depend upon a mixture of fresh and salt water. It was an environmental disaster. Instead of a living eco-system, the road was now flanked for miles by a post-apocalyptic landscape of branchless dying trees. As we drove west, a blood-red sun was setting behind this ghostly dead forest, like a scene from *Mad Max*. Suddenly there was a sharp crack, like gunfire. The windscreen of the bus exploded into a shower of flying glass. Everyone dived under their seats. The driver hero-ically remained at his post and slammed on the brakes.

'Don't panic' he laughed, as if this happened all the time. 'It's only the wind.'

High winds blowing off the ocean had shattered the windscreen. The driv-er and his mate punched the remaining glass out of the windscreen and we carried on.

****

Barranquilla

Barranquilla is the industrial centre of the north coast. It has none of the historical associations of Santa Marta and Cartagena. It's more like a Colombian version of Liverpool: a dirty, run-down northern city that claims the country's best football team, Junior, and its friendliest people. Little more than a hundred years old, already it's seen better days. In fact, the only reason for tourists to come here at all was Carnival, which everyone said was the maddest in Colombia. If they'd said the maddest in, say, Belgium, then we wouldn't have expected much. But in Colombia there's *serious* competition.

But it was pretty quiet when we arrived. Most shops had shut early for the

weekend and the city centre was deserted. Discarded newspapers and bottles littered the streets and plastic bags swirled everywhere, picked up by
the wind and blown into our faces. Beggars, street-kids and mumbling
dossers kicked their way through the rubbish or slept beneath piles of
newspaper in shop doorways.

We'd agreed to meet Mark at 'The Hotel California'. We'd chosen it mainly
because we knew we wouldn't forget the name. It was the most depressing
hotel I've ever seen. Occupying the second and third floors of a run-down
office block, the rooms were separated by flimsy cardboard partitions that
didn't reach the ceiling and were smeared with a shit-brown paint layered
with grease and dust. At least, I hope it was paint. Lines of drying clothes
filled the reception. A faint, murky echo of daylight was all that penetrated the grime-covered skylights. You'd need to be desperate to stay there,
although I was sure Mark would have. But there was no sign of Mark.

We found a better hotel, whose only drawback was that the fan would
have sliced the top two inches off my head if I'd stood up straight. The
lobby was full of businessmen watching the Colombian soccer team play
another World Cup warm-up match. My eyes lit up. Melissa groaned.

****

own goooooooooooooaaaaa! a tale of soccer, cocaine and yankees
Colombians love soccer. They were far more interested in the approaching
World Cup than in the Presidential elections due just before the tournament. The national team had thrashed Argentina 5-0 in Buenos Aires – a
sensational result followed by wild celebrations in which many died. And in
keeping with a Colombian tendency towards either abject despair or ram-
pant bravado, everyone was convinced that they would win the World Cup.
They hadn't lost for 30 games. Even Pele was tipping them. Carlos
Valderrama – a Junior player and Barranquilla's local hero – was the play-
maker, a familiar figure with his blond afro and dapper brown moustache.
But the Colombians were struggling for form. In El Prado in Santa Marta, I'd
watched them draw their last game, together with a teenage boy who
drunk a whole bottle of rum in the first half and spent the second face
down on the floor, sobbing.

Colombia didn't go on to win the World Cup. They were knocked out in the
first round, losing to Romania and the USA. Being eliminated was bad, but
losing to the USA was a national humiliation. For one thing, the United
States didn't even have a professional soccer league. But worse still, it was
. . . the *United States*. The hated gringos.

Colombians are sore at the States. Sore about Panama, which was a province of Colombia until 1903, when the US funded an independence movement to create a client state for the Panama Canal. Sore at US domination of their economy. Sore at US pressure to stamp out cocaine – refusals to give their politicians US visas; threats of trade embargoes; US troops flying into Colombia, US-funded aerial spraying of coca fields with toxic chemicals.

Cocaine is less unpopular. Legendary Medellín cartel boss Pablo Escobar cultivated a Robin Hood image, building sports centres and a complete *barrio* for poor families. (He was also a psychopathic ex-hitman.) Cocaine sold to the US feeds many Colombians, poor as well as rich. Even the good health of Colombian soccer is due to cocaine. Colombia's big clubs were all saved from bankruptcy in the 1980s by the drug-cartels (while providing ideal money-laundering opportunities) and are now among the richest and most successful on the continent. Nor has cocaine reduced Colombia to anarchy. Less than 1% of the country's murders are over drugs: there are more drug-related killings in the United States than in Colombia.

'I hate gringos,' our taxi driver said, turning to face us while overtaking the car in front.

'But *we* are gringos,' I said nervously.

'No, you are English.' He explained. 'That is not a gringo. A gringo is *norteamericano*. A yankee.' He spat out of the window and simultaneously whistled at a girl across the street.

The Colombian team had a chance to beat the yankees: for every peasant struggling to survive when the price of coffee dived; for every street kid sniffing glue to escape his hunger. And they blew it. The United States won 2-1.

One of the American goals was an own goal by a Colombian defender, Andrés Escobar (no relation to Pablo). Soon after the tournament, Escobar was leaving a restaurant near his home when a man walked up to him, pulled a gun and fired twelve shots into his chest, killing him. Newspaper reports said that the man shouted '*Gol*' each time he fired a shot.

Whether this was simply an act of Colombian football fanaticism, or something more, remains unclear. It was rumoured that a lot of drug-cartel money in Colombia had been backing the national team, but that substantial money had also gone on a US victory. And once eliminated, the Colombians improved dramatically to beat Switzerland 2-0 in their remaining group match, a performance which only served to fuel speculation about their abject form in the two earlier games.

****

carnival!

Carnival began. The whole of Barranquilla lined the procession route. We found a spot between a food-stand and a beer tent, both belting out salsa. Everyone was dancing, drinking, throwing water. 'Barranquilla girls are the most beautiful in Colombia,' the man beside us confided and offered us some rum. Little boys twisted through the crowds, selling boxes of chalk powder for people to throw. Youths ran past, firing water pistols at any girls they saw.

The procession itself was a disappointment, perhaps because we were at the end of the route and the dancers looked exhausted. They passed to noisy cheering but without music, and most of the floats were just big adverts for rum or beer companies. But it didn't matter. By the time the floats arrived in mid-afternoon, everyone was too drunk and drenched in chalk and water to care. Teenagers wore cheap plastic masks: gorillas or demons or one-eyed zombies. Men threw live snakes (with their mouths sown up) around the neck of a terrified 'victim', inevitably a pretty girl. Drunken duos roamed through the crowds dressed as Rambo with wooden machine guns, or blacked-up as Indians or African warriors with toy bow-and-arrows, staging mock hold-ups. You were supposed to give them a few coins to go away. Transvestites minced past. All over town, men strutted about in blonde-afro Valderrama wigs and yellow Colombian soccer shirts, beer cans in hand.

The carnival lasted four days. The processions were almost immaterial. It was simply an excuse for one big, swaying, staggering, drunken binge. As the days wore on, water and chalk flew with greater abandon, supplies being quickly topped up by the entrepreneurial young chalk-sellers. The Rambos and African warriors became drunker and more belligerent in their demands for money, eventually becoming openly threatening. The numbers of drunks sleeping in doorways grew daily.

In the evenings, clubs put on special concerts. We went to one, featuring the great Celia Cruz. Actually, we just hung around the car-park, which was a mini-festival in itself, full of stalls and temporary bars. We went with a German called Rainer – who, with his long, unfeasibly blonde hair and sleeveless denim jacket, looked like you'd imagine a German heavy-metal guitarist – and Jackie and Jennifer, a couple of outdoorsy Canadian girls who were staying in our hotel.

Jackie and Jennifer had been in a bar the night before when a drunk staggered in, pulled a gun and began shooting randomly. Everyone dived under the tables. The drunk fired a few more shots, swayed in the door-way for a moment, then staggered out. Everyone got up and carried on drinking.

We played drinking games for a while, then decided to try a few differ-ent bars and dances. Somewhere along the way a drunk Colombian and a young Venezuelan attached themselves to us.

'Colombian girls are the most beautiful in the world,' the drunk Colombian told us proudly. Melissa rolled her eyes. The Venezuelan boy said he was a businessman, by which he meant he was at the carnival to sell Chiglets, a brand of chewing gum. Eventually, at a nightclub some-where in the early hours, Jackie found herself alone in the ladies' toilet with the by-now drunk Venezuelan Chiglet-seller. In order to make his feelings towards her clear, he dropped his trousers and pants. Jackie ran out crying. The Chiglet-seller was perplexed.

'Do you think she likes me?' he asked me anxiously.

We found Jackie and took her home, drunk and tearful, in a taxi.

'I only wanted to have some fun.' she sobbed.

The carnival climaxed with the *Festival de Orquestas*, a two day concert in the baseball stadium, televised live across Latin America, featuring top salsa stars from Cuba, New York and Puerto Rico, as well as the best Colombian bands like Joe Arroyo and Grupo Niche.

Salsa is a Caribbean music and, although never exclusively so, it is essen-tially a black music. Its popularity lies in the parts of Spanish America with black or *mulato* populations: Cuba, Puerto Rico, Panama, Venezuela, Colombia, the coast of Ecuador, The term *salsa* was probably first applied to the music in 1973 by Jerry Masucci, a Jewish New Yorker who owned Fania Records – the Motown of salsa.[40] But its roots lie in the 19th centu-ry 'son' of black Cuba and it uses African percussion and the African call and response pattern – solo and chorus – common to all black American

music. We were a long way from the airy melancholia of the Andean
Indians' flutes and pipes.

We could see half the stage from a nearby flyover, which saved us paying
to go in. From there we watched the bands perform their sets of elegant
sensuality, sliding horns and smooth singing mixed with explosive bursts of
percussion. Many were big, twelve or fifteen-piece bands, all smartly
turned out with snappy suits and synchronised dance steps, a fashion that
went out in the West with The Temptations. Most bands looked as if they'd
bought job-lots of suits, usually with a fat trumpeter ridiculously con-
stricted by an outfit three sizes too small. The award for the best band
was won by the *Gran Combo de Puerto Rico*, an aggregate that first saw
the inside of a nightclub way back in 1955. The local *vallenato* bands,
though, drew the wildest response with their earthier, rougher sound.

On the last evening of the carnival, we went to a big finale (free, naturally), featuring many bands from the *Festival de Orquestas*. We bumped
into the young Venezuelan Chiglet-seller of the previous night. 'The
Canadian girl. Do you think she likes me?' he asked again. Maybe he
sensed that he'd gone wrong somewhere. The area in front of the stage
was submerged in water. Anyone approaching the stage was met with a
barrage of water and chalk bombs. Shrieking teenagers chased each other
through the crowds, soggy T-shirts stuck to wiry bodies. On either side of
the main stage stood two enormous sound-systems playing competing
records. They continued to do so even while the main bands were in full
swing, making it impossible to hear the bands unless you braved the full
onslaught of water and chalk to get to the front.

The next morning, the streets looked like a war-zone. The shops still had
their metal shutters pulled down. The pavements and roads were buried
beneath plastic bags and discarded beer cans. Newspapers blew in the
wind. Dossers and street kids slept off the previous night's drink and glue.

Things, in other words, were back to normal.

****

costeños

The *costeños* are warm and friendly, quick to laugh and smile. But I
sensed a sadness too, as if they knew theirs was a paradise lost. Such a
beautiful country. *Que rico*. So rich, so full of potential. Yet such a mess.
The Indians of the Andes also went on drunken binges to forget their hard
lives for a night. But at least they had the dignity of knowing who they

were and who had robbed them. The *mestizo* Colombians, neither fully European nor fully indigenous, didn't even have that. They are the dispossessed *and* the dispossessors; the victims and the perpetrators.

'I love Colombia,' a German backpacker in the Miramar told me. 'This country is just being born. It's not like Europe. Europe is declining: *our* culture is old. Dead. Here, something new is emerging, out of all these bits. The Spanish and the Indians and the blacks. There's life here, and energy. In the music, the people.'

We caught the bus back past the dead mangrove forest to Santa Marta. This time the movie was a sort of 'Carry On Salsa', a 1960s comedy about a woman who was a classical cellist by day and a wild *salsareña* by night, in nightclubs populated by shady Latin men with droopy moustaches, wide-lapelled suits and florid purple shirts. It was just about the only film we saw in South America in which no one got killed. We checked back into El Prado, where fat Alberto welcomed us emotionally and enveloped Melissa in a sweaty embrace.

'Ah, hello, beautiful, beautiful,' he sighed.

section 4
Arrecifes

"Breathe, breathe in the air!
Don't be afraid to care
Leave, but don't leave me
Look around and choose your own ground
For long you live and high you fly
And smiles you'll give and tears you'll cry
And all you touch and all you see
Is all your life will ever be"

PINK FLOYD, 'BREATHE'

Chapter 7
Arrecifes

Louis

After Barranquilla, it was nice to be back in the relative calm of Santa Marta. There was still no sign of Mark, so we decided to go to Arrecifes and hang out on the beach until he turned up. We left a message to that effect in the Miramar, addressed to The Party Animal.

We'd heard a lot about Arrecifes. Every backpacker in Colombia was either going there or had just been. The only problem was that Arrecifes was inside the Tayrona National Park, and this was closed, apparently because of the mess left by partying Colombians over the Christmas holidays.

But, after all, this was Colombia. The Miramar manager explained, between chess moves.

'Yes, the Park is shut. Rook takes Knight. No, it is no problem. Hmm, good move. You must take a guide who knows how to get past the guards. Check. You need a guide? Yes, we have guides here, of course . . . checkmate.'

We assembled at six that evening with a bunch of other backpackers and a guide called Louis, who was perhaps the only person in the tropics, other than Englishmen who remember the Raj, to tuck his shirt inside his shorts and iron his socks.

'Ze main thing is to 'ave fun,' he announced as he collected his guiding fee from each of us. The minibus roared out of Santa Marta at the usual suicidal speed. To avoid the park guards, we were going in at night. This meant a two-hour hike through the jungle in the dark, as Arrecifes was some distance from the road. Louis was, I'm sure, simply bribing a guard, but he made a big play of having us all tiptoe quietly past the main entrance and park office with our torches turned off. Then he led us along a winding path through the moonlit forest, climbing up rocky slopes and dropping into dry creek beds. It was an atmospheric walk, full of shadows and strange bird calls.

After two hours of darkness and jungle, we heard the sound of breaking surf. A few minutes later, we emerged before a funky beach restaurant, tables lit by flickering candles, a floor of sand and a roof of palms, the air thick with the sweet smell of ganja. Travellers and hippies sat smoking, drinking, playing chess or cards, reading books and talking. Outside, hammocks were slung between coconut trees. A Doors tape was playing. Louis sat us down triumphantly, waiting for someone to buy him a beer, and chatted to some of the other travellers. We pitched our tent outside in the dark.

****

Arrecifes

In the morning we saw why we'd come. The beach at Arrecifes was said to be the most beautiful in Colombia. It would be hard to imagine a more beautiful beach anywhere, and there was no trace of the litter that was the reason for the park's closure. An arc of white sand curved away to two rocky headlands. Waves crashed against these twin sentinels, while the beach itself was dotted with giant charcoal grey boulders lying in clusters like outsized natural still-lifes.

Behind the beach, coconut palms waved in the breeze. Behind them were steep hills, covered in forest that looked like giant broccoli. These impenetrable foothills eventually soared to the alpine peaks of the Sierra Nevada de Santa Marta. Nabusímake lay just over the mountains, only about 60km as the condor flew but a three day journey around the sierra by road.

It was the sort of place you dream of when you travel. Not a seedy hovel of a hostel in some dirty Third World city, but a wild empty beach with waves pounding the shore and palm trees swaying behind you. A place that made you feel alive.

Although it often looked deserted, there were in fact about thirty locals somewhere among the palm trees, and a similar number of tourists. Some stayed only a few days, others a few months.

All the strands of the Gringo Trail came together in Arrecifes. Fresh-faced innocents on their gap year; seasoned travellers who'd been on the road for so many years they could hardly remember where home was; New Age mystics practising yoga positions and coke-snorting Party Animals.

Because of the way the forested hills enclosed the beach, it felt like being on an island. The lack of a road and the long walk through the forest meant no day-trippers. There were hardly any Colombians. Maybe they couldn't afford to bribe their way in.

Arrecifes itself consisted of three restaurants. We'd arrived at the imagi-
natively-titled 'Arrecifes Restaurant'; the funkiest and most popular with
travellers. Next to it was 'El Paraíso', slightly smarter and favoured by the
few Colombians who made it to the park. El Paraíso had huge numbers of
under-employed staff who spent most of the day doing nothing. There
were the donkey-handlers who brought in supplies from Santa Marta; a
couple of serving-girls in a little shop which didn't sell much except biscuits and candles; two receptionists; three cleaners; two waitresses and a
cook.

The third restaurant was run by a fat man, his wife and his equally fat
twelve year old son. Set back a little distance from the seafront, among
the coconuts, it was a simple place with no decoration or frills. Just a few
rows of wooden tables inside a small fenced compound. It was always
empty, although the menu was identical in content, price and quality to
the other two restaurants.

There was also a dirt football pitch on which gringos were sometimes
tricked into playing barefoot soccer matches against the locals. It was a
trap. The Colombian team was a mixture of fat old men and children, but
always won. Long before the end of the game the soft soles of the gringos'
feet were worn raw and none of them could walk, let alone run. You
could tell if there'd been a game because of all the gringos limping
painfully for the next week, nursing terrible blisters.

This little trio of restaurants was the centre of the action – although
'action' is perhaps the wrong word to describe a bunch of stoned backpackers sitting around listening to Bob Marley tapes.

We camped a half mile along the shore. I like to think of such places as
embryonic cities. The restaurants were downtown. Anyone who needed to
be within close staggering distance of a bar camped in the 'inner-city'
beside the restaurants. Our new spot was the suburbs.

This is where the longer-term 'residents' ended up, when they wanted to
establish a proper little camp and do their own cooking. From here, the
five-minute stroll along the beach to the restaurants became a minor
expedition, to be planned from the comfort of your hammock.

There were one or two hard-core types who had to go that bit further
than everyone else, finding a remote spot in the bushes to sling their
hammock. Every so often a bronzed and emaciated hippie would mysteri-

ously emerge from some tangled undergrowth, machete in hand.

I'm convinced that one of the attractions of Arrecifes for such types was the chance to walk around with machetes. While it might be a natural thing for a Colombian farmer, I've been wary of travellers with unnecessarily dangerous weapons ever since an Indiana Jones wannabee from Idaho demonstrated his black-widow catapult by firing a toffee clean through a Nairobi hostel wall, two inches above my temple. Even he looked shocked at the size of the hole.

****

Peublito
We set up our tent and hammocks and built ourselves a driftwood windbreak. We collected a pile of firewood and coconut husks (which burn very slow and hot) and scavenged a collection of old pots and pans from those left whenever someone summoned up the energy to leave Arrecifes. Soon we were nicely settled. Melissa and I had covered a lot of ground over the last few months. Mountains, jungles, remote treks. We were both glad of a rest.

The only local sight was a ruined Tayrona Indian village simply called Peublito. It was only a few stone stairways and raised stone platforms, the wooden buildings themselves having long since been reclaimed by the jungle. A couple of Kogi Indian families, descendants of the Tayrona, had been encouraged to live there in reconstructed homes, thatched and circular – much like the one we'd stayed in on our way to Nabusímake – to give visitors an idea of what the town once looked like.

The Tayrona had occupied the slopes of the Sierra for centuries. Peublito was just one of a network of towns which included the enormous Ciudad Perdida, the greatest archaeological find in South America of recent years. Skilled astronomers and mathematicians, they resisted the Spanish for over a century. Peublito was a lovely two-hour climb inland from the beach, shaded from the heat of the sun by the forest. Half-way there was a huge, flat boulder where you could rest and drink in a lush panorama of jungle and ocean.

****

Colombian grass
We spent the days lying in our hammocks, reading, writing letters, wandering to the restaurants for coffees, chatting to other travellers, gathering firewood . . . And trying to build a fire.

This proved trickier than it should have done, with the wind blowing in from the ocean and the moist sea air dampening the wood. We stopped offering people coffee, as Melissa complained that she ran out of conversation before I got the water to boil. When we did get a fire going, we bought fish from the local fishermen and fried it in coconut milk, followed by bananas cooked in rum.

We varied between sleeping in the tent or in our hammocks, until we woke up one morning to find four threads of rope hanging from the trees. We replaced the hammocks – the restaurants hired them out – but noted that if Arrecifes was paradise, it was not a completely crime-free one.

There was always a bit of dope floating around. Kogi Indians would sometimes bring some down from the hills. Colombian grass was good, and Santa Marta supplied much of the dope smoked by American troops in the Vietnam War, its contribution to the anti-colonial struggle. After a couple of spliffs, the already-relaxed pace of the beach wound down a few more notches.

There was an outside possibility of the two local policemen raiding the beach, so everyone buried their grass in the sand. It had to be fairly well-hidden – that was the whole point of burying it, after all. All you had to do was carefully note The Spot, and dig it up later.

The problem was you always buried the dope just *after* you'd smoked a spliff. And just after a spliff is, of course, not the best time to make a careful note of anything. A vague approximate guess, yes. ('It's . . . er . . . in the sand. I think.') But a careful note? When the time came for the next spliff, it was impossible to find The Spot. I scraped back the sand where it should have been, and found . . .

It wasn't there.

We'd stare at The Spot for a while. We'd look around the camp to work out where else it might be. Were we looking at yesterday's Spot, perhaps? Maybe today I'd put it somewhere different? I'd ponder this for a while, forget what I was looking for, look out to sea, remember that I was trying to remember something, spend a few minutes wondering what it was that I had been trying to remember and then wonder if it was time for another spliff. Which would jog my memory and I'd finally come back to The Spot.

'This *is* The Spot, isn't it?' I'd ask Melissa.

'Yes, just there, where your hand is,' she'd reply.

Except that it wasn't.

We'd start digging up the sand to look for it. The little hole would grow wider and deeper until we'd dug a trench that almost circled the tent. We'd stop to reassess the situation.

'It's no good. I can't find it anywhere.'

'Find *what* anywhere?'

'What?'

'Find what anywhere'

'No, what did you say?'

'No, it was *you* that said it. What have you lost?'

'Weren't we looking for something?'

'The Dope. The DOPE.'

'Oh. I've got *that* right here. I've been holding it for ages.'

'You've had it for ages? Why didn't you say something?'

'I didn't know you were looking for it.'

We'd skin up another joint, kick back and watch the surf rolling in for a while.

'I guess we'd better bury this again. Just in case.'

'OK. But make a *careful note* of where you're putting it.'

We sat back and looked around. At the camp behind us, a whole load of people seemed to be crawling around on their hands and knees, digging up the sand.

Like I said, Colombian grass was pretty good.

163

****

the swimming pool

Arrecifes wasn't quite perfect. The beach directly in front of us had a deceptively dangerous undertow. People had drowned only a few metres from the shore. Carlos, an Italian who'd been camped on the beach for five months, told us that twelve people had drowned in the last year. He'd witnessed the last of these fatalities, a Colombian on his honeymoon. The man's new bride got into trouble and he'd rushed out to save her. Somehow, she made it back, but he didn't. There was no life-saving equipment and the only warning was a small sign nailed to a tree in front of one of the restaurants.

About twenty minutes walk along the shore was another bay, protected by a ring of rocks and coral that formed a natural semi-circular swimming pool, maybe a hundred metres across. A family of fishermen lived behind the pool, with a sun-dried old grandmother who spent all day cooking fish for tourists. Fishing nets lay spread out on the beach.

The main event of each day at Arrecifes, apart from cooking and the daily forage for firewood, was the trip to the swimming pool. It was a lovely place. You could swim in warm, calm water, while powerful waves battered the protecting ring of rocks and plumes of white spray burst into the air. We'd float for hours, looking back at the beach and the broccoli hills.

The walk to this bay was just as beautiful, through coconut palms and around two enchanted little coves. At high tide, you had to clamber over huge boulders that blocked the thin, golden beaches of these bays. A shipwrecked fishing boat half-blocked the entrance to one of them.

****

smugglers

Until recently, drugs were the main business here. Conditions were perfect: a remote location cut off by the Sierra Nevada de Santa Marta and hidden by jungle; a direct route across the Caribbean to the United States; and a perfect climate. The densely-forested seaward slope of the Sierra remains one of Colombia's main marijuana-growing regions. Since its peak in the 1960s and 1970s, however, Santa Marta's marijuana production has declined, as the country's drug cartels concentrate on the more lucrative cocaine business. To the families in Arrecifes, it must have all seemed much the same: dope, cocaine, fish, coconuts; all just something else to bring in a few *pesos*.

164

****

Helena

Melissa and I were camped just behind the beach, among the coconut palms. Beside us were three English boys – who I never saw move further than from their hammocks to the water – and Helena.

Helena had been in Colombia for a year, surviving by selling jewellery that she made from seashells and leather. Since arriving in Colombia, she'd been arrested three times, held up by gunmen twice and kidnapped twice. She said that she'd been on one bus that was stopped by guerrillas, who'd lined all the passengers up against the bus and lectured them on the people's struggle. When the lecture finished, the line of passengers burst into 'spontaneous' applause. A few sub-machine guns does wonders for one's appreciation of the finer points of rhetoric. Then the guerrillas waved the passengers back onto the bus. They didn't even rob them.

She told us the story of her first kidnapping. She was hitching – either a very brave or very foolish thing for an eighteen year old blonde English girl to be doing in Colombia. A middle-aged man pulled up and offered her a lift. It seemed safe enough, because the man's elderly parents were in the back of the car. After a while, he stopped in a village and dropped his parents off, then suddenly produced a gun and told her to do as he said. They'd head for the border with Venezuela and she would drive the car across, loaded with cocaine. He locked her in his house and went to arrange the cocaine. But Helena somehow found and hid his car keys. He cursed and threatened her but she held firm. She said she'd wait till he fell asleep, then drive to the mayor of the village.

'Go on then,' he said, 'the mayor is my brother.'

But she refused to give him the keys. After more threats and curses, but no physical violence, he decided to let her go and call the whole thing off. It was a typically Colombian tale: drama, fear, incompetence and farce all in one.

****

Carlos

Carlos was camped just behind us. He was Italian. He had the tidiest camp in Arrecifes, and he even swept the dust every morning. Carlos was forty, but he was in the best shape of anyone on the beach; densely muscled, not an inch of fat, and with a tidily cropped jet-black beard.

Everything about Carlos was tidy. He'd only recently left the French Foreign Legion, which perhaps accounted for his fitness and the military mania for orderliness. He would get up every morning and clean the area around his tent, brew some coffee and then retire to his hammock to read until exactly midday, when he would brew up another coffee and smoke a bamboo waterpipe. Then he would sit back for an hour or two, before spending the next two hours spearfishing with his harpoon. After that, he would collect firewood or go for a run along the beach, and then cook supper. He was a man of fixed habits.

He also knew how to live on a beach. His fire jumped into life at the merest poke, as I glanced across from within the billowing cloud of smoke that marked my own attempt. He could open coconuts with two sharp slices of his machete. I discovered that this, too, was not as simple as it sounds, the machete bouncing back at me with life-threatening velocity when I tried. I suggested to Carlos that he ought to run 'beach-survival skills' tours for wealthy tourists. He could take them to a deserted beach and allow them to fulfil their Robinson Crusoe fantasies for a couple of weeks. Finishing up, of course, with a slap-up lobster dinner. He could charge a fortune.

It all required practise, of course, and Carlos had plenty of that. He went to a beach for four or five months in the way the rest of us might go for a two-week holiday. He'd grown up in a fishing family in Naples and periodically earned a living as a diver. He was an expert harpoonist, living off fish and coconuts and buying only a few necessities, such as rice and cooking oil. To make life interesting, he only went after specific, hard-to-catch species of fish.

'Issa no sport iffa you jus' shoot any ol' fish,' he said. 'I rather come back witha nothing.'

If he had a good day, he would sell fish to other tourists: grouper, mackerel, red snapper, octopus and lobster, all fresh from the sea. Of course, we could buy the same fish more cheaply from the local fishermen if we could be bothered to walk that far.

One day, Carlos caught a giant lobster, which he placed in a bucket 'for sale' outside his tent, and asked 10,000 pesos. It was the biggest lobster we'd ever seen, so we decided to splash out.

The lobster was dead. I knew you were supposed to cook them alive, but this one sat lifelessly in Carlos's bucket. We decided to bargain.

'It's dead, Carlos.' Melissa told him.

'No, issa not dead.' said Carlos.

I picked it up for inspection. One of its legs fell off.

'It certainly looks dead to me,' I said.

'No, no, issa jus' resting.'

'*Just resting!?* This, Carlos, is a dead lobster.'

'No, no, they always sleep inna da afternoon, you know.'

I thought Carlos was simply running through Monty Python's parrot sketch, but he swore that he'd never heard of Monty Python. 'Monty Pyfon, 'oo is zis Monty Pyfon?' We bought the lobster anyway, and feasted on it for hours – or rather, spent hours trying to break it apart with my penknife, grabbing the odd mouthful here and there.

Carlos, with his brooding Mediterranean looks and trim black beard, could have been Ulysses himself, transposed in time, stranded far from home on a distant shore, travelling for so long that he could probably never go back to a 'normal' life.

He said he'd been on the road for the last fifteen years. Wherever we'd been, Carlos had been there five times longer. He'd spent fifteen days in the little village of Aguas Calientes, the hot springs with the floating turd at the foot of Machu Picchu – a place where most travellers only stop for as long as it takes the train to arrive. Apart from five years fighting forgotten colonial wars for the French in Chad and Djibouti and other obscure parts of Africa, he'd lived for six years in India. There, he'd adopted the lifestyle of a *sadhu*, a wandering Hindu holy man who has no home or possessions except a symbolic trident. He grew his hair and learnt Hindi and spent his time smoking chillums and living off alms and food from pilgrims.

When his visa ran out they threw him out of India. But he kept coming back. So they threw him out again. And again he returned. Eventually they put him in prison, where there were forty men in one room and you had to fight for floor space to lie down at night.

'But that was the cell for foreigners, you know,' Carlos expanded. 'The cell for Indians was the same size, but maybe it 'ad two 'undred men in it.'

Despite his experience of Indian prison, Carlos loved India and Indians. What he really wanted was to go back and live there. He told us how he'd been in an Indian hospital where the patients were fed on intravenous drips attached directly to coconuts. When the milk from a patient's coconut was used up, the nurses would simply replace it with a fresh one. His love of Indians was surprising, as in all other respects he was an old-fashioned racist.

'I never trust a Jew.' he told me, when he saw me wearing a Star of David, 'anna I never trust an Arab either.' He ranted about lazy blacks and the arrogant French, and the miserable, lazy, ignorant South Americans, and everybody else. Except the Indians.

'Butta the most important thing, you know. Never trust an Italian,' he confided one day, just before selling us the dead lobster. And just after Melissa said that Carlos kept trying to chat her up.

'He wants to know what a beautiful woman like me is doing with . . . you,' she revealed.

I looked over at Carlos. He gave me a neighbourly wave.

'He said all the other girls on the beach are just silly kids. He wants to see me in high heels.'

It must have been hard for Carlos to find a suitable woman. Here was a man who was fluent in English, Spanish, French, Italian and Hindu – who could read philosophy in any of them while simultaneously carrying out a conversation in two others. Who was superbly fit, could harpoon fish and open coconuts and no doubt knew how to kill a man with his bare hands. Yet not many women would have wanted to share the life of a wandering Sadhu *and* dress up in high-heels.

'Tella me somefing,' Carlos asked me one day. 'Why all Englishmen are so obsessed with their arseholes?' I didn't know. So Carlos explained. 'Inna da Foreign Legion, these English 'squaddies', they always do 'the Flaming Arsehole'. You know? Issa song. They stick a rolled-up newspaper uppa their arse, anna set fire to it, an' they gotta sing-a this song, The Flaming Arsehole, before they can put it out. You tella me why, eh?' Carlos the multi-lingual philosopher was unable to fathom this strange English behaviour.

****

Michel

Carlos had acquired an apprentice, Michel, a young Italian who'd decided to hang out at Arrecifes and learn the art of living on a beach from a master. Wherever Carlos was, Michel was normally somewhere a few yards behind him. He was learning to harpoon, to climb palm trees and open coconuts, to build fires and gut fish and everything else needed for a life by the sea. It was a tempting proposition; abandon the rat-race for a life of rugged self-sufficiency in a beautiful wild spot, living virtually for nothing, selling some fish for a bit of cash, and then moving on to another wild and undeveloped tropical beach somewhere else along the way.

Michel was even copying Carlos's chat up lines.

'Michel asked if I would give him lessons in sex,' Melissa told me one day. 'He wants to know what a beautiful woman like me is doing hanging out with . . . you.'

Maybe it just came with being Italian.

****

Lionel and Pascale

Carlos had been on the beach for five months but a French couple, Lionel and Pascale, were approaching their first anniversary there. Pascale had taught the wife of one of the fishermen to bake French bread to sell to tourists. In return, the family let them camp for free on their bit of beach.

They'd fenced off their tent within a thick circle of branches and created a cosy campsite, although with none of the regimental tidiness of Carlos's camp. They'd fashioned a table and seats from lumps of driftwood, enjoyed a ready supply of coconuts from an overhead tree and had even dug an oven in the earth bank behind the beach. Lionel would go harpoon fishing with the local fishermen and Pascale would bake the fish in the oven, along with delicious bread and coconut cake. Before Arrecifes, they'd spent a year on a tiny island in Honduras that was so small that fresh water had to be fetched by canoe from the neighbouring island.

One day, Lionel was arrested.

The two local cops, stationed a couple of kilometres up the coast, realised they'd landed a cushy number, and usually turned a blind eye to a little bit of dope and cocaine. But after we'd been there a couple of weeks, the senior cop – who everyone called *el jefe* ('the boss') – was replaced by an enthusiastic, baby-faced twenty year old, eager to show everyone who was in charge. The new *jefe* rode into Arrecifes on his horse and arrested Lionel for smoking a joint. The other cop shrugged apologetically as the officious youngster led Lionel away without even let-ting him grab a pair of shoes, and drove him off to Santa Marta to throw him in jail.

Unfortunately for the junior *jefe*, but luckily for Lionel, it was the day of the Colombian general election. Hundreds of people had been murdered during the last elections, so the Santa Marta police chief was understand-ably pre-occupied. He asked *el jefe* why the hell he was wasting his time on this, the tensest day in four years. The manager from the Miramar came and bailed Lionel out. As it happened, the election passed without violence (a minor miracle in Colombia) and was won by Ernesto Samper, a Liberal. Samper was soon fighting for his political life after it was alleged that his election campaign had received huge donations from the Cali drug cartel.

When Lionel got back to Arrecifes, the owner of the Arrecifes Restaurant, roaring drunk because his wife had walked out, chased him with a machete for talking to her the day before.

****

Phillipe
El jefe wasn't ready to give in. A few nights later he launched a raid on Phillipe's camp.

Phillipe, plus a Swiss boy with dreadlocks called Christian and a quartet of French and Italian travellers, were the other 'long-termers'. They'd been there for two months when we arrived. (We only thought of it as 'Phillipe's camp' because we'd met Phillipe already, in San Agustin, where we found out, in turn, that he'd just spent a month with Mark in Vilcabamba in Ecuador.) Phillipe's camp didn't do much fishing, but instead a lot of sniff-ing coke, smoking dope and relaxing.

One evening, when they were doing just that, the two police charged through the trees on horseback and rode directly into their camp, too fast for them to hide the incriminating evidence.

'We know you have ganja, and we will find it,' *el jefe* announced, and turned the camp upside down. The two cops dug up the sand around the fire, looked inside the cooking pots, opened all the packets of food, shook all the hammocks and made everyone open their rucksacks.

But no dope.

Finally they gave up and left, mystified. Phillipe and Christian and the others were mystified too. Where was the ganja, then? Then Phillipe saw it, lying in plain sight on the sand in the middle of the camp, so obvious that no one had noticed it.

****

surfing pigs and other animals

Arrecifes was full of animals, mainly of the farmyard variety. There were three bloated pigs, who would snuffle their way up and down the beach, looking as if they might explode at any second. The oddest sight was see- ing them roll in the surf to cool down. There was an ugly, angry turkey- cock. Puffing up his neck, flapping his saggy red jowls and spreading his wings, he would charge anyone who crossed his patch of dust, which he'd inconveniently decided was half-way along the path between the Arrecifes Restaurant and the toilets. A desperate spider-monkey was tied to a near- by tree, with just enough string to climb the first branch before being yanked back in frustration.

There were dogs and chickens and cats, all competing with the pigs and the turkey for scraps. A Brazilian traveller brought along a pet squirrel. There were lizards, frogs, crabs and crows, and three storks in a freshwa- ter pond just behind the beach, half-way between our camp and the restaurants. There were parrots and vultures and little brown birds not spectacular enough for anyone to care what they were. Out at sea, of course, there were all sorts of fish, lobsters, squid, eels and sharks.

And there were donkeys. These were used to carry food in through the forest, there being no road. The restaurant owners had discovered that the cheapest way to feed them was simply to turn them loose among our campsites. They'd eat anything. You had to hide your food in impenetrable bags or suspend it high in the trees. Otherwise you'd be woken in the night by the sound of chomping and, shining your torch, you'd see a donkey munching through supplies that you'd spent a whole day fetching from Santa Marta. Nights would be punctuated by regular cries of '*burro!*' ('donkey!'), followed by a barrage of coconut husks. As these thudded against its solid flanks, the donkey would look up, consider the situation and then amble away. They were especially fond of cardboard and paper. Helena, an English girl camping next to us, sheepishly returned a book I'd lent her.

'I hope you've read this. A donkey ate the first page,' she apologised. 'And the last.'

I hadn't. Still, I was lucky. One English backpacker had his passport eaten. We imagined him explaining that to the British Consulate. '. . . erm, yes, that's right, eaten by a donkey.'

Phillipe tried riding one of the donkeys. It didn't like being ridden at all and charged off with Phillipe hanging on grimly. Than it screeched to a sudden halt, launching Phillipe over its head directly into his own camp fire. Luckily, the fire was only smouldering.

There were, too, armies of ants and a few too many flies and mosquitoes. Most of the long-termers – with the exceptions of Lionel, Carlos and Melissa – developed festering wounds on their ankles, where flies had infected scratched mosquito bites. Phillipe developed a sore on his knee that became a deep hole. He sought advice from one of the fishermen, who applied a gungy green paste of pulped plant, which at least controlled the infection.

****

the rape

There was one nasty incident. After a drunken night at the bar one of the locals, a man who worked for the coconut plantation which surrounded the restaurants, groped his way into the tent of a sleeping Swiss girl and raped her. The next day, when the other Colombians heard about it, they beat him up and forced him to go to the police. The rapist was a rather pathetic, sad old man. I felt a little sorry for him, having to watch a string of half-undressed Western women. Rich, sophisticated creatures from countries he could never afford to visit, they'd hardly notice a poor, uneducated, not-so-young and not-so-good-looking peasant like him. So he'd got drunk and frustration and desire got the better of judgement. He'd lost his job, and with it his home.

****

shopping

We made trips to Santa Marta to buy food. I was growing to love the walk through the cool shady forest, getting to know the dips and twists of the path with increasing familiarity.

Getting back meant finding our way past the park guards. Once, we calculated an angle through the forest that would by-pass the entrance and rejoin the path about half a mile beyond. But walking quietly through a jungle in the dark is not easy, especially when you don't want to make any noise. I imagine our clumsy thrashing was audible far beyond the guards' hut, as was Melissa's scream when she walked into a huge black spider's web. We gave up before we got completely lost, and decided to talk our way in. The guard was not surprised to see us.

'I am the park manager. You were having a little trouble in the bushes?' he said, amiably.

'Us?' we protested. 'An animal, perhaps.'

We felt we should offer a bribe of some sort. But how, exactly, do you do it? Despite everything you expect of South America, we hadn't had to bribe anyone yet. Should I drop a note and see if he picked it up? Should I enquire obliquely if there were any 'special entry fees'? Or should I just come right out with it and ask, 'Look, how much do you want, mate?' In the end we thought we'd wait for him to bring up the subject, figuring that he'd make it clear if he wanted something. But he was more interested in discussing his English correspondence course. We dwelt for a bit on verbs and tenses. Then moved onto nouns. After personal pronouns, pronunciation and gender, he relented.

'OK, you can go in,' he said in Spanish. (His course didn't appear to have taught him any actual English yet.) 'But it is dangerous to walk after dark. My staff patrol the park. In the night they must shoot. To kill. There are many criminals here. Smugglers. It is safer if you come with me.'

He beckoned us into his jeep and drove us as far as he could along the path. He told us that the park stretched for twenty kilometres along the coast and back into the mountains, and he had a staff of four, which was why the clean-up operation was taking so long. He left us where the track became too narrow for the car. We still had to walk for an hour through the jungle.

'I hope he wasn't serious about the guards.' Melissa muttered.

****

a place to live

When we woke on that first morning, to our first sight of the beach at Arrecifes, we thought we'd stepped into a holiday-brochure picture of a tropical paradise. After a month, the picture had come to life to reveal a place rich in characters and little dramas. We could begin to see it not simply as a romantic place for a holiday, but as a real place where people lived.

It was even more beautiful that way.

Chapter 8
a full moon trip

'More precious than the news of the anti-neutrino, more full of hope for humanity than the detection of new quasars, is the knowledge that certain plants, certain compounds, unlock forgotten doorways onto worlds of immediate experience . . . '
TERENCE MCKENNA, FOOD OF THE GODS

lightweights
We'd been at Arrecifes for over a month when Mark turned up. It was another late, lazy, morning. I was writing a letter in the restaurant behind the beach, which as usual was mysteriously deserted.

I looked up to see Mark striding out of the trees towards me. With him was Helena, who was returning from an overnight shopping trip to Santa Marta. She had to run to keep up with Mark. He was wearing his Clint Eastwood hat and a sweat-drenched, sleeveless T-shirt. Sweat poured down his face. He smiled at me, as wild-eyed and intense as ever. He had the beginnings of a beard.

I wondered how things would go this time. Mark looked at me in the same way. More arguments and tension, or would the easy pace of beach life mellow him out?

Instead, I said, 'I guess you could do with a drink.' I called for a beer. Mark downed it in one gulp and ordered another. While he drank, I filled him in on the beach scene. An trickle of exhausted new arrivals stumbled out of the trees behind him.

'Lightweights.' said Mark.

I took Mark to our camp. Melissa laughed. 'Here comes trouble,' she joked as Mark plonked his rucksack down in the dust and began to roll up a joint. Mark smiled back enigmatically. Melissa and I showed off our little campsite like regular suburban home-owners, pointing out the fire and the pots and pans and the view. I warned Mark about the dangerous current and the coconuts falling on his head in the night. Neither was a joke. A coconut is as hard as a cricket ball and five times the size. People have been killed by falling coconuts. Mark looked at the water. Rolls of surf broke invitingly a few metres from the shore with a steady roar. He

175

stripped to his shorts, strode down to the water's edge and plunged head-first into the oncoming waves. Seconds later, he was marching back.

'Time for a pipe,' he decided.

A couple of pipes slowed things down. Mark began settling in. He put up his tent and found a spot to sling his hammock. It formed a nice protective flank to our camp: we now had tents and hammocks on three sides and the firepit at the front. It looked very cosy. Mark had brought rice, lentils, onions and garlic.

'A gourmet selection, as usual, I see,' I said.

'Ahh, but I have also got . . .' He fished around in his rucksack and produced a carefully-wrapped plastic bag. Inside the bag was a rum bottle filled with a thick, sludgy-brown syrup. He held it up for us to inspect, '. . . this.'

'OK, what is that?' Melissa asked.

'Ah ha,' Mark replied. He climbed into his hammock and fell asleep.

'This,' he explained when he woke up, 'is twenty doses of San Pedro from Vilcabamba. Fully tested and approved. I reckon half for me and I can sell the rest. There might even be some in here for you two, if you're lucky.'

'What's it like?' I asked.

'Aah,' said Mark, 'now *that* depends what you mean. On the one hand everyone agrees that San Pedro is the most disgusting thing they've ever tasted. No matter how you take it, it really tastes like dogshit. Not that I've ever eaten dogshit, but you know what I mean. People have tried to snort it, inject it, cook it, put it in tea – anything to make it less unpleasant – and it still tastes like shit. On the other hand, it's one of the strongest hallucinogenics known to man.'

Melissa eyed the bottle uneasily. 'You two can do that psychedelic stuff, but not me.'

****

Vilcabamba
We made a half-hearted attempt to tell Mark about our journey through

Colombia. As always, Mark waited impatiently for us to finish so he could get onto what he was really interested in: *his* travels.

After we'd left him at the pool table in Quito, he'd headed for Vilcabamba, a tiny village in a fertile green valley in southern Ecuador, surrounded by parched brown hills. It sits at that ideal mid-range altitude – in this case about 1500m – that produces a perfect warm-but-mild climate. The valley is famous for the supposed longevity of its inhabitants, many of whom were claimed to live to 120. This was attributed variously to the climate, the yoghurt or a stress-free life. It turned out to be because they were using their grandparents' birth certificates.

It's not the yoghurt, nor even the promise of living to 120, that attracts most travellers, but the San Pedro cactus which grows in the surrounding hills. When boiled down for about eight hours, it produces the foul green slime that Mark had shown me.

Melissa and I already knew some of this from Campbell, the Kiwi who had passed out in the Gran Casino II bar back in Quito. He'd travelled down to Vilcabamba and then up through most of Colombia with Mark. But he'd left Mark in Santa Marta and arrived at Arrecifes a week earlier. Two English girls, Sandra and Kim, has also been with Mark and Campbell in Vilcabamba and had also turned up in Arrecifes. They'd all agreed to meet here when they left Vilcabamba.

In Vilcabamba, the four of them had managed to find an apartment with a television, stereo, kitchen and all-fairly-mod-cons. Just like home. They stayed for a month, hunting for San Pedro, cooking it and taking it, watching TV, listening to tapes, reading, drawing and recovering from the last trip so that they could start over again. (Also just like home, for Mark at least.) They'd also met Phillipe there.

Mark managed to sneak in a few extra San Pedro trips while the others were having days off. He said he'd taken it fifteen times during the month, which was pretty intensive going when you consider that each trip lasts fourteen hours. Mark liked Vilcabamba.

'It's one of the most beautiful places on earth,' he enthused. 'It's a Power Place. Weird things happen. A lot of shamans live there. It's probably like places where ley-lines cross in England, or something. You know, I never really had much time for all that stuff when I was in England, but now I can see how there might be something in it after all.

177

'There was a stream, and it always rained on one side, and never on the other. It was just a trickle, so you could stand with one foot on one side and one foot on the other side. And one side of you would be getting wet, while the other side would stay dry. Every time.

'Then there was a hill called Mandango, which looks just like an Indian woman lying on her back with her knees bent, with her face looking up at the sky. When you did San Pedro, it looked exactly like that. The local legend says she was the woman who gave birth to the world.'

He paused to let this information sink in, then continued, 'One thing about San Pedro, which anyone who has done it will tell you, is that you become really tuned into animals. Like the cat around our apartment. You don't want to talk to people much, but you can sit for hours and watch spiders or birds, even frogs. It's as if you're tuned into some more natural wavelength.'

They'd rented the apartment from a Swiss guy called Jan, a traveller who'd decided to stay. Jan knew the best, most secret San Pedro spots. He took Mark and Campbell out into the hills to harvest some cacti. 'You can buy it in the village,' Mark explained. 'But if you buy it, it doesn't have the same effect. For the best trips you have to find the plants yourself or be given it as a gift.' Jan took to Mark like a long-lost brother. Phillipe (who spoke English with a true comedy French accent) said. 'Ee always talk about Mark. Jan always like ze, 'ow you say, ze exceptional people like 'im.'

****

Guardian of the Threshold
'This is San Pedro,' Mark explained, sketching a tall, slightly spiny, tubular cactus. Mark liked to be precise about the science of drug preparation. 'You throw away the outer husk and green centre, then boil the white flesh for seven or eight hours until you get a milk-shake thick liquid. An elbow-to-wrist sized chunk makes enough for one. Its main psycho-active ingredient is mescaline, the same as peyote.'

Hallucinogenic plants are central to South American shamanism and San Pedro has probably been used for over 3,000 years. Drawings of god-like figures holding San Pedro cacti have been found on ceramics and reliefs at Chavín de Huantar in Peru, dating from around 1200BC.

San Pedro was banned as heretical by the Spanish Inquisition. Users were tortured and/or killed. But its use persisted, especially on the north

Peruvian coast. The plant was renamed after Saint Peter, who in Christian mythology was known as the Guardian of the Threshold. An apt choice for a plant believed to open a gateway into an alternate reality.

****

The Edge
I once asked Mark why he did this sort of stuff.

'I've got this image,' he replied. 'I imagine a huge cliff-top in a world of darkness. Above the cliff there's a tribe of cave-dwellers, who keep a fire burning in the mouth of the cave.[41] The fire lights up the cave, but obscures everything outside. The cave-dwellers wonder what's outside, but are afraid to leave the safety of the cave and eventually forget the outside altogether and take the cave for the whole world. But a few crawl out onto the dark cliff-top, inching forward, feeling for The Edge. Because edges define. Think about it. How can you picture a thing if you can't see its edges?

'There are always people who go beyond the everyday. Mystics, shamans, meditators, scientists, artists, mountaineers, acid-freaks, masochists, perverts . . . But it's interesting that shamans say you need to confront fear if you want knowledge. That's what I think. It's fear that holds most people back from exploring the universe around them. That just seems such a waste to me.

'If I've got an aim in life, I guess that's it – to find The Edge.'

****

cops and robbers
From Vilcabamba, Mark and Campbell made their way up through Ecuador and Colombia, following us along the Gringo Trail through San Agustin, then on to Cali and Bogota.

There are two ways to travel through Colombia. Despite its reputation, Melissa and I had discovered it was possible to travel the length of this beautiful country with scarcely a whiff of drugs or trouble. Mark did it the other way.

For a start, he'd been arrested in Cali buying coke from a dealer who turned out to be a plain-clothes policeman. The choice was a Colombian prison full of desperados, murderers and God-knows-what, or a fine. And how much was the fine? The policeman made it clear he'd accept whatever Mark happened to have on him. He made a quick body-search. As always, Mark was almost broke. Finally he found $100 in his sock. To show it was nothing personal, he let him keep the coke. It still worked out cheaper than buying it in England.

It was a familiar scam, and I was surprised that Mark had been suckered. Buying cocaine from a stranger in the main plaza in one of Colombia's most notorious drug-cities was asking for trouble. We'd met a Spanish traveller who'd fallen for the same trick, except he'd been carrying $2,000. Typical of Mark to get off cheaply. The Spanish guy had also been allowed to keep his coke, although I doubt that he considered it particularly good value.

Sometimes the police didn't even bother trying to sell you the drugs first. We met two Australian girls who'd also been in Cali. They'd been sitting quietly in a cafe waiting for their bus, when the police burst in and arrested them for possession of cocaine. One of the cops emerged from the toilets brandishing a bag of white powder as 'evidence'. The cops dragged them off to the police station and told them to pay a $2,000 fine or get used to prison food. The girls demanded a lawyer. The cops kept them locked up for two days, beating them up occasionally.

'Do not worry,' the cops told them. 'We will not rape you. We are not barbarians. We are honourable men.' Eventually the girls paid the fine and were released.

They got in touch with the British consulate, who said Cali was notorious for this sort of thing. The consulate asked them to bring a complaint. To their surprise, the complaint led to a hearing and – even more surprisingly – the policemen were sacked. As they were led away one of the girls gave vent to her feelings, shouting, 'Now you can't even support your families, you bastards.'

****

the hand-grenade

Mark and Campbell's next stop was Bogota. Melissa and I ('the Hill People' as Mark had called us) spent as little time as possible in the big cities, and headed for the mountains as often as we could. But Mark, the Party Animal, revelled in the vibrant unpredictability of Colombian city life.

'We met this guy Hernando in Bogota,' Mark said, 'who invited us back to his apartment for a little party. We were sitting there, smoking a few spliffs, drinking a few beers, doing a few lines of coke, listening to some salsa, talking. Then there was a hammering at the door. Hernando went downstairs to answer it. We could hear shouting and swearing.

'Suddenly, Hernando's mate grabbed a machete which just happened to be lying around, and charged downstairs. So Campbell and I grabbed the other two machetes, which also happened to be lying around – you know, your typical house, with three machetes lying around in the living room.

'Downstairs, there was a big argument going on. We managed to work out that the two blokes at the door, both blind drunk, were actually friends of Hernando. They'd just been kicked out of a bar for being drunk, and they knew Hernando had a live hand-grenade. They wanted to go back and blow up the bar. Hernando refused to give it to them, of course. At this point Campbell decided to back off, gave me his machete and went upstairs.

'There I was in the middle of Bogota, coked up to my eyeballs, in a hall-way holding two machetes, while some drunk Colombians argued about whether or not to blow up a bar with a live hand-grenade.

'And I thought 'yep, this is Colombia, just like I imagined it'.'

****

Campbell, Sandra and Kim

They'd reached the coast. Mark went to a Caribbean Music Festival in Cartagena, which turned out to be a disappointment. Campbell couldn't be bothered with the festival, and had come straight to Arrecifes. A tall, lean, soft-spoken New Zealander with long, flowing blond hair and rugged surfer-type looks, in New Zealand he worked on his family's farm near Queenstown. He spent a few months each year working on repair crews on the London Underground, and in between he travelled.

Sandra and Kim, the two girls from Vilcabamba, had also turned up in Arrecifes. They looked like typical hippie-ish travelling English girls; long straight hair, tie-dye dresses, sarongs, leather bracelets, silver ankle chains, pierced noses, a few silver rings, funky Guatemalan caps, the odd tattoo. Sandra was solid and healthy-looking. Kim was thin and strung out from too much cheap travelling, bad food and good drugs.

The three of them had moved into a ready-made camp in front of the Arrecifes Restaurant, with a rough wooden fence at the front and a bush at the back. One half of this little compound consisted of a flimsy whicker cage the size of a bus shelter, with room for a couple of hammocks inside. A tree-stump seat and a makeshift table stood outside. Books, plastic bags, empty rum bottles and half-burnt candles lay around, and fingers of melted wax crawled across every surface. No more than twenty paces from the restaurant, it was close enough to hear the music from the bar late into the night and, more importantly, close enough to find no matter what state you were in. A dozen other hammocks hung in the dusty clearing in front of the restaurant. It was definitely inner-city.

****

a full-moon trip
'To fathom hell or soar angelic,
Take a pinch of psychedelic . . .'

Mark wasted little time and took some San Pedro the next day. Campbell and Kim both seemed nervous about it. Campbell said that he thought the San Pedro was bad luck. Since leaving Vilcabamba, all his gear had been stolen and Kim had been sick.

A French backpacker called Robert asked Mark if he could try some San Pedro. It had a strange effect on him. About two hours after taking it he was sitting in the restaurant when he suddenly turned ashen-grey and slid to the floor. We carried him down to the beach for more space and air, where he slowly came round. He was convinced that he was dead.

'It is OK, I feel fine. Don't worry. But I am dead. I know it.' He kept repeating, 'I am dead.' He remained such a ghostly shade of grey that no one was quite sure that he wasn't. Robert wandered off in a trance for most of the afternoon, eventually coming to sit at our campfire as night fell. Melissa cooked him some food and sat with him as the trip wore off. He fell asleep curled up in the sand beside our fire. The next day he didn't remember anything about being dead.

'San Pedro,' Carlos said, 'I try it once. Never again. Itta was the wors' day inna my life.'

He didn't say why, but I'm sure Carlos had his demons. He had, after all, spent the last six years in the Foreign Legion. He'd been in real battles. Who knew what he'd seen and done?

True to his Vilcabamba schedule, Mark took a day off, then suggested the three of us take some San Pedro the next day.

We took it at midday. Mark was right about one thing – it tasted foul. For a couple of hours we sat around our camp, waiting. I'd slung my hammock low so that Melissa and I could sit sideways with our feet on the ground, like a collapsed old sofa. I felt a spine-tingling anticipation. Mark lay in his hammock and dozed.

It came on slowly.

I felt a vague strangeness. Not that I felt odd myself. Rather, it was the beach, the palm trees, the sea, the sand; everything seemed at once to recede and become more vivid, more alive. I felt myself drifting away from the people around me. Other people no longer seemed entirely real; just ghostly or imagined objects that inhabited my vision.

I recalled a childhood fantasy, in which I imagined that only certain people were real. These were people I knew or saw regularly, or whose eyes met mine in a crowd. The rest – unnamed human shapes brushing past in busy streets, never to be seen again – I imagined to be something less real. Robots maybe, or ephemeral phantasmagoria, fleeting images without names or souls.

Now the beach was full of such simulacra. A few familiar faces remained here and there: Carlos sitting behind us tidying his campsite, Phillipe and his mates chatting around their campfire. And then, drifting further, they too were gone, left behind as the San Pedro came on stronger.

I waited for hallucinations – for giant lobsters to march out of the water or elephants to leap from the trees. But I could see exactly what I had seen every day for the last month.

Except that it was all different. Now everything glowed and pulsated with a wonderful radiance and beauty. Some strange magical energy seemed to light up everything. Not like the stark glare of car headlights, but a luminescence that was as much felt as seen, and seemed to emanate from the very heart of things. It was as if I had been looking through a dull, opaque film, and now this film had been pulled away, the true vividness of the world was suddenly dazzling. I felt I was seeing things as they really were. *This* was true reality. Within everything, transcending everything, was an all-embracing energy. The life-force, the underlying reality.

My flatmate in England, Eddie, called LSD a 'psychic enema' for its ability to flush out this sort of feeling. Strangely, Mark, with his recently-acquired Jesus beard and long hair, had begun to look remarkably like Eddie. Eddie was a flute player, and Mark was now wandering along the beach playing his queña, seawater washing over his bare feet. I had the odd sensation that I was seeing two familiar people merged into one.

I watched the Mark/Eddie person. Mark had immersed himself completely in the 'traveller' image. It was hard to imagine him returning to England.

'What are you thinking?' I asked Melissa.

'It's beautiful,' said Melissa. 'The coconut trees have got faces.'

'Friendly or frightening?'

'Friendly. They're smiling at me.'

She lent her head on my shoulder. I felt her closeness and our mutual support.

Mark wandered back to the campsite. We sat watching the waves break, listening to the crash of the surf and the great sucking whoosh as the water rushed out again, like the steady breathing of a vast living organism. Mark gazed out to sea, listening, lost in thought.

'It's as if the sea is calling me to come out and join it,' he said after a while.

'Like the sirens calling to, erm . . . Jason?' said Melissa.

'And which Jason would that be, Melissa?' Mark asked.

'Jason and the Astronauts?'

'I *knew* I could rely on you,' Mark laughed.

Mark and Melissa were looking at one other. I could see what they were thinking.

'No. I *don't* think we should swim. I know you think you can handle it, Mark, but we've been here a month, and the current is definitely getting stronger. We were out there body-surfing every day at the start of the month, and it was powerful then. But now it's . . . different. It's too strong. I told you that twelve people have drowned here – right here in front of us – in the last year.'

'It's the moon,' said Melissa, 'the tide gets stronger as the moon becomes fuller.'

Mark weighed it up. He knew it was dangerous. He knew that twelve people had drowned in the last year, because I kept telling him. On the other hand, he always thought he could go that bit further than most people. Which, generally, he could.

'It's as if there are invisible strands of energy, like a spider's web, reaching out from the ocean, pulling me towards it,' Mark said. 'I feel as if I can actually see them. Fine silver threads.'

'It's the moon,' Melissa repeated. 'Like the pull of the tides, reaching us too.'

Both of them were staring at the surf. I knew Melissa would have enough sense to resist. I wasn't sure about Mark.

'Just remember that if you get into trouble, no one's going to come and pull you out. There's no lifesaving equipment on this beach, and you're a stronger swimmer than me. If you can't swim out of it, I'm not going to be able to drag you out. Especially not when I'm tripping.'

Mark smiled ruefully and said nothing, but I could see he was convinced. I relaxed.

The afternoon was beginning to cool. I decided to take a stroll along the beach while it was still light. Unlike the ayahuasca trip with the Cofans, I had no problem walking. I stopped to chat to Campbell, but just as Mark had predicted, I had little desire to talk to anyone. People seemed distant. I felt cut off from them, as if I was looking into a room from outside a window. I carried on to the end of the beach, where it swung out towards the headland. The surf was uneven, buffeted by the curve of the bay. I looked back along the beach. The white lines of surf rolled in and the coconut palms waved in the wind. Everything was wild and untamed – the sea, the jungle-covered hills, the giant boulders on the beach, the jagged headland. The air itself. Then I noticed a middle-aged man with silver hair beside me. He glanced nervously at me, and kept flaring one nostril.

'I like wild places,' I said, by way of explanation. He seemed startled that I'd spoken.

'Ah, *si, si,*' he gushed with sudden recognition, as if he'd only just discovered why he was standing here himself. He flung his arms wide to embrace the view. 'I too, love nature.' He peered at me knowingly, as if he'd cracked a code, and flared his nostril again.

Now I remembered where I'd seen him. He was the coke dealer from the Miramar. Immaculately dressed as always, he probably wasn't standing in this deserted, windy spot because he loved nature. I felt I ought to leave him to his business. I started to head back. The silver-haired coke-dealer looked puzzled. He'd cracked my enigmatic code, but I still hadn't bought anything.

I wandered back to the camp. Neither Melissa nor Mark were around. A bird perched on the end of a piece of firewood, perfectly still with its head cocked sideways, looking directly at me.

'I know,' the bird seemed to say. 'You're in our world now,'

Later on, a cat appeared. I'd never seen a cat around our camp before but it, too, stopped directly in front of me and looked into my eyes. 'I know, too,' it said. The approaching dusk infused the air with an orange-pink softness, fading into twilight. The beach felt even more magical. Mark, now back at the camp, was on hand with a scientific-sounding explanation.

'In twilight, our vision switches gradually from the cones that the eye uses to see colour to the rods, which only see black and white but are more sensitive to shapes. It really is a time of visual transformation. That's why you get that weird things-are-not-quite-what-they-seem feeling.'

We sat by the fading fire in the moonlight, our minds drifting into the night, listening to the waves and animals and people around us, until finally the San Pedro, too, began to fade.

****

it's communication, Jim, but not as we know it
Mark began telling me about a book he'd picked up in Vilcabamba. Food

of the Gods, by Terence McKenna. Melissa was inside the tent, skinning up. We knew this because she was holding her hands right next to the torch, which had the effect of projecting a magnified shadow-show of the whole process onto the side of the tent, rather defeating her attempt at discretion.

McKenna's book was another take on the whole 'lack of respect for nature' aspect of Western culture. He proposed that hallucinogenic plants (he suggests psilocybin mushrooms) were the catalyst that led to the sudden appearance of self-consciousness in early humans. Picture, if you will, our proto-human ancestor, accidentally swallowing a few magic mushrooms and . . . feeling a bit weird. Into her mind pops the question people have been asking themselves while tripping ever since: 'Where the bloody hell am I?' - thus inventing consciousness, language, philosophy, psychology, geography, religion and a whole tool-kit of other -ys and -ologys. OK, McKenna's version is a little more sophisticated than this but, basically, the black monolith in the movie 2001 should have been magic mushroom-shaped. Mushrooms turned on the human race. For whatever reason, there clearly was a sudden explosion of human intelligence. Self-awareness, spirituality, language, the birth of everything that makes us uniquely 'human', all appeared in an evolutionary split-second.

McKenna went on to argue that these magical plants, with their mysterious power, would surely have been considered sacred. He produces some evidence to suggest that early religions revolved around ritual use of such plants. This hallucinogenic sacrament would have constantly renewed our ancestors' direct experience of the magical energy of nature all around them, cutting straight through to its sacred heart in a way no theological text ever could.

The third step in McKenna's theory says that it was when we in Europe stopped using such plants (for whatever reason) that our attitude to Nature began to change. The plants were our connection with that underlying natural energy, and that connection was severed.

Underpinning all this is the idea that plants such as San Pedro contain a sort of 'voice-within-nature' that reveals the beauty and power pulsating through the universe. This all probably sounds extremely silly to you. Perhaps it should have to me. Except . . . today I'd heard that voice: the chemical imprint of San Pedro in my brain had shown me something magical. The holy energy of nature.

'Are you two going to talk crap all night?' Melissa called out from inside the tent.

****

Silver moon

It was past midnight. The moon was high, the brightest full moon I'd ever seen. A glowing white orb filling the night with metallic, silver light.

A beautiful full moon trip.

It was over twelve hours since we'd taken the San Pedro. We were sitting around the campfire, still coming down from the trip. Melissa had emerged and was boiling water for some tea. Suddenly, I felt a great rush of affection for both Mark and Melissa. I lay back in the sand and looked at the moon and the coconut palms dancing above me. I knew that this moment contained whatever it was I'd been looking for when I came to South America. It felt like freedom.

'You're two good people to travel with.' I said.

All the arguments and trivial tantrums melted away. It was all worth it.

Chapter 9
the fishboy

'someone gonna die . . .'

We spent the next day recovering and lazing around the beach. It was much like any other day at Arrecifes. We collected firewood, brought a large grouper from Lionel and fried it with rice, followed by bananas sautéed in rum and sugar.

There was one piece of drama. Carlos, returning from his daily fishing trip, said that he'd just saved a Colombian boy from drowning. He was still pumped-up and excited.

'These Colombians, these bloody kids, they can't even swim, but they gotta go out, you know. The current now, issa too strong. It getta real strong, this last week, you know, stronger than I ever seen before. I almost die, trying to get 'im out. You know, I almost die today. Two hours it take me to get 'im out. I 'ave to knock him out, you know, because 'e was so frightened. Never again. Next one, I let 'im drown. I almost die. Really. This Easter holiday is comin', with all these dumb Colombians gonna come. I tell you, someone gonna die on this beach this week.' It was the first time I'd seen Carlos get excited.

'I tell you, someone gonna die.' he repeated.

****

a dull morning

The next morning Mark and I went to the empty restaurant to write letters. It's strange to look back on those few moments, knowing now what was about to take place. It was an ordinary, sleepy morning, like any other. Just hanging out, nothing much to do, no hurry to do it. In hindsight, a whole number of little things had a strange resonance to them, but as we sat waiting for breakfast and chatting, I had no premonition that anything was about to happen. I doubt that Mark did either.

We hadn't yet decided if we were going to travel together or split up again. After a month at Arrecifes, Melissa and I were refreshed and just about ready to move on.

'So what do you think you're going to do now?' I asked Mark.

'I think I'll be staying here,' he said.

It was only natural that Mark would want to hang out at Arrecifes for a while. After all, it was the perfect spot. It was a beautiful place to finish the San Pedro and party with other travellers. He could live for next to nothing, too, which was a major attraction, given Mark's financial situation. We idly discussed ways in which he might make some money.

'I was thinking of sending coke back to England. If it was very thinly spread inside a letter, I could send it back to, say, John Peacock's address, but put the wrong name on it. So he'd keep the letter and not open it for a month or something. If the police turned up, he could say it wasn't anything to do with him. And with coke at, what, $5 a gram here, for almost pure stuff, well . . . '

We laughed at the idea. We both knew he wouldn't do it, of course, not because of the risk but because in the end he wouldn't be bothered. I'd never met anyone as lazy as Mark, or with so much potential, or with such complete self-belief. He was the classic case of the brightest kid at school who gets into trouble because everything is too easy. He could have done anything, except nothing seemed worth doing. Sometimes I felt that he never really *cared* about anything. I wondered how much he really cared about himself.

Mark was writing to Andrea, his girlfriend in England. He wanted to persuade her to come to South America. It was always hard to tell with Mark and women, but I got the impression that he was genuinely fond of Andrea. Secretly, I suspected, Mark really enjoyed the company of women, but he found it hard to admit this, even to himself, and kept up a misogynistic, laddish front. I suspected, too, that this stemmed from his troubled relationship with his mother: his parents had separated when he was young and he'd very much sided with his father. (So much so that when we lived together in London he didn't see his mother once in three years, even though she lived less than two miles away.) Whatever the cause, Mark rejected anything he considered 'soft' or 'feminine'. But now he seemed willing to relent a little, to let a little softness show through.

Maybe this was just the effect of travelling, loosening him up and allowing him to be a bit more expressive. It had that effect on me, although this was partly due to Melissa. I pushed Melissa into thinking more, and she pushed me into feeling more. But the 'traveller' persona definitely allowed – required, even – a little more softness than that of 'homeboy-slacker'. In a London suburb, a bloke got funny looks and the sofa all to himself if he went on about 'feelings', but to be a cool beatnik travellin'-man, a hint of rugged sensitivity was positively de rigour, and even sexy. Out here you could even say you liked poetry, for Christ's sake. Mark was getting into the role.

Or maybe it was that 'Saturn Returns' thing Melissa had talked about, a new level of maturity. I didn't imagine that Mark was suddenly going to transform himself overnight into some sort of tearstained luvvie but, whatever the reason, he seemed in a more relaxed and conciliatory mood. Maybe we could chill out on the beach for a while and patch up our differences. Our relationship went deep enough to cut through a few months' bullshit, and I still wanted to travel with Mark – for his vitality, his humour, his insights that came at you from unexpected angles.

Maybe the San Pedro trip was a fresh beginning: the real start of our travels together. I felt a pulse of optimism. A fresh beginning. Things were going to get better between us.

'By the way, you've got to read this book,' Mark said to me, interrupting my thoughts. 'Campbell's got it. It's called 'Fishboy', about this boy who drowns and lives under the sea. It's like an extended poem about the sea. You've must get it off Campbell and read it.'

****
not waving . . .
We walked back to the campsite, where Melissa was boiling some water. Helena and a couple of German girls were there, chatting to Melissa.

'I'm just going for a quick swim to freshen up,' Mark said. I knew he fancied one of the German girls and wanted to impress her. He took off his T-shirt, stretched his body and strode purposefully down to the water.

'Even on a beach, Mark still marches around everywhere,' Melissa remarked and we all laughed. I lay back in the hammock and listened to the palm leaves rustling against each other in the breeze and to the girls talking. Melissa was explaining the meaning of 'Chi'. A few Colombians had started to arrive – the park was now officially open again for the Easter holiday – and a group of them were playing frisbee on the beach.

'How's that tea doing?' I asked Melissa. But Helena interrupted me.

'There's someone waving out there.'

We looked out to sea. A handful of people were playing in the surf. Then, just beyond them, I saw someone waving their arms. Not frantically. Just signalling calmly. If he was calling, we couldn't hear him over the sound of the surf.

Melissa jumped up. 'Hey, it's Mark.' He was about twenty metres off-shore, which meant about forty metres from us. I couldn't see his face clearly from that distance. I guessed he was doing what you should do, if caught in a rip tide, which was to remain calm, attract attention, not try to fight the current. Instead, you should let it carry you out and then swim sideways out of it.

But this was not a rip tide.

Where he was swimming, piles of boulders beneath the surface created a deadly turbulence which dragged you down, not out.

We ran down to the water's edge. But what could we do? Should we swim out to try to save him? I remembered the Colombian honeymoon couple, and Carlos saying even he had almost drowned – and I always figured Carlos, who spent two hours harpooning every day, was the champion swimmer. I remembered my conversation with Mark, saying that if a strong swimmer couldn't swim out of the current, how could someone pull them out? I looked wildly around for something – anything – to spring forward and suggest itself. I suppose everyone else was doing the same.

In the few seconds it took to think all this, a Colombian man had leapt into the water and was swimming through the surf towards Mark, who was still treading water and waving.

The Colombian reached Mark. The two appeared to speak, two heads bobbing up and down between the waves, appearing and disappearing from view. Then the Colombian turned and struck out for the beach. Mark began to follow him, obviously summoning up his energy for a last big effort.

He took a couple of strokes, riding up onto the surf and closer to the beach. The Colombian broke the surf and was safe, now back on the beach side of the breaking waves. That was all it took. Just three of four purposeful strokes would take you through the one, critical, breaking wave, and suddenly you were safe. And conversely, that was what made it so dangerous; that the journey from safety to treacherous water was only a couple of steps. But cross that fine line and suddenly your feet were swept up and you were in very big trouble. I had felt it, too, playing in the surf. That sense of being only a tiny miscalculation away from disaster. It scared me.

We watched Mark fighting the waves. My stomach tightened. We were helpless, like spectators at a closely-fought sports event. But this was no game. This was a deadly serious struggle. A matter of life or death.

For a moment, it seemed he was safe. He was getting back. Even as I watched, I could picture Mark striding up to us, a broad grin on his face, triumphantly flourishing another story of adventure and escape. That was what he lived for: you could see it in his eyes sometimes.

But there were to be no more narrow escapes. Suddenly, a big, churning wave crashed over him and, instead of coming in, he was dragged back out again. The next wave was big too. It broke, the aerated white remnants washing towards the sand of the beach. When it receded, there was nothing.

Nothing.

We stood, shocked.

'He's gone,' Melissa said quietly. It had taken no more than a couple of minutes.

****

the fishboy

We knew it instantly. He was gone. Dead. Drowned. We felt it with a stone-cold certainty that grabs you in the stomach, like a punch to the solar plexus. That's were it hits you, in the stomach. A lurching, sinking, tightening sensation, like going over the edge of a rollercoaster.

Phillipe and a few others had seen what was happening and had joined us on the shore. Carlos was not around. I wondered if, had he been, he would have gone out to try to save Mark.

We stood for a moment that felt like an age. No one knew what to do. What could we do? It was already over. It was already too late. The

Colombians along the beach were still playing frisbee, oblivious to the drama that had just unfolded a few yards away from them. I tried to focus my mind. Should I be doing something? Should I be angry? Should I be crying? Should I feel guilty for not trying to save him? But I couldn't think of anything. Except that it was already over, already too late.

Humans are designed for action. Our instincts have evolved to respond to danger, to send adrenaline pumping around our bodies in a crisis. But the crisis was already over. All our lives, we are on the lookout, consciously or subconsciously, for danger, ready to spring into action at the merest snap of a twig in the undergrowth. Now the worst had happened. But the thing was over. Panic and adrenaline were no longer appropriate.

But I couldn't think of anything that *was* appropriate.

Except that it was already over, already too late.

The older of the two policemen who patrolled the park rode up on his horse. What use was a horse, I thought. He was talking to the Colombian who'd swum out to Mark. The Colombian was saying that Mark was yellow, his face was yellow. He said that Mark had told him to get back and save himself. It seemed that the Colombian, a man in his early forties, had at first thought that Mark was his son, which is why he'd dived in to save him.

I asked the policeman if he had a boat. No, he said, he had a horse. I knew it was pointless anyway. By now, most of the people on the beach had figured out that something had happened and were crowding around the policeman on his mount, to find out what it was. The would-be life-saver quietly disappeared, no doubt wanting to stay out of any police business. In Colombia, witnesses tend to melt away. I'd heard that the police often arrested witnesses to a death and accused them of the mur-der, demanding, of course, a bribe to 'drop charges.' Whether this was true, or just out of shock, the man vanished from the beach. We never saw him again.

'Your friend?' the policeman asked. 'Did he have any credit cards? American Express? Travellers cheques?'

I caught sight of Lionel. 'Maybe we can get the fishermen's boat,' I said. Lionel shrugged. We could try, but we both knew it was too late. 'OK, let's go,' he said.

We ran along the beach, through the coconut trees, barefooted, dodging fallen palms and sticks. It felt better, at least, to be doing something, however hopeless it was. Just to be running, out of breath. Maybe, just maybe, Mark was still out there somewhere, somehow. Maybe he had resurfaced, had found something to cling to, had struggled onto a lonely rock or some hidden stretch of beach out of sight. We had to make sure.

We reached the fishermen's place. Pablo, who owned the boat, was not there. The sun-dried old grandmother pointed behind her with a vague wave, and told Lionel that Pablo was collecting coconuts. We ran back, shouting Pablo's name. Eventually, an answer floated out from within a thick mass of trees. Pablo followed, machete in hand.

Lionel explained the situation, I said that we'd pay for petrol, and we set off. The three of us jumped into Pablo's tiny dugout canoe. It had taken twenty minutes to get this far. On the way out of the fishermen's sheltered bay, we had to stop and rescue four teenagers, two girls and two boys, who were floundering in the water off the headland. They barely knew how to doggy-paddle. God knows what they would have done if we hadn't turned up. Mark's death probably saved their lives.

We decided I would jump off and run back to the beach to see if Mark had somehow got back there. If not, I would wave a white flag to tell them to carry on looking. As I ran back through the shallow water up onto the beach, I still half-expected to find Mark waiting for me, with his big, tri-umphant grin. But it was not to be. I grabbed a white T-shirt and waved it at Lionel and Pablo. I knew we were just going through the motions.

Lionel and Pablo searched the coast for a while before giving up. The Colombians went back to playing frisbee. So, someone had died. A gringo had died. People die every day. They'd seen it all before. Maybe they'd even been here when the last person drowned. Word spread among the gringos and we sat in shock, not knowing what to say, not wanting to say very much.

'We should get rid of the San Pedro,' said Campbell. 'It's bad magic, if you ask me. Everyone who's taken that load of San Pedro has had something bad happen to them. I had all my gear ripped off and Kim got sick, and now this.'

As sunset approached, we climbed up onto the rocky headland of the bay. Melissa, Campbell, Kim, Sandra, Phillipe, Helena and myself. The rocks rose about ten metres above the water, and it required some scrambling to get out to the furthest one, jumping over narrow chasms between the boulders, which the inrushing sea filled with foaming spume and then drained with a sucking rush. The tide was coming in and the waves smacked the base of the rocks, sending geysers of spray high into the air, reaching up almost to where we sat.

Out here, perched on the rocks of the headland, there was no deception; no doubting the power of the ocean. Waves rolled in relentlessly from across an infinite expanse of water. Through each flowed the limitless energy of an interconnected universe – that same energy that we'd felt during our San Pedro trip. Against it, a human was nothing but a piece of helpless flotsam.

Campbell took the bottle of San Pedro, still three-quarters full. He held it in his hand for a moment. Then he stood up and hurled it as far out into the sea as he could. It landed with a tiny splash far below us and disappeared. Campbell stared after it for a few seconds.

'It's a sad day,' he said.

'Mark really is the Fishboy now,' said Sandra.

We sat in silence, each thinking our own thoughts.

Melissa gazed out towards the horizon.

'The sea looks beautiful after a kill.' She spoke softly, as if to herself.

****
slacker-shaman
I sat on the rock and thought about what Mark meant to me. There'd been so many narrow escapes that everyone who knew him always half-expected something like this would happen. Yet Mark was one of those people you always assumed was charmed; who'd always emerge grinning triumphantly.

Beyond the numb shock of the moment, I could already sense an emptiness within me – the void that Mark's death would leave in my own life.

Mark and I hadn't always seen eye to eye, especially on this trip. But he'd remained a special person for me. Perhaps it was because, almost alone among my friends, he'd rejected all that hypocritical, poisonous 'career' shit. To most people, it looked like apathy and idleness, but I saw it differently. Mark had refused to sell his mind – his soul – to some bland, evil, world-fucking corporation just so he could smarm and backstab his way to self-important middle-management middle-age. I'd seen the vitality sucked out of too many other friends as they signed that Faustian pact. But Mark remained free. Alive. He'd refused to let the System's projects and values become his projects and values. To Mark, music and drugs and having the time to think always came before money and respectability and a career. And he was right. They do. They should. I respected him for it. I respected him for not caring about things that were not worth caring about.

Mark' s sights were set on the vast wild regions of reality that lay beyond the confining walls of normality and respectability. He was outside the cave, searching for the Edge. He was our cosmic warrior, our psychic explorer, our slacker-shaman. And his house – with its mouldy coffee-cups and chaos-strewn carpets – was our sacred space. Our suburban gateway to an alternate reality.

Mark had told me many times, too, that he wasn't afraid to die. That was an important thing. It meant that he was free to live. The fact that he was prepared to go out into the surf, to accept risks, made him the person he was. If you'd taken him away from the Edge, you would have taken the Edge out of him. Taken away his life and vitality, like brainwashed Alex in *A Clockwork Orange*.

I thought of a line in another film, *Deliverance*, when tough-guy Burt Reynolds takes Jon Voight and some city-slickers on a back-country rafting trip that goes horribly wrong. In one crisis, Voight defends the fat, useless member of the party to Reynolds.

'He's highly respected in his field, you know,' says Voight.

'And what is his field?' Reynolds asks.

'Insurance,' Voight replies.

'Insurance?' sneers Reynolds. 'Sheee-it.'

I always associated that line with Mark. He never believed in insurance.

****

a pirate sea

I thought, too, about the little things that suddenly seemed strangely prophetic. Melissa's disturbing horoscope before we left. Carlos saying someone would drown. Mark mentioning the book about the boy who drowned, the Fishboy, just before his death. And saying he would be staying at Arrecifes. Our San Pedro conversation about no one coming to save Mark if he went swimming. Above all, I remembered him talking of the sea calling him to come out and join it. To be at one with it, at one with nature. In the end, he'd been seduced by the Sirens' song.

Were these just coincidences, only invested with significance by a tragic accident? Probably. Or was there some strange magic here? Maybe *all* events have presentiments, like ripples in time stretching backwards as well as forwards, so faint that only a few tuned-in people can detect them. Maybe something as powerful as a death sent ripples big enough for even me to detect. Albeit only with hindsight.

What were the last seconds like for Mark? Those last seconds of life that must always remain a mystery to those still living. Suddenly realising that . . . *this was it*. The end. Probably, given Mark's self-belief, he would have been sure that he was going to escape, even when he told the Colombian to go back, right up until the last seconds. I imagined him, even as he struggled, running through the great story he would be able to tell when he got back to the beach. Then, the sudden realisation that this time there would be no story, no escape. I only hoped the time between that moment and losing consciousness was short. It had been so, so quick, plucking him from the cosmic dance in mid-leap. That, at least, was a blessing.

There may be worse ways to die. Out in the surf, revelling in existence even in the instant of death. Is it better to die when we are old and worn out, life slowly ebbing away while the cold face of infinity gazes down on us and we wait for the end? I remembered my dying grandfather, the summer before, barely able to speak, whispering, 'When will it end?'

My grandfather had been 94. His death filled me with a terrible, cold dread that took an age to leave. He had been a wonderfully strong person, who had lived a long, full and worthwhile life and had remained alert and healthy until the very last weeks, full of enthusiasm and outrage and sharp intelligence. I watched him at the end, thin and wasted, begging for a release, even while the strength still in his body refused to let him go. 'When will it end,' he mouthed. All I could think was 'This is the best we can hope for.' His life was as long and fulfilled as anyone could reasonably ask. And yet still it ended in pain, still too soon.

Maybe Mark was lucky. Not to die so young – he was three months short of thirty – but to die quickly, unexpectedly. In action, so to speak. In a way it was a warrior's death, cut down in battle, rather than eaten away by age or illness. In warrior cultures, an active death was always the only honourable, desirable way to die. Mark's fight was with the elements, of course, not with a human opponent. It was also with himself: he knew the risk and yet still felt drawn to take it.

It was a beautiful place to die. A beautiful, romantic place, far away from home. This was the Caribbean, but not the holiday-brochure Caribbean of tourists sipping pina coladas beside limpid, turquoise waters. Instead, it was a wild, pirate sea, where breakers relentlessly assaulted the beach and the ceaseless roar of the surf pounded like artillery on some distant battlefield. It was the ocean of the Spanish Main and ruthless, murderous buccaneers like Francis Drake and Captain 'Bluebeard' Morgan. To die in such a place had a romantic poetry to it. Such an elemental death, dragged back into the savage ocean womb of the world.

I looked back along the beach. The last thing Mark would have seen was this beach. The piles of giant boulders. The coconut palms rocking in the wind and the palm roofs of the restaurants, and behind it all the hills, with their mantle of thick green jungle, reaching up towards the unseen snow of the mighty Sierra Nevada. Could there be a more beautiful image to carry into eternity?

We watched the orange orb of the sun disappear behind the hills and stain the sky with streaks of bloody red. The gathering darkness made it dangerous to stay on the rocks much longer, and the incoming tide threatened to cut us off. We climbed down and retreated back to the beach.

'How do you feel?' Melissa asked.

'It's funny, but I really don't know. Like an actor waiting for some lines. I just feel . . . empty.'

Melissa put her arms around me and rested her forehead against mine. She looked into my eyes. The moment didn't need any words. I closed my eyes and felt tears on my cheeks, but they were tears of gratitude – of relief that I wasn't alone.

Chapter 10
afterlife

a walk in the forest

I watched the sea fade into the darkness. It seemed as if a thousand heads appeared and then disappeared as the waves rose and fell. But it was only the silver light of the rising moon, still nearly full, catching the white foam crests and making them shimmer in the fading twilight like – a sparkling sea to mirror the emerging stars above. Melissa and I lay together in one of the hammocks and fell asleep holding each other.

I expected nightmares. But none came and in the morning I felt vaguely guilty about having slept easily. I'd been grateful for the little ceremony on the rocks. The throwing away of the San Pedro; sitting there silently with the waves smashing against the rocks and the spray around us. It felt right, as if fulfilling a basic need for some sort of ritual to say goodbye to a friend.

Should I have tried to save Mark? Logic told me the attempt would have been both unsuccessful and suicidal. I remembered a little basic lifesaving at school: a feeble backstroke doggy-paddle, pathetic even in a calm swimming-pool. But this treacherous ocean was a different proposition. And yet . . . shouldn't I still have tried? Even if I'd died trying. Action, they say, speaks louder that words, and when it mattered I'd done nothing. Maybe – probably – I'd been right. But in that moment, I saw my true colours. Cautious and afraid. Just as I'd been afraid to let myself go fully on the ayahuasca trip with the Cofans. Just as Mark wasn't afraid. To take things to the Edge. And now, finally, over it.

The next morning there was still no sign of Mark's body, so I left the beach and headed along the path through the jungle into Santa Marta. I had to report his death, and then . . . Then I had to phone Mark's father. To tell him that his son was dead.

As I walked, I searched my mind for avenues of doubt we might have overlooked. How could I tell his father if there was even a tiny possibility that it wasn't true?

But, however many times I relived the moment in my mind, I could see no other outcome. Could he have been swept in on the surf and be lying in an unseen corner of the bay? No, we'd searched every inch of beach, and then searched it again. Could he have resurfaced further out to sea and swum to another bay, or been washed there, unconscious but alive? No. He could only have come up in our bay – the others were simply too far away. Too many people had seen it happen.

There was no chance that Mark was alive. No chance at all.

Yet I couldn't shake the feeling that it just wasn't real. It couldn't be. What I'd seen must have been a trick of the light, a hallucinatory hangover from the San Pedro trip. Even now, certain as I was of Mark's death, unable to find any lingering lifeline of hope, I still half-expected to return to our camp to find Mark there, laughing at my confusion.

I tried to lose myself in the rhythm of walking. To draw strength from the cool beauty of the forest and the privilege of being in this magical place. Rich layers of greenery enclosed the narrow path. Dappled light and birdsong filtered through the trees into the shady interior of the forest. The path eased between natural gateways of giant boulders, so narrow that I had to turn sideways to get through, and switchbacked gently; up over small hills and down across almost-dry creek beds.

Mark was the first person close to me to die like this. It was true that I'd watched my grandfather and grandmother die, slowly, in hospital beds. But Mark's was the first sudden and unexpected death; the first close friend of my own age who'd died.

A strange feeling swept over me. Freedom. Almost elation. I remembered Terry Hall (the ex-Specials singer) saying in an interview that when his father died he'd woken up the next day feeling like Superman. Mark's death was the one moment that I'd always dreaded, rehearsed somewhere in the back of my mind for as long as I could remember. Not Mark's, in particular, but someone's. Sooner or later it had to happen. We know that those close to us must die and, if we outlive them, we must watch them go. Just as the anticipation of tragedy can be unbearable, the fact itself at least brings release from that dreadful tension.

Maybe I'd found what I was looking for. If I'd come away looking for Life with the capital letter, then this was surely it, although in a way I hadn't wanted or expected. But this was something real; something that mattered; something that went far beyond the petty vanities and artificial ambitions of our ordinary life and touched on the existential basics of what it is to be alive. In Mark's death, I felt myself more alive than ever.

Had Mark found what *he* was looking for? Did he take the risks that he did because part of him had sought this outcome all along; sought the ultimate truth of death? I couldn't say.

All I knew was that the forest felt more wonderful and beautiful than ever, its preciousness sharpened by the poignancy of loss, its presence at once peaceful yet pulsatingly alive.

The forest survives each falling leaf, each dying tree; humanity outlasts each human life. If we let go of transient forms, then we can open our minds to the underlying, interconnected energy that fills our universe. Let go. Shamanic ecstasy. The Buddha's basic teaching. And the hardest to follow.

I walked on.

I felt that I was seeing a basic truth for the first time with perfect clarity. It was something that had been forming in my mind throughout the trip. Now this moment – and specifically, the way that the forest seemed to ease the pain of Mark's death – brought it home to me. It was simply this: that we need Nature, not just for the raw materials it yields, but also to nurture our spirits. To keep us 'grounded'. We *need* that sense of Nature as sacred. Without this connection to Nature we will never find peace. Perhaps that's why we Europeans are so restless, always travelling and building, striving for something that seems forever just beyond our grasp. We're searching for that lost connection. The connection I'd felt in the vast, still silences of the mountains; in the magical life-energy of the Amazon; on the beach during the San Pedro trip.

I thought again of my grandfather's death, which in the sterile, utilitarian setting of a London hospital had filled me with such dread and hopelessness, when his death should have been the cause for celebration, of a life lived long and full. But here, with boundless life all around me, death seemed somehow easier to bear – an inevitable part of the endless natural cycle – even though Mark's death, so young and with so much left to offer, was surely the greater tragedy of the two.

It seemed so obvious. This lost connection was what I'd been searching for all along. The beating heart that was missing from my material world. And now I'd found it.

I realised that none of this would make any sense to Mark's father, coming

over the end of a telephone from Colombia on a dull March day in suburban England. The thought sobered my mood, and the contrast between
the near-euphoria of the previous moment and the chilling prospect of
that phone call only added to the unreality of it all.

****

reporting a death

I reached the road and caught a bus into Santa Marta. I decided that,
before phoning Mark's father (and mainly to delay that task) that I would
report his death to the police. The policeman at Arrecifes had already
said that he couldn't – or wouldn't – make the report. At the police station
in Santa Marta, I approached the officer at the desk.

'I wish to report the death of my friend,' I began. The policeman held up
his hand and pointed to an open door. Inside was a small, grimly functional room. There was one plain table with a chair either side of it. A couple
of other chairs rested against the wall, below a high, small window.

The cop at the desk was interviewing a middle-aged woman. He was no
more than nineteen. A big ape of a boy, a fat kid who'd spent too much
time at the gym, with a podgy face, military crewcut and a neck buried
deep inside pumped-up shoulders. His uniform was two sizes too small,
the tight armpits forcing him to hunch his shoulders and hold his arms
slightly away from his body.

The boy smiled insinuatingly at the woman, and made a hand gesture
under the table. It was clear that she'd have to put some money in it to
get any further. The woman hissed in disgust, got up and walked out. It
didn't look too encouraging. I sat down in her seat and began to explain.

'My friend has drowned.'

'Why are you telling me?' He replied evenly. He looked at me for a
minute, trying to decide if he could get anything out of the dirty-looking
gringo in front of him.

'Because I want to report his death.' I said.

He shrugged. 'Why?'

I wasn't expecting the question. Why did I want to report his death? He
was dead, after all, whether I reported it or not. What difference would it

make if I didn't report it? But surely someone couldn't just . . . die. Not after all those years of filling in forms. Birth certificates, school exams, job applications, driving licenses, bank accounts, tax forms, mortgages, medical forms, insurance forms. Everything must be recorded. I knew I had to report Mark's death. But why?

'In my country, we must report deaths,' I ventured, lamely.

'And how do you know he is dead?'

'I saw him drown.'

'And where is the body?'

'There is no body. It has not been found.'

'If there is no body, you cannot report him dead. You can only report him missing,' the ape-boy pronounced. He looked pleased with himself at having outwitted a gringo. 'You must go to the office around the corner for that, under the arch.'

I began to get up to leave.

'One minute please,' The ape-cop said. 'Your friend. Did he have any . . . credit cards?'

I left.

Following his instructions, I found the second office.

'I want to report my friend's death.' I began.

'Ah, yes.' The cop behind the desk was older and had a kinder face. He looked at me sympathetically for a moment, then smiled. 'But we are the traffic police. You must go to another office. You must go to the DAS, the immigration office.'

If Mark needs immigration papers, I thought, they won't be Colombian ones. I imagined Gabriel, standing in front of the Pearly Gates, stuffed into a uniform two sizes too small as he examined the passports of the dead. It took me an hour and a half to find the DAS office, a badly sign-posted building on the other side of town. It was a modern office with a waiting room like a doctors' surgery. I had to wait an hour for the queue of people to reach me.

When my turn came, the woman on the desk looked puzzled.

'But why are you telling me, *señor*? He hasn't left the country. Maybe you should try the coroner's office.' Reporting a death in Colombia was proving harder than actually dying.

She gave me the address of the coroner's office. It was back across town, near the police station, in an office block above a small, run-down shopping mall. It was closed for lunch.

My Spanish was struggling to cope with circumstances that weren't in the phrase book, but I found a cafe and returned to the coroners' office after lunch. This room was large, with a number of desks and filing cabinets and bare white walls. About ten people were huddled around one of the desks, on which a travelling salesman had opened a suitcase full of jewellery. I explained that I was looking for the coroner. A woman looked up.

'The coroner is at lunch, if you'd like to wait.'

I sat down to wait. One of the girls began to chat to me. She'd visited a relative in Australia once and spoke a little English.

'I am sorry your friend is dead.' She paused, smiled sympathetically and continued. 'Are you from Australia? I went to Sydney and Melbourne five years ago, to see my auntie. Australia is very beautiful, don't you think. Very clean.'

No one was doing any work. There was no evidence, on the empty desks or in the bare office, of work ever having taken place. At last, a white-haired man marched in, with an air of authority.

'Yes, this is the coroner's office. But it is not the right office to report a death. You must see Dr Lopez in the *Fiscalia*.'

I had no idea where or even what the *Fiscalia* was, and I was beyond wondering why no one else had bothered to point that out that I was in the wrong office during the hour I'd been sitting there. I expected him to tell me that the *Fiscalia* was on the other side of town next to the DAS office, but this time it was in the same building. I followed his directions up a concrete stairwell. On the landing above, the doors were protected by iron bars. A security guard sat behind a small table.

'I want to see Dr Lopez,' I said. The security guard scrutinised his list slowly. Then he looked up and scrutinised me slowly, as if about to deliver a judgement of great wisdom.

'There is no Dr Lopez.'

'He is the coroner. I must see him. I, er . . .' I struggled to think how exactly to continue, but the guard saved me by saying,

'Oh, the coroner. The next floor, on the right.'

I opened the door. Another office. Five people sitting at desks. This time there was a bit more evidence of activity and paperwork lying around.

'I wish to see the coroner . . .' I started.

'No, this is not the coroner's office.'

I tried again.

'I want to see Dr Lopez?'

'Lopez? He is in the next room. But he's not the coroner.'

A young man in his early twenties looked out through the open door of the adjacent room.

'I am Dr Lopez. I *am* the coroner. How can I help you?'

I explained the situation. To my surprise, instead of directing me to another agency on the other side of Santa Marta, he took me into his office and showed me a thick file of reports and photos of missing people, as if to demonstrate that I really was in the right office at last. Then he produced a photocopied sheet resembling a multiple-choice exam. The form asked for details of the incident. What type of nose did the missing person have? How many eyebrows did he have? Did it matter how many eyebrows he had?

After I'd filled this out, Dr Lopez called three assistants from the front room. They spent the next twenty minutes amending the form, tippexing over things, asking me questions and incorrectly copying what I'd written onto a duplicate form, in pencil.

'So that we can change it later, if we want,' they explained disarmingly.

I looked over their shoulders and pointed out the mistakes, and they rubbed them out and wrote them down incorrectly again. Eventually, we arrived at an approximate version of what I'd written on the original form. Dr Lopez assured me that the police and coastguards would be notified. Everything, he announced, was now in hand and under control.

****

a tough call

I caught a cab back to the Miramar. My foray into the labyrinthine corridors of Colombian bureaucracy had managed at least to delay the dreaded moment that had to come, but it could be postponed no longer. I had to telephone Mark's father.

It was too late to return to Arrecifes by now, so I booked myself a bed at the Miramar. The usual motley crew of travellers sat around the courtyard in various states of degeneration, chatting, reading, playing chess, drinking beer and fruit juices. A few were slumped in front of the TV in the corner, watching some second-rate bloodfest on the cable channel – *Die With a Hard-On* or something.

I circled the phone for at least an hour, summoning up courage. Finally, I made the call. My heart was pumping as I dialled. It was the most difficult thing I'd ever had to do. It was Mark's stepmother, not his father, who answered. Now I had to actually say what I'd been rehearsing all day.

'Denise, I'm afraid that something terrible has happened, Mark has drowned.' So simple, yet so devastating. I heard myself speaking the words that every parent must dread above any others. Your child is dead. The most terrible news of all.

There was a silence.

'Is this a joke?' she asked, eventually.

'I'm afraid not, Denise. I wouldn't joke about something like this.'

The very speaking seemed to make it a step more real. Are things true before they are spoken? Maybe they remain in the same state of unresolved potential as Schrödinger's famous philosophical Cat, which cannot be said to be either in or not in its box until we open the lid to look inside. My call lifted the lid on the often-surreal 'travelling' world, and made Mark's death a reality at home as well. Until now, it had been confined to Arrecifes and Santa Marta. And as long as it stayed there, it was as if there was something not quite definite about it. Mark might be dead in our dream-world of hammocks and San Pedro and surfing pigs, but once we were back in the dull English suburbs and the drizzle and rush-hour traffic jams, things would return to normal. For his family, it was true in a way: for them Mark was still alive until this phone call. For them, this was the moment of his death, and I felt like the executioner.

Mark's father came to the phone. He tried to talk, but his voice went and he was unable to speak. I gave him my number at the Miramar. I waited, watching people moving about in the hotel, not wanting to think about what it felt like at his end of the phone. After a few minutes he phoned back, a little more collected. Was there any hope, any possibility? I told him that there wasn't, but of course we were looking anyway. Mark's father searched for a lifeline of hope. But I could offer none. I could see no way in which Mark could have survived.

We agreed that I'd go back to Arrecifes and arrange for a boat to search the coast. Then I'd return to Santa Marta and phone again. I said that he should decide if he wanted to come to Colombia. Not to search for Mark, but to see where it had happened; to know the place where his son had died.

To me that seemed important.

****

a pelican
I spent the night in a room with a group of beautiful, sun-tanned Chilean hippies, two boys and two girls, who sat on their beds and got stoned and did lines of coke and slowly worked on jewellery to sell. One of the boys strummed a guitar softly. In the morning, I searched through a bag of Mark's, which he'd stored in the hotel safe room. Campbell had said that Mark might have a left a stash of coke somewhere and we ought to get to it before the police did. But I couldn't find anything, so I returned to the beach.

In Arrecifes, Melissa filled me in on what had been happening. With nothing to do, she'd just been sitting, talking about Mark's death to Helena and Campbell and Carlos, waiting for me to return.

'The young policeman rode down and demanded to search Mark's tent. He wanted to confiscate everything. He wanted to know if Mark had any credit cards or cash. Helena was around and refused to let him into the tent, which led to a big argument. Finally, he gave in, but then he produced a typewriter from somewhere, sat on the beach and typed a letter saying that Helena goes to jail if anything is moved, and made her sign it.'

I searched the tent for the missing cocaine. A couple of soft-porn magazines were the most incriminating evidence I could find. I set a couple of Mark's notebooks aside to give to his father. Inside one, he'd written the lyrics of a Pink Floyd song that he was learning to play on his *queña*,

'Long you live and high you fly,
But only if you ride the tide,
And balanced on the biggest wave,
You race towards an early grave.'

As I'd promised Mark's father, I walked down to Pablo, the fisherman by the swimming-pool bay. I said I'd pay him a hundred dollars, which I hoped was a lot by local standards, to search for Mark's body. I asked if I could come out with him.

I quickly regretted it. Pablo's boat was nothing more than a hollowed-out tree trunk with an outboard motor. As we passed through the narrow gap in the ring of rocks that sheltered the bay, we hit the swells of the open sea with a jolt. The tiny boat rose on each crest and plunged into troughs deep enough to obliterate all sight of land. I suddenly felt a long way from the shore – especially now that I knew just how dangerous the sea really was. Pablo steered into the waves with long-practised skill, ensuring that they broke over the bow and didn't knock us sideways. We followed the coastline for an hour in both directions. On either side of Arrecifes, black sea-cliffs rose out of the ocean, and to be sure that we wouldn't miss Mark's body if it was stuck on a rock, Pablo steered perilously close to these imposing ramparts. The ocean pounded their base with a hollow boom, sending spray high above our heads. This flimsy contraption seemed a very insignificant thing to have entrusted with our lives.

Some other fishermen were fishing nearby, so we motored over to ask if they'd seen anything. Pablo pulled up alongside their equally fragile-looking boats, cutting the engine as they talked and letting the boats drift together, rising and falling on the swells. I marvelled at the everyday courage of these men, who face these seas in such tiny vessels without even a spare paddle in case their ancient outboard motors fail. Everybody had lost someone – a father or brother or cousin – to the sea. Yet still they went out to fish, from necessity but also with a deep love of the ocean.

As the fishermen talked, a solitary pelican flew past, close in below the cliffs. It flew only inches above the water, skimming the waves. Its wide, white wings waved slowly, as if in slow motion. Such gracefulness. Such a contrast to its comical gawkiness on land. I began to throw up, out of a mixture of sea-sickness and fear, and prayed for dry land.

****

easter

For the next week we waited to see if the tide would bring Mark's body back. I hoped that it wouldn't. Better, I thought, that it should remain at sea. The sea had claimed it and the sea should keep it. I made another trip to phone Mark's father. He'd decided to come to Colombia and had booked the next available flight, which was the following week.

In the meantime, it was Easter weekend, the country's main holiday. Arrecifes was transformed from a laid-back travellers' retreat to a full-scale Colombian beach party. Suddenly, there was a hammock strung from every tree. The restaurants were packed with noisy, laughing faces. Lines of *Latino* hippies sat cross-legged beneath the palm trees, selling jewellery and pipes on sarongs spread out in the dust. A few strummed guitars. A Brazilian girl sold extravagant earrings made from the exuberantly-coloured feathers of tropical birds. Salsa blared out from dozens of ghetto-blasters.

Most of the new arrivals couldn't swim but, with typical Colombian bravura, men and boys doggy-paddled out into danger. In Pablo's boat, we'd twice had to stop to pull struggling swimmers out of the water. They had big grins on their faces as we dragged them into the boat. Melissa and Helena rushed up and down the beach.

'Don't swim, don't swim. It's too dangerous,' they shouted. The Colombians laughed and ran out into the waves. One teenage boy collapsed unconscious on the beach after he was rescued. Thinking he had died, his frightened friends ran off and left him. When he came round,

Melissa was the only person there to look after him. A group of surfers had arrived and spent the whole weekend charging out on their boards to rescue one floundering swimmer after another. The surf boards were the only real means of negotiating the breaking waves and the surfers had a deal with the owners of the restaurants, who let them stay for free during these big holidays in return for this voluntary life-saving service. If they'd been here a few days earlier, they might have saved Mark.

The holiday-makers crowded into every space around us. They played salsa at full volume on huge ghetto-blasters and drank and sang and partied. The beach began to fill up with rubbish and empty beer cans. The idea of low-impact camping clearly hadn't reached Colombia yet. Faced with this invasion, we found ourselves transformed from dirty backpackers into indignant residents moaning about the disturbance to our peaceful little idyll, like some retired Home Counties major complaining about the local rock festival.

'These-a workin'-class people,' Carlos fumed, 'They donna know 'ow to respect the beautiful places, you know. They shouldna be allowed on the same beach, you know.'

'Workin' people.' he pronounced the term with contempt, as if work was the least reputable thing he could think of. 'There shoulda be a special beach forra them, made of concrete, you know, and leave the nice beach to us.'

****

being and becoming
The Colombians next to us were a bunch of young guys determined to be drunk for the duration of the holiday. They dug a pit, filled it with rubbish, doused it liberally with petrol, stood back and threw in a match. Toxic, choking black smoke billowed up and engulfed our campsite.

My mind went back to the little girl on the way to Nabusímake, who'd built our fire so naturally and simply. I thought of the contrast between the Indians and the *Latinos* we'd found throughout our trip. The Colombian boys and their noxious fire were the inheritors of a *Latino* culture that was ultimately European. A culture that has cut its ties to the land and no longer respects nature; that has sacrificed the natural world on an altar of materialism. Their culture was my culture. The sons and daughters of European *conquistadores* and the children of those who stayed behind in Europe: we were much the same.

Someone, in a BBC TV series on the Wild West, neatly summed up the difference between Indian and European world-views (although he was referring to the whites and Indians of the *North* American plains and specifically, if I recall, to General Custer and Chief Sitting Bull).

The Indian, he said, was in a state of *being*, content simply to be in his natural environment, because he thought it was perfect. The white man, on the other hand, was in a state of constant *becoming*, always striving to change himself and his environment. He didn't know what it was to be at peace with the world around him.

****

the donkey
Three nights after Mark's death, I was sitting in our camp. Mark's tent and hammock still stood untouched, to one side. One of the troublemaking donkeys lopped over towards me, stopped right in front of me and looked directly at me. I was surprised because this was the first time I'd seen any of the donkeys take an interest in anything except food. Normally they ignored anyone who wasn't actually hitting them or throwing coconuts at them. I had a peculiar feeling that it was not the donkey looking at me, but Mark, saying goodbye. I stared at the donkey, looking for some sign of confirmation, although I knew it was an absurd thought. The donkey eyed me impassively.

'Didn't I tell you?' it seemed to say. 'Didn't I say I'd take you further?'

****

a torso
At the end of the week, Melissa and I went back to Santa Marta to meet Mark's father and brother, Eric and Iain. I'd stopped expecting his body to reappear. 'They-a come inna seven days, orra never,' Carlos pronounced. Lionel, the fishermen and everyone with any claim to knowledge of the sea agreed that after a week or so, bodies were rarely found. Almost a fortnight had passed since Mark's death.

Eric and Iain arrived by taxi from the airport. We met them outside the hotel that I'd booked for them. Mark's father was a big, balding man with a friendly, jovial manner. But now he looked grey and gaunt, the trauma of the last two weeks etched in his eyes.

Iain was, like Mark, athletically built and ruggedly handsome. One year younger than Mark, the two of them had been intensely competitive all their lives – an often petty rivalry that was only just beginning to mature into a genuine mutual respect. Whatever Mark had done, Iain had bust a gut to go one better. If Mark had been in the school rugby team, Iain had to be captain of next year's team, and his team had to be more successful than Mark's. As always with brothers, the rivalry mattered much more to Iain, the younger, than it did to Mark.

Once they'd checked into the hotel, we all went to see the coroner.

'Dr Lopez? No, he is not the coroner. He is just a photographer who comes here sometimes.'

Dr Lopez came out of his office and waved us in.

He expressed his condolences to Eric and Iain and showed us an advert he'd placed in the local newspaper, announcing Mark as 'missing' and asking for any information. He was clearly pleased to have some proof that his office had actually done something.

The next thing was to take Eric and Iain to Arrecifes. We caught a taxi to the park entrance and began the two-hour hike to the beach. We'd been walking for ten minutes when we saw six men approaching, carrying a stretcher. One was the baby-faced police chief from Arrecifes.

'Great news,' the young *jefe* beamed, 'We have the body. Now, who wants to identify it?'

The short answer was . . . nobody. Having accepted in our minds that Mark's body was lost, its sudden appearance needed some mental adjustment. We looked uneasily at the lumpy mass on the stretcher, hidden beneath a sheet. *El jefe* continued,

'*Señors*, it is many days in the water. It has now no arms and legs, and nothing . . .' he tapped his own head, '. . . nothing here. Maybe fish eat it. Or against the rocks. You understand?'

We nodded lamely. One of us had to inspect the body. Melissa looked at me.

'I don't want to see it,' I mumbled, 'not like this, without warning.'

'Well, someone has to identify it,' Eric said. He stepped forward and the policeman pulled back the sheet. Eric looked at whatever was under-neath. He turned to us, at a loss as to what to say.

'I can't identify it.'

What was there to identify? The thing on the stretcher was a grey, blood-less, limbless, headless torso. Around the hips hung a thread of black material. Certainly, this might be the remains of Mark's black shorts, and the torso was the right size for a six-foot man. Who else could it be?

Yet there were stories that Colombian gangs sometimes disposed of incon-venient bodies by palming them off as accidental deaths. They would, I'd heard, scan the newspapers for mention of a missing person that matched their own corpse, then dump it during the night in the spot mentioned in the announcement. So it seemed a little suspicious that a body should have reappeared the day after Dr Lopez's advert in the paper, and in exactly the spot where Mark had drowned. The policemen, too, seemed a little too pleased with themselves.

As we wondered what to do, one of the other men stepped forward and identified himself.

'I am Señor Hernandez. I am a funeral director from Santa Marta.' He showed us a badly-printed business card and smiled ingratiatingly at Eric.

'It is very, very sad. So young.' he said. Then, getting quickly to the point, he brought out a piece of dog-eared typewritten paper. 'If you will sign this, we can prepare the body for the funeral. Make it very nice. You only pay one thousand dollars.'

I translated for Eric. The vultures didn't waste much time gathering: we'd been with Dr Lopez (who as far as we could make out really *was* the coro-ner) only a couple of hours before and he didn't know that the body had been found. Yet the funeral director had got to the scene at least three hours before us, so he must have known at least five hours ago. And it was only 11am now.

'You must sign,' he insisted, 'We must work fast or it will be too late. The body will decay. If you sign now, we can make it very nice. But if we wait, it will be too late.'

Very nice?

214

Was he mad? How nice can you make someone look with no arms, legs, blood or head? Was the man some sort of miracle worker? And surely, after fourteen days, another day or so wouldn't matter. Anyway, we still had no way of identifying it. Eric was understandably reluctant to commit himself to burying the wrong body.

Realising we weren't going to sign the undertaker's contract, *el jefe* said they'd take the body back to Santa Marta. Two of us could follow in the police car.

We decided that Eric and I would continue to the beach as originally planned. Melissa and Iain would follow the body and find out what they were going to do with it in Santa Marta. We would meet at Eric and Iain's hotel in Santa Marta in the evening.

****

'issa piece of meat . . .'

Eric and I watched the body and its entourage disappear along the path, and then set off. I clung to the notion that the raw beauty of Arrecifes would have the same healing effect on Mark's father that I was sure it had on us. Luckily Eric was still a fit, strong man. Years behind a desk hadn't leached away the obvious athleticism of his youth. His head, however, was turning an alarmingly bright pink.

At the beach I asked Campbell and the girls about the body. They said it had washed up the night before at the end of the bay, where I'd met the silver-haired coke-dealer and just beneath the rocks where we'd held our little funeral service. We went to the restaurant and sat with Sandra, who talked about Mark. It turned out that Eric knew Sandra's father in England. For a moment the conversation took a rather bizarre 'what a small world' turn, like idle chat at a dinner party.

I showed Eric our camp and Mark's tent. Carlos, sitting by his fire behind us, expressed his sympathy. His own father, he said, had drowned at sea when he, Carlos, was a young boy in Naples. His father had been a fisher-man and his family had always lived beside the sea. Carlos knew how treacherous it could be.

'But this body. Issa not Mark, you know. Issa piece of meat, you know, a piece of meat.'

I wondered if this was exactly the right thing to say to a grieving parent,

but Eric took it in his stride. We carried on through the coconut plantations to Pablo's house in the swimming-pool bay. I explained that Eric
had come to thank him for his efforts in looking for Mark's body. Pablo
was fishing, but the grandmother and a couple of other men were there.
'*El padre, el padre,*' they murmured. The normally-grumpy old grandmother stopped scrapping fish, waddled forward and embraced Eric, like
a mother hugging her child. Eric was a big man and she had to stretch
up to reach his chest. It was the first real physical expression of sympathy since Eric and Iain arrived. We'd consoled each other with words but
this natural and simple gesture conveyed more than words ever could –
even, or maybe especially, from a stranger. We asked her to pass on our
thanks to Pablo.

I wanted to leave Eric alone on the beach to absorb the place, but he
didn't really want to be left. Stepping straight off a plane from England,
it couldn't mean what it meant to us. It takes time to tune in to the natural when you've been in an urban or suburban environment for so long.
Eric was videoing the beach 'for the rest of the family to see,' and
spent much of the time walking around with his eye pressed to the
video camera.

'But Mark was just so young, just so young,' he kept repeating. 'Don't
you think twenty-nine is much too young to die?'

Of course I did.

****

car chase

It was getting late, so we headed back. The policemen had told us that
near the entrance, along a separate fork in the path, was a cafe and a
bus-stop, neither of which I'd known existed. A few people sat around,
waiting for a bus. I asked a smartly-dressed man when it was leaving.

'Half an hour. Have a drink, I will call you. Don't worry, I am the owner
of the bus. I know about your son – I am very sorry. I am also the owner
of the restaurant on the beach. I will call you.'

Around a bend in the path we found a small thatched bar, and ordered
cold drinks. I wondered if I should point out that, if he owned one of
the beach restaurants, perhaps he ought to organise some sort of life-
saving facilities. If Colombia had been the United States, we would
probably be suing him for a lot of money. But what was the point?

Colombia *wasn't* the United States.

After fifteen minutes we wandered back to see if there was any sign of the bus. The bus/restaurant owner looked puzzled to see us.

'The bus? No, it has just left. Five minutes ago.' he said.

His manner implied we'd asked a silly question. There were no more buses until morning.

'What about us?' Eric asked. 'I must get back tonight. We've got our flight booked.'

The bus/restaurant owner turned to the people behind him. An animated conversation ensued, with a lot of hand waving. After a couple of minutes, a middle-aged black man, wearing shorts and a pink T-shirt that said 'Mr Joe – best burgers in Florida', waved us into a battered car. Then he jumped in and, wheels spinning in the dust, we screeched away.

Mr Joe hurtled down the track. He threw the car around onto the main road, its rear end sliding outwards like a car-chase in a Hollywood movie. We swerved wildly to overtake a couple of run-down vehicles and caught sight of the bus ahead. Mr Joe roared up behind it, one hand jammed on the horn, while we leant out of the windows, shouting and waving frantically. The bus driver took no notice – after all, it wasn't all that different to normal Colombian driving. Perhaps he thought we were simply trying to overtake him too. We rattled on like this, waving and shouting and hooting, bouncing over potholes and trailing clouds of dust and exhaust fumes. Finally the bus driver realised we were trying to stop him, and braked. Mr Joe waved us goodbye with a grin.

'Ah, *el padre*,' the bus driver said, brushing aside our offer of payment. The incident was a perfect vignette of Colombia: chaos, inefficiency and frustration, and then, just as you're about to go mad, people going out of their way to help you.

We returned to the hotel to find Melissa and Iain waiting for us.

****
'keep smiling . . .'
'You won't believe what a day we've had.' Iain spluttered. I could almost see the steam rising from him. He said that he and Melissa had followed

the body back to town. On the way the two cars had got separated and when they arrived in Santa Marta there was no sign of the body. The police took them to the funeral parlour, where the funeral director again tried to get Iain to sign the $1,000 agreement. Iain, struggling to recall his O-Level Spanish, said he just wanted to see the body.

Ah, yes, the body.

No, it wasn't actually there, but at the company's other parlour – on the other side of town.

So the police had driven them across town to the other parlour. When they got there, nobody had heard of the body, or had any idea where it might be.

'Don't worry,' the policemen told them. 'We'll find it.'

They spent the next four hours searching Santa Marta: funeral parlours, police stations, government offices. Iain and Melissa were becoming increasingly agitated in the back of the car, while the two policemen tried to soothe them. They stopped to have some sandwiches in the car while they considered their next move. Finally, they found the body at the cemetery, dumped unceremoniously on the lawn and lying in the sun.

Dr Lopez was there already. Seeing Iain and Melissa, he pulled on a pair of gloves, bent down, ripped open the chest of the torso, and pulled out a pair of black lungs.

'Was your friend a smoker?' he asked Melissa.

There being no morgue or facilities to store the body in Santa Marta, Dr Lopez instructed that it be temporarily buried beneath the lawn to pro-tect it from further decay in the sun.

And that was where things now rested.

Iain's eyes bulged with exasperation as he recounted the story. Eric, though, managed to take the frustrations and peculiarities of Colombia in his stride. He'd worked for a long time in Nigeria, and he knew the difficulties of trying to get anything done in a Third World country.

'You learn to be patient. The main thing is, keep smiling and never lose your temper,' he said.

****

'tourist eaten by sharks . . .'

We ate pizza in a restaurant along the sea front. We gave the leftovers to a scrawny boy sitting in the road outside, dressed in shorts and torn rags that were once a T-shirt. Next to him, two other boys lay sprawled across the pavement in glue-induced slumber. The boy looked shocked for an instant, then beamed at us and started to shake his friends to give them some pizza. The street kids in Santa Marta shared everything.

The next day we went back to see Dr Lopez in his office. It was Sunday, but he'd come in on his day off because he knew Eric and Iain had to leave. Once again, here was that extra bit of kindness to balance all the frustrations. He showed us the morning papers. Mark had made the front pages of two local newspapers. In the finest journalistic tradition, they'd managed to get his name wrong – some things are the same the world over. Still, as we struggled to translate the reports, we agreed among ourselves that Mark would have appreciated their sensationalism.

Corpse of tourist found
Dead Englishman appears, mutilated by sharks
The corpse of the Briton, who disappeared on the beach at Arrecifes at 11am on the morning of the 28th March, has been found, totally unrecognisable and missing various limbs and its head. It appears that 'while it was under the water, the white meat of the corpse was eaten by the fish,' a police spokesman explained . . .

We, or rather Eric, still had to decide what to do with the body, and there still remained the problem of how to identify it. Eric and Dr Lopez decided that a sample of bone would have to be flown to England and its DNA tested against a sample of Eric's own blood, to see if they matched. A positive result, Dr Lopez said, would make it pretty certain that the body was really Mark. If so, Eric would have the body cremated and the ashes flown back to England for a memorial service. The testing would take a couple of weeks. Meanwhile, the torso itself would go to Barranquilla, where there was a morgue and a crematorium. We'd spoken to the British Consulate on the phone and they'd promised Eric they would make sure that everything went as planned.

There didn't seem anything more to be done. Eric and Iain had a plane to catch. They collected their things from the hotel and we stood on the pavement outside and watched them leave in the taxi. Tomorrow they would be back in England, wondering if it was all a terrible dream.

****

a last fruit shake

Melissa and I still had to make one trip back to Arrecifes, to break up our camp and collect our things. I'd been back and forth between the beach and Santa Marta so often – it seemed strange to think this was probably the last time I'd ever see it. We said goodbye to Campbell and Sandra and Kim, to Carlos and Michel and Phillipe. I took one final, long look around. The beach at Arrecifes was one of the most beautiful places I've known: despite what had happened, I felt a pang of sadness to be leaving it. Then we began the trip back again, along the path through the jungle.

We decided that we'd go down the coast to Cartagena, and from there fly to Guatemala. Our first thought had been to return to England. But what would that achieve? It wouldn't bring Mark back. We had nothing to do there, no real reason to return. Better to carry on travelling, to find other strange landscapes and cultures in which to immerse ourselves.

We checked out of the Miramar and had a last *maracuyá* fruit shake on the sea front. In a still-deserted bar a salsa band was playing a song called *Siempre Alegre*, by Raphy Leavit.

'Hay que pasar la vida siempre alegre, despues que uno se muere de que vale . . .' they sang.

The sun was setting over the bay and the evening was just beginning to come to life. Young couples and beautiful *costeña* girls, with long tanned legs and long dark hair, were hanging about on the promenade. A few dealers sat around, quiet but sharp-eyed, waiting for customers. We recognised some of the regulars jogging along the beach in the cool of the early evening.

' . . . hay que gozar de todos los placeres, cuando uno va a morir, nadie lo sabe . . .' The music's sweetness disguised the poignancy of the message, in a country where life is cheap. 'Always be happy in life, after you're dead what's the point, taste every pleasure, who knows when death will come.'

'We'd better find our bus, I guess,' I said. 'We've got a plane to catch too.'

' . . . *vive la vida, mira que se va y no vuelve* . . .' the singer wailed.
'Live your life. It's passing, and it's never coming back . . .'

'Guatemala?' asked Melissa. 'Where's that?'

Footnotes

1. *These clothes and hairstyle were imposed by King Charles III of Spain in the 18th century, in imitation of the Spanish peasantry of the time.*

2. *Jesus, for instance, is identified with the Inca Sun God; the Virgin Mary with the Moon or with Pachamama, the Andean earth-goddess. The Inca God of Thunder became linked to Saint James of Santiago, the patron saint of the gunpowder-equipped Spanish soldiers. Ayamarca, the Inca Month of the Dead, survives in the Day of the Dead on November 1st, when people visit family graves.*

3. *Campesina, mestiza and blanca are simply the feminine versions (the -a ending indicating feminine gender in Spanish). There are also a few black communities, mainly along the Pacific coast, plus a few scattered 'others'—Chinese, Japanese, Lebanese. As all generic terms for the indigenous people of the Americas are colonial impositions—there was no need for a collective description before the Spanish arrived—I'll stick to the most recognisable one, Indians, despite its obvious problems (i.e. they don't come from India).*

4. *Find out what it means yourself—be careful who you ask!*

5. *The dispute between the two countries dates from 1941, when Peru annexed half of the then-Ecuadorean Amazon. This was instigated, it is rumoured, by certain US oil companies, after the Ecuadorean government decided not to allow them to exploit the region's vast oil reserves. Ecuador has never accepted the loss.*

6. *I recommend* The Conquest of the Incas, *by John Hemming, for a detailed account of these extraordinary events.*

7. *Huayna Capac was said to have 500 male descendants (presumably by different women) but only sons of the 'coya'—who was both queen and sister—counted as heirs.*

8. *Firearms only became decisive with the much later invention of the repeat-fire rifle. As for dogs, the Indians only had small, docile breeds, kept mainly for food. According to Bartolomé de las Casas, 'The Spaniards have a number of wild and ferocious dogs which they have trained especially to kill the people and tear them to bits...to feed these dogs, they ensure that wherever they travel they always have a ready supply of natives, chained and herded like so many calves on the hoof. These they kill and butcher as the need arises.'*

9. *To put this into perspective, in 1992 the combined population of Peru, Bolivia*

and Ecuador was 41.1 million. Between 1542 and 1570, the population of the Americas as a whole fell from perhaps 100 million to 10 million: the 90 million dead would have represented about one-fifth of the entire human race. As there are no accurate records, these figures are only estimates. Some historians believe the pre-contact population was much lower—but that doesn't alter the central point that this was a human nightmare of almost unrivalled proportions. (The same caveat applies to the figures for the Potosí mines in the next chapter.)

10. Along with China, India, the Middle East, Egypt and Mexico.

11. So much so that Mathew Parris made it the title of an entertaining book about Peru.

12. Cabildo of Jauja, quoted in Hemming, p 120.

13. Their success also helped the Spanish. The Incas destroyed other Andean military forces and established an infrastructure of control, so the Spanish simply took over an existing empire.

14. See Reay Tannahill's fascinating Food in History for the answer.

15. And there were certainly plenty going in Hackney. A survey of one local school, for instance, found over 170 different first languages amongst its pupils.

16. The people of northern Bolivia are mainly Aymara. Those in the south are mainly Quechua.

17. There are higher lakes in Peru, but Titicaca is the highest that has regular traffic.

18. The historical material on these pages is drawn mainly from Eduardo Galeano, Open Veins of Latin America.

19. See Reay Tannahill, Food in History.

20. Ministerio de Prevision Social y Salud Publica, 1991-92 (quoted in Duncan Green, Silent Revolution p7).

21. The pre-Conquest population of North America was much lower anyway, and the Indians were either killed or forced onto reservations. The invading Europeans wanted the land to farm. In South America, and especially the Andes, European settlement was limited: the Europeans needed the Indians to work the mines and plantations. It was largely a question of timing. South America was settled first, at a time when Europe was, if anything, underpopu-

lated. By the time of the mass European emigration of the 19th century, the best land in South America was already 'owned' by established Latino elites. What wasn't—the Amazon, for instance—was less inviting than the 'empty' prairies of North America. So the poor and hungry masses of Europe went north, not south.

22. In fact, Coca-Cola still uses small quantities of coca leaves from which it extracts flavoring coca after leaching out the cocaine and other alkaloids (source: <u>The Andes Cocaine Industry</u> – P Clawson & R. W. Lee).

23. Nine out of every ten dollars spent on cocaine in the USA remains in the States (source: Latin American Newsletters). The US government, incidentally, estimates its citizens spend $49 billion on illegal drugs every year (Latinamerica Press, March 7th 1996): Bolivia's official GDP in 1992 was only $6.7 billion.)

24. In 1992 the US budget for such operations in South America was $1.2 billion. As General 'Mad Max' Thurman, head of US Southern Command, put it, 'The Latin American drug war is the only war we've got.'

25. Technically, 'jungle' is only one part of a rainforest eco-system. The branches of large trees form a high canopy that blocks sunlight and limits the plantlife below. When a large tree falls, it lets sunlight in through the gap in the canopy, stimulating thousands of plants to grow and fight for the space. These impenetrable sections are 'jungle.' Eventually, one tree will win through and grow tall enough to close the canopy gap. The Amazon as a whole, though, is a rainforest, not a jungle.

26. Poverty statistic from Judith Kimerling: 'Oil, Lawlessness and Indigenous Struggles in Ecuador's Oriente', in <u>Green Guerrillas</u>, - ed Helen Collinson. Other information from Judith Kimerling: <u>Amazon Crude</u>.

27. A Quechua word meaning 'vine of the soul' or 'vine of the dead'. (In many Indian languages, the same word is used for 'dead', 'soul', 'spirit', or 'shadow'.) Under it's other name, yage, ayahuasca achieved cult status in the 1960s with William Burroughs' and Alan Ginsberg's 1963 book, <u>The Yage Letters</u>.

28. After <u>Shamanism - Archaic Techniques of Ecstasy</u>, the title of Mircea Eliade's seminal study.

29. Europeans were animists before becoming Jews and Christians-—and indeed, Christian imagery such as Heaven and Hell, angels and demons, the Devil and the cross all derive from older animist beliefs. So what caused the great change to monotheism? One possibility is that it was due to the development of agriculture in the Middle East, which made us feel that we'd 'mastered'

Nature. Of course, agriculture also developed in the Andes and they remained animists, but they had plenty of volcanoes and earthquakes to remind them that Nature was still boss. For a different theory, see Raine Eisler's briliant _The Chalice and the Blade_.

30. Nevill Drury, _The Elements of Shamanism_.

31. In Spanish, Doña and Don are terms indicating respect, not first names.

32. The CUT (Columbia's TUC) reported that in the same period 1,542 trade-unionists were murdered, yet not one of their killers has been convicted. The Committee to Protect Journalists rates Colombia as the world's most dangerous country to report the news, with 98 journalists dead in two decades.

33. 'Survival International' newsletter, no. 32, 1993. They were Luis Napolean Torres, Angel Maria Torres and Antonio Hugues Chaparro.

34. They actually live in farms dotted around the hills. Most families have two farms, a winter one in the valley and a summer one higher up the hillside.

35. These are called poporos. They're used to crush sea-shells, to make an alkaline powder that reacts with coca to create a more narcotic effect. For the Arhuacos, coca is a symbol of fertility—the stick and poporo represent the penis and the womb respectively.

36. The term mulato indicates an African-Indian or African-Spanish ancestry (or all three combined) as distinct from mestizo, which means a mix of Indian and Spanish.

37. Coffee is both Colombia's second biggest export and the world's second most widely-traded commodity (both after oil and excluding illegal drugs).

38. Manufactured goods as a % of total exports: Bolivia 7%, Colombia 18%, Peru 12%, Ecuador 1%. Developed nations (average) 76% (source: 1987 'World Bank World Development Report').

39. The report also noted that the gap between rich and poor had doubled in the two decades from 1970 to 1991. In 1991, the planet's richest 20% received 85% of all income, the poorest 20% a mere 1.4%.

40. Although there are various other explanations for the origin of the term.

41. Philosophical dudes will recognise this as a reworking of Plato's famous 'Simile of the Cave.'

Bibliography

HISTORY

A VERY BRIEF ACCOUNT OF THE DESTRUCTION OF THE INDIES, Bartolomé de las Casas (1st printed 1552)
OPEN VEINS OF LATIN AMERICA, Eduardo Galaeno (Monthly Review Press, New York, 1973)
THE CONQUEST OF THE INCAS, John Hemming (Macmillan, London, 1970)
FOOD IN HISTORY, Reay Tannahill (Eyre Methuen, 1973)
SÍMON BOLÍVAR, Denis Wepman (Chelsea Harbour Publishers, New York, 1985)

MODERN ECONOMICS

THE ANDES COCAINE INDUSTRY, P. Clawson & R. W. Lee (St Martin's Griffin, New York, 1996)
SILENT REVOLUTION, Duncan Green (Cassell, London, 1995)
THE ANDES: A QUEST FOR JUSTICE, Neil MacDonald (Oxfam Report, 1992)

SHAMANISM AND RELIGION

THE TAO OF PHYSICS, Fritjof Capra (Wildwood House, 1975)
THE ELEMENTS OF SHAMANISM, Nevill Drury (Element Books, Dorset, 1989)
THE CHALICE AND THE BLADE, Raine Eisler (Harper Collins, London, 1990)
SHAMANISM: ARCHAIC TECHNIQUES OF ECSTASY, Mircea Eliade (Arkana, 1989)
FOOD OF THE GODS, Terence McKenna (Rider, 1982)
SHAMANISM, COLONIALISM AND THE WILD MAN, M. Taussig (1987)

ETHNICITY

THE INDIGENOUS VOICE: VISIONS AND REALITIES, ed. Roger Moody (International Books, Utrecht. UK distribution by John Carpenter Publishing, PO Box 129, Oxford OX1 4PH. Tel: 0865-790 715) (Section 2 quote is taken from this anthology, p582)
THE RETURN OF THE INDIAN, Phillip Wearne (Latin American Bureau, Cassell, London, 1996)

OIL

GREEN GUERRILLAS, ed. Helen Collinson (LAB, 1996)
AMAZON CRUDE, Judith Kimerling (Natural Resource Defence Council, New York, 1991)

SALSA

SALSA: HAVANA HEAT! BRONX BEAT, Hernando Calvo Ospina (LAB, 1995)

TRAVELOGUES

The Fruit Palace, Charles Nicholl (Heinemann, 1985)
Inca Kola, Matthew Parris (Ulverscroft, 1992)
Cut Stones and Crossroads, Ronald Wright (Viking Press, 1984)

SONGS

Lyrics to 'BREATHE', by Pink Floyd (from Dark Side of the Moon).
Lyrics to Raphy Leavit's 'SIEMPRE ALEGRE' reproduced from Salsa: Havana Heat! Bronx Beat

ORGANISATIONS

COLOMBIA FORUM - contact details tbc
LATIN AMERICAN BUREAU 1 Amwell St, London EC1B 1TW. Tel: 0171-278 2829
SURVIVAL INTERNATIONAL - contact details tbc
TOURISM CONCERN - Stapledon House, 277-281 Holloway Road, London N7 8HN. Tel: 0171-753 3330 http://www.gn.apc.org/tourismconcern

ALSO AVAILABLE AT
YOUR LOCAL BOOKSTORE

GREETINGS FROM
CANNABIS COUNTRY

BY ANDRE GROSSMAN
GREETINGS FROM CANNABIS COUNTRY is
a must have for enthusiasts! The
book contains a collection of 30
beautifully detailed photo-postcards,
taken by Andre Grossman at
Trichome Technologies—the world's
most sophisticated and largest
marijuana growing operation.
Fourteen of the potent strains of
marijuana are displayed in both a
colorful and playful way. The safest
way to send pot through the mail!
$11.95

THE MARIJUANA
CHEF COOKBOOK

BY S. T. ONER
THE MARIJUANA CHEF COOKBOOK gives a
whole new meaning to cooking with
herbs. With more than 40 first-rate
recipes, this wonderful cookbook
offers a multitude of ways to turn
humble leaf into culinary treats that
everyone can enjoy. In the mood for
something sweet? Try Decadent
Chocolate Bud Cake washed down
with a delicious Mary Jane's Martini.
A heady blend of theory and technique, THE MARIJUANA CHEF COOKBOOK
is filled with delicious easy-to-follow
recipes that will take you and your
dinner guests on a natural high.
$12.95

CANNABIS CULTIVATION

BY MEL THOMAS
Easy-to-follow, step-by-step directions enable anyone to grow and harvest the highest quality marijuana using simple techniques and inexpensive, everyday gardening tools. An experienced grower, Mel Thomas pens a comprehensive manual that is both interesting and informative. The book covers all of the important factors which can influence growth rate, yield and potency: lighting, planting mediums, pH, nutrients, water systems, air and temperature, and CO2. CANNABIS CULTIVATION will help you turn almost any space into a high-yielding garden.
$16.95

STEVEN CERIO'S ABC BOOK: A DRUG PRIMER

DON'T MISTAKE THIS ONE FOR A SIMPLE CHILD'S ALPHABET BOOK! Steven Cerio's ABC BOOK: A DRUG PRIMER is a must-have for Ravers and Stoners alike. Come along for the ride from A-Z, and read the poems that accompany Steven's colorful psychedelic illustrations. Each letter represents a different type of drug, and its effects are stated in an accompanying poem. A lighthearted and amusing piece of work, this ABC book is pure fun!
$12.95